Pieter van Reenen

Phonetic Feature Definitions

Their integration into phonology and their relation to speech

A case study of the feature NASAL

1982
FORIS PUBLICATIONS
Dordrecht - Holland/Cinnaminson - U.S.A.

Published by:
Foris Publications Holland
P.O. Box 509
3300 AM Dordrecht, The Netherlands

Sole distributor for the U.S.A. and Canada:
Foris Publications U.S.A.
P.O. Box C-50
Cinnaminson N.J. 08077
U.S.A.

ISBN 90 70176 46 7

Printed in the Netherlands by Intercontinental Graphics, H.I. Ambacht.

Before we can accomplish the happy
marriage between phonology and phonetics
we have to work out the rules for
predicting the speech event given the output
of the phonological component of grammar. To me this is the central, though
much neglected, problem of phonetics...

Gunnar FANT

Acknowledgement

The present study was intended to be part of an analysis of vowel nasality in Old French, a subject suggested to me by L. Geschiere.

In the course of my investigations - and after fundamental discussions with R. P. Botha and the late H. Mol - I decided to tackle theoretical problems in a separate publication.

Valuable comments and criticisms on both style and content, given by B. Siertsema, M. van Veelen-Bosma and K. H. van Reenen-Stein, have improved this study considerably.

I have also profited from comments of and discussions with N. S. H. Smith, J. J. Spa and W. H. Vieregge.

To compose the manuscript I have used a microcomputer. J. Portier, M. C. H. Dekker and P. J. Siderius (the latter two from the Computer Science Department of the **Vrije Universiteit**, Amsterdam) converted the output of my microcomputer into the format required by the publisher.

Amstelveen, October 1981

Contents

Introduction

Phonology may be characterized as the study of the sound patterns of human
language; experimental phonetics as the study of the production, perception
and acoustic properties of human speech. Phonologists emphasize the theoretical, descriptive and distinctive aspects of sounds, phoneticians study the
properties of speech sounds by means of experimentation. Phonologists and
phoneticians study the same object from different angles. This complementary
approach of the phenomenon of LANGAGE (in the Saussurean sense of the word) in
the two disciplines is very valuable: results in the two domains may have
reciprocal fruitful effects.

The reality is often different, however. There are not many phonologists
who are more than superficially interested in the results obtained by means of
phonetic experimentation. And quite a lot of phoneticians ignore phonology,
because they consider it an intuitive and introspective practice. Indeed, as
far as phonology is concerned with the theoretical framework which accounts
for phonetic transcriptions of speech utterances but not with the speech
utterances themselves, and phonetics is concerned with speech utterances and
phonetic transcriptions without being really interested in the question how
these phonetic transcriptions relate to phonological theory, it is obvious
that these phonologists and phoneticians have the view that their fields are
separate.

There are also phonologists and phoneticians who do not share this view and
who are interested in integration. They regard the results of phonetic experiments as relevant to phonological theory. It is my opinion that this integration should be pursued. The more general aim of this study is to explore the
possibilities of a closer integration of phonology and experimental phonetics.

The linguistic framework adopted in the present study is that of transformational generative theory, more specifically its phonological component as it
is described in Chomsky and Halle's **The Sound Pattern of English (SPE)**, still
the standard work in the field. Occasionally, more recent works are quoted,
especially Anderson (1974), but also Hooper (1976) and Kenstowicz and Kisseberth (1979). Yet, to my mind **SPE** still offers the best starting point for
attempts to relate phonology to physical properties of speech.

In this study I will outline an empirical framework for generative phonology slightly different from that in **SPE**. In addition, I will make proposals as to the form of phonetic feature definitions, the way they are integrated into phonology and their relation to speech. As this task is too extensive to be carried out for all or even several features, I have selected just one: the phonetic feature NASAL. The more specific aim of this study is to present a detailed view of the relationship between phonology and experimental phonetics, illustrated by the feature NASAL.

Existing publications on nasality will be referred to, but a complete summary of the bulk of the existing literature is not provided. Studies on the phenomenon of nasality are found in too many different fields: oto-rhinolaryngology, dentistry, acoustics, logopaedia, phonetics and linguistics. And for over a 100 years scientists have published on the subject. As recent and extensive but far from complete bibliographies may be mentioned: Ohala (1975), Entenman (1976), Trenschel (1978), Almeida (1978).

Though in some cases I will reanalyse or further analyse results of phonetic experiments, it should be kept in mind that the present study is phonological in nature and it does not describe any experiment I have carried out myself. The methods used for my reanalysis and further analysis of results of phonetic experiments have been adapted to the various experimental results produced by others. These methods will be discussed in the chapters where they are introduced or in the appendices at the end of this study. And although it will be possible to derive testable hypotheses from the conclusions I will arrive at, it is outside the scope of this study to test them experimentally.

Chapters one and two serve to introduce and develop the theoretical framework for this study. The other chapters concern the phonetic feature NASAL, its integration into this framework and its relation to speech. The appendices mainly contain data collections.

CHAPTER 1

The framework in **SPE** and some criticism

In this chapter I give an outline of the framework of generative phonology as
it is found in **SPE** (section 1.1). This framework is criticized in section
1.2. In section 1.3 I discuss two different attitudes towards **SPE**.

1.1 AN OUTLINE OF THE FRAMEWORK IN SPE

The phonetic feature NASAL belongs to the category of entities which together
form the level of phonetic representation. Both the feature and the level of
representation are constructs in transformational generative theory. Below I
give an outline of their place and function within this theory. The outline is
based upon Chomsky and Halle (1968).

A transformational generative grammar consists of a syntactic, semantic and
phonological component. The lexicon is part of the syntactic component and
consists of lexical formatives and lexical redundancy rules. As far as their
phonological form is concerned, lexical formatives are represented as so-
called lexical matrices, of which Chomsky and Halle (1968:166) provide the
following examples:

(1)		(a) inn		(b) algebra						
		i	n	ae	l	g	e	b	r	ae
consonantal		–	+	–	+	+	–	+	+	–
vocalic		0	0	0	+	–	0	–	+	0
nasal		0	+	0	0	–	0	–	0	0
tense		–	0	–	0	0	–	0	0	–
stress		0	0	0	0	0	0	0	0	0
voice		0	0	0	0	+	0	+	0	0
continuant		0	0	0	0	–	0	–	0	0

In lexical matrices as in (1) the rows represent features, the columns the
phonological segments out of which the lexical formatives are constructed. In

the original version of generative phonology in **SPE** three specifications occur
in this kind of lexical matrices: positive ("+"), negative ("-") and zero
("0").

   When lexical matrices leave the lexicon, they are converted into phonological matrices by means of the lexical redundancy rules, which replace the zeros
("0") by binary terms: positive ("+") or negative ("-")(p.171). Application of
the redundancy rules to (1) would give the following results, a diagram not
presented in Chomsky and Halle [1] :

(2)	(a) inn		(b) algebra						
	i	n	ae	l	g	e	b	r	ae
consonantal	-	+	-	+	+	-	+	+	-
vocalic	+	-	+	+	-	+	-	+	+
nasal	?	+	-	-	-	-	-	-	-
tense	-	-	-	-	-	-	-	-	-
stress	+	-	+	-	-	+	-	-	+
voice	+	+	+	+	+	+	+	+	+
continuant	+	-	+	+	-	+	-	+	+

Phonological matrices as in (2) occur in syntactic surface structures, which
form the output of the syntactic component and in phonological surface structures, which form the input to the phonological component. Phonological surface structures are usually referred to as phonological representations.

   After the phonological rules of the phonological component have been
applied, the following phonetic matrices are formed (cf. Chomsky and Halle
1968:165):

(3)	(a) inn		(b) algebra						
	i	n	ae	l	g	e	b	r	ae
consonantal	-	+	-	+	+	-	+	+	-
vocalic	+	-	+	+	-	+	-	+	+
nasal	2	+	-	-	-	-	-	-	-
tense	-	-	-	-	-	-	-	-	-
stress	1	-	1	-	-	4	-	-	4
voice	+	+	+	+	+	+	+	+	+
continuant	+	-	+	+	-	+	-	+	+

Phonetic matrices as in (3) are found at the level of phonetic representation. At this level distinctive features have a phonetic function, whereas the lexical matrices in (1) and the phonological matrices in (2) are classificatory matrices, i.e. the features do not have a phonetic, but a classificatory function. In phonetic representation distinctive features are multivalued, i.e. they may be specified positively, negatively or in terms of integers. In other words, a phonetic feature may be present in different degrees. In (3) [1 stress] is paraphrased as "main stress", [4 stress] as "stress of the fourth degree", and [2 nasal] as "partial degree of nasalization" (p.165). Phonetic representations may be viewed as series of concatenated lexical formatives, which consist of linearly ordered phonetic segments. The segments are composed of phonetic features.

Phonetic features are physical scales "which may in principle assume numerous discrete coefficients" (p.298; cf. p. 297) or "a fixed number of values" (p. 298; cf. p.5). They have articulatory, acoustic and perceptual correlates, but for practical reasons Chomsky and Halle usually describe them in articulatory terms only (cf.p.298-299). Phonetic features form a universal set (p.4), independent of the grammar of any particular language (p.164). They represent the phonetic capabilities of man (p.295,cf.297). The output of the grammar of any particular language consists of phonetic representations which are constructed out of the same universal set of phonetic features, but the manner in which the values or coefficients of the phonetic features are distributed in phonetic representations is language-specific.

In the phonological component "all grammatically determined facts about the production and perception" (p.293) of a sentence are added to the phonological surface structures by means of phonological rules, which interact with "certain universal phonetic constraints" (p. 293) or "universal rules" (p. 295).

Chomsky and Halle do not discuss these universal rules or universal phonetic constraints in any detail. They seem to view them as articulatory constraints on sound sequences, as a kind of universal smoothing rules between segments. Their role may be that of changing the segmented phonetic representations into quasi-continuous entities more like the physical reality of the speech signals and the articulatory movements which produce them. These constraints are not included in phonetic representation, see the following quotation from Chomsky and Halle (1968:295): "phonetic transcriptions omit properties of the speech signal that are supplied by universal rules. These properties include, for example, the different articulatory gestures and various coarticulation effects - the transition between a vowel and an adjacent consonant, the adjustments in the vowel tract shape made in anticipation of subsequent motions, etc." As we will see below, instead of "phonetic transcription" we may read "phonetic representation".

As we have seen above, phonological rules interact with "universal phonetic

constraints" or "universal rules". Since the results of the application of
these constraints are not included in phonetic representations, it follows
that phonetic representations do not contain **all** linguistically relevant facts
about the production and the perception of a sentence.

For Chomsky and Halle the constraints are marginal, but in this study they
play a more central role. Another scientist who mentions them is Anderson
(1974:5-6): "each segment is characterized in terms of a state of the vocal
organs, and the transitions between these states are assumed to be predictable
in terms of very general linguistic and physiological laws." I assume that the
expression "linguistic and physiological laws" refers to one kind of laws,
which is physiologico-linguistic in nature. Halle and Stevens (1964:605) probably provide the clearest description of the constraints: "Because of the
inertia of the structures that form the vocal tract and the limitations in the
speech of neural and muscular control, a given phonetic parameter cannot
change instantaneously from one value to another; the transitions from one
target configuration to the next must be gradual, or smooth." (Descriptions of
such constraints can be found in the older literature as well.)

Although it is not made clear, Chomsky and Halle (1968:295) seem to leave
open the possibility that phonological rules interact with language-specific
"phonetic effects" as well. Among these language-specific phonetic effects,
Chomsky and Halle (1968:295) mention the "articulation base", e.g. "in French
the mobility of the lips and forward position of the tongue". [2] However, the
position of Chomsky and Halle is not entirely clear on this point, since these
language-specific "phonetic effects" are explicitly excluded from phonetic
representations on page 295, and they are not mentioned on page 293 among the
grammatically determined facts about the production and perception of sentences in the same way as the universal phonetic constraints. Whether this is
an oversight, I do not know. It may be that Chomsky and Halle regard
language-specific "phonetic effects" as not linguistically relevant at all.

1.2 PROBLEMS WITH THE TESTABILITY OF PHONETIC REPRESENTATIONS AND PHONETIC FEATURES IN SPE

If we consider generative phonology to be an empirical science, phonetic
representations should be testable. However, it is doubtful whether phonetic
representations in **SPE** are testable indeed (see 1.2.2). The status, the testability and universality of phonetic features will be discussed in 1.2.3. In
1.2.1 I will deal with a few terms.

1.2.1 TERMINOLOGICAL ISSUES

In **SPE** several expressions occur which play an important role in the present study and which need some comment. These expressions are "phonetic transcription", "physical or acoustic reality" and "perceptual reality".

In **SPE** the expression "(phonetic) transcription" is synonymous either with "phonetic representation", i.e. output of the phonological component, or with "system of transcription", "device for recording facts observed in actual utterances" (pp. 293-295, ix). In the present study I will use the expression "(phonetic) transcription" in the latter sense only. Phonetic transcriptions are made by "the skillful transcriber" or "the careful and sophisticated impressionistic phonetician ... who knows the language" (pp. 293, 25). For English, for instance, Chomsky and Halle (p. ix) follow transcriptions of the sort presented in Kenyon and Knott (1944).

In the expression "physical or acoustic reality" (p.25), I take it that Chomsky and Halle do not use "physical" and "acoustic" as synonyms. Since they use also expressions as "physical articulatory system" (p.65), I interpret "acoustic" and "articulatory" as the more specific terms, "physical" as the more general term. Acoustic phenomena, such as sound waves, are physical phenomena, just as articulatory phenomena, such as movements of the tongue, are physical phenomena. The acoustic reality and the articulatory reality are parts of the physical reality.

The "perceptual reality" is distinguished from the "physical reality" (cf. p.25). Since "speech perception is an active process, a process in which the physical stimulus that strikes the hearer's ear is utilized to form hypotheses about the deep structure of the sentence"(294), I take it that the perceptual reality is part of the mental reality of a speaker-hearer and that physical and mental reality are complementary in the speech process.

1.2.2 THE TESTABILITY OF PHONETIC REPRESENTATIONS

Botha (1971:191-204) has dealt with the testability of phonetic representations in **SPE**. I mainly follow and summarize his exposé of Chomsky and Halle's position.

According to Chomsky and Halle (1968:25, 65, 294, 297-8, 381) phonetic representations have relations with (a) independent elements of a physical or acoustic reality (p.25) and (b) independent elements of a perceptual reality.

(a) The relationship between phonetic representations and a physical or

6

acoustic reality is quite indirect. Chomsky and Halle (1968:25) observe "that there is nothing to suggest that ... phonetic representations describe the physical or acoustic reality in any detail". They reject the view that phonetic representation is "a device for recording facts observed in actual utterances. That the latter view is not tenable, in any very strict sense, has been known at least since mechanical and electrical recordings of utterances have revealed that even the most skillful transcriber is unable to note certain aspects of the signal, while commonly recording in his transcriptions items for which there seems to be no direct warrant in the physical record" (p. 293). As linguists they "are primarily concerned with the structure of the language rather than with the acoustics and physiology of speech" (p.293). Therefore Botha (1971:195) concludes: "since phonetic representations do not directly refer to a physical reality, evidence about this physical reality is not directly relevant to the testing of these representations."

(b) In **SPE** phonetic representations describe or refer to independent elements of a perceptual reality of the speaker- hearer. Chomsky and Halle distinguish two kinds of data which are relevant to the testing of phonetic representations. (i) Intuitive judgements which phonetically untrained native speakers are able to make about perceptual properties of utterances and (ii) phonetic observations made by trained phoneticians about perceptual properties of sentences.

Unfortunately, according to Chomsky and Halle (1968:25-6) phonetically untrained speakers are largely unaware of such perceptual properties and their judgements are impressionistic. The same holds with respect to the judgements of trained phoneticians. In addition, Chomsky and Halle (1968:26) observe that the phonetic transcriptions made by trained phoneticians may be influenced by "arbitrary convention and irrelevant cognitive limitations". To these considerations of Chomsky and Halle themselves Botha (1971:196) adds a third one which concerns systems of phonetic transcription: "it is rather doubtful whether observations on which agreement can be reached only by trained phoneticians WHO MUST OPERATE WITHIN THE SAME SYSTEM OF CONVENTIONS can be regarded as independent evidence about what a native speaker is supposed to hear". This is the more important because Chomsky and Halle (1968:ix) think "A system of transcription ... not "refutable" by evidence". As phonetic representations cannot be tested against physical properties of speech utterances (since the latter are irrelevant) nor against intuitive judgements of native speakers and phonetic observations by trained phoneticians (since they are both irrelevant and unreliable), it is doubtful whether phonetic representations are empirical. Chomsky and Halle (p. 25) themselves arrive at this conclusion in connection with a notoriously difficult aspect (stress contours) of phonetic representation: "There may be no empirical sense to the question of whether the resulting representation is correct in full detail".

For the working linguist this situation is unsatisfactory. In chapter 2, I
will make some alternative proposals.

1.2.3 PHONETIC FEATURES

Phonetic representations of utterances are constructed out of phonetic
features. Phonetic features cannot be tested directly, since they need at
least one segment in order to be actualized as a sound, i.e. the shortest possible phonetic representation. We have seen above that it is doubtful whether
phonetic representations can be tested (see 1.2.2 above), but the testability
of phonetic features is doubtful as well. The following observations concern
phonetic features with respect to their ontological status, their correlates
and their universality.

According to Chomsky and Halle, phonetic features "provide a representation
of an utterance which can be interpreted as a set of instructions to the physical articulatory system, or as a refined level of perceptual representation"
(p.65); and they represent "aspects of the vocal tract behaviour that are
under the voluntary control of the speaker" (p. 381). I think it self-evident
that expressions such as "set of instructions", "voluntary control", "perceptual" refer to aspects of the mental reality of the speaker-hearer and that
the expression "aspects of the vocal tract behaviour" refers to aspects of the
physical reality. If this is accepted, it follows that phonetic features are
not only part of the mental reality of the speaker-hearer but also belong to
the physical reality.

The same conclusion may be drawn from the fact that a phonetic feature has
three correlates: an articulatory, an acoustic and a perceptual correlate
(p.299). It is natural that the articulatory and the acoustic correlates
describe aspects of the physical reality and that the perceptual correlate
describes aspects of the perceptual or mental reality.

As we have seen in 1.2.2 above, in **SPE** phonetic representations do not
describe the physical reality of utterances in any detail. Therefore, the
articulatory and acoustic correlates of the phonetic features in terms of
which phonetic representations are constructed do not describe the physical
reality in any detail either.

Chomsky and Halle stress that phonetic representation describes a **perceptual** reality (not a physical reality in any detail). However, they do not
assign a special status to the perceptual correlate as compared to the physical correlates, since they consider the correlates to be equally important and
interesting as appears from the following quotation: "We shall describe the
articulatory correlate of every feature ... We shall speak of the acoustical

and perceptual correlates of a feature only occasionally, not because we regard these aspects as either less interesting or less important, but rather because such discussions would make this section, which is itself a digression from the main theme of our book, much too long" (p. 299). Apparently, Chomsky and Halle consider the three correlates to be **equally** important and interesting, without assigning a special role to the perceptual correlate. I do not understand why they do not regard the perceptual correlate as **more** important and interesting than the two physical correlates.

In addition, what they say in this quotation is not in agreement with what they do. It is true that Chomsky and Halle speak of the acoustic correlate of a feature occasionally, but they never mention any perceptual correlate. It follows that phonetic representations are described in terms of physical correlates only. This makes the physical correlates completely untestable, since (a) phonetic representations in which they occur do not describe the physical reality of utterances in any detail; (b) there is not even a relation between physical and perceptual correlates of a feature, since the perceptual correlate has not even been provided.

Therefore, we have the following situation in **SPE**: the physical correlates which are provided are not testable, whereas it is stated that the perceptual correlate, which is not provided, is testable. And even the testability of the perceptual correlate is doubtful (see 1.2.2 above).

A last observation concerns the universality of phonetic features. In 1.1 we have seen that phonetic features are supposed to be universal, i.e. they are the same for all languages. With respect to the physical or the acoustic reality they describe this is easy to accept. However, the question may be raised whether the perceptual reality described by the perceptual correlate is the same for speakers of different languages. In an experiment described by Bondarko (1979) a difference has been found in the perception of French nasal vowels between a group of French listeners and a group of Russian listeners. The French listeners perceive the nasality, the Russian listeners do not perceive the nasality. (But neither Russian nor French listeners perceive the alleged nasality of Russian vowels followed by nasal consonant, cf. Bondarko 1979:71; since the point is not at issue, I do not develop it here.) This finding strongly suggests that the perceptual reality of the French speakers is different from that of the Russian speakers. If the perceptual reality of speakers of different languages is not the same, it is difficult to claim that the perceptual correlate of a phonetic feature describes the same aspect of the perceptual reality in these different languages. If the perceptual correlate of a feature describes various aspects of perceptual reality, depending on the languages, the feature cannot be said to be universal. Unfortunately, in Chomsky and Halle (1968) this problem is not even hinted at.

1.3 TWO ATTITUDES TOWARDS SPE

In the preceding sections I have introduced the phonological framework of
Chomsky and Halle (1968) and signalized some deficiencies. These deficiencies
are rather fundamental and it is not entirely surprising that a phonetician
like Kohler (1978:113) in his review of Ladefoged (1975) observes that the
reader "should study carefully what the book (of Ladefoged, PvR) presents on
coarticulation and targets, but should forget most of what it says about the
phoneme and generative phonology", i.e. about **SPE**.

Yet, other phoneticians adopt a more positive attitude towards generative
phonology than Kohler does. As a motto for this study I have taken a quotation
from Fant (1973:173): "Before we can accomplish the happy marriage between
phonology and phonetics we have to work out the rules for predicting the
speech event given the output of the phonological component of grammar. To me
this is the central, though much neglected, problem of phonetics ..." and, as
we may add, of phonology. Fant's observation continues: "... it (this problem, PvR) is of the same magnitude as that of generative grammar in general
and will require a similar set of transformational rules ... The derivation of
the rules of this 'phonetic component' of language aims at describing the
speech production, speech wave, or perception correlates of each feature given
the 'context' in a very general sense of co-occurring features within the phonological segment as well as those of following and preceding segments."

Like Kohler, Fant reacted to the proposals of Chomsky and Halle (1968). But
instead of rejecting generative phonology, Fant described the outlines of an
extensive research programme. Though Fant's quotation dates from 1969, the
implementation of the research programme has hardly made any progress since.
And, as we have seen above, the few scientists who work on it such as Ladefoged and Ohala - a few other references can be found in Hewlett (1981) - are
actually white crows whose efforts are not always appreciated.

The phonological framework of Chomsky and Halle (1968) needs a number of
inevitable changes, but there is no need to reject it. The framework I will
propose in chapter 2 is different from that of Fant, but I agree with Fant's
view and feel we should not leave the field lying fallow **which** he outlined
twelve years ago.

NOTES TO CHAPTER 1

1. The "?" specification of the feature NASAL in the [ɩ] segment of **inn** is
    not an official symbol. I have introduced it because I do not know the
    intention of Chomsky and Halle on this point. The problem will be

discussed in chapter 2.

2. Language specific constraints are mentioned by Fant (1973:173) as well:
    "one set of sequential constraints is expressible as coarticulation rules
    which may be both universal and language-specific."

Modifications and extensions of the **SPE** framework

In this chapter I propose some modifications and extensions of the **SPE** framework. In 2.1 I will deal with phonetic features, in 2.2 with speech utterances, phonetic transcription and phonetic representation, and in 2.3 with
interferences between features in sounds. In 2.4 I give a summary of the
chapter.

2.1 PHONETIC FEATURES

In this section I will discuss phonetic features, especially their correlates,
their physical scales and the question in what respect they are universal.

According to Chomsky and Halle (cf. p.299) the definition of a phonetic
feature consists of a pair of antonymous terms as definiendum and three correlates as definiens. In 1.2.3 above we have concluded that these three correlates describe or refer to speech properties belonging to two realities: the
perceptual correlate describes or refers to aspects of the mental reality of
the speaker-hearer, while the articulatory and acoustic correlates describe or
refer to aspects of the physical reality of speech sounds.

I will argue (a) that in Chomsky and Halle's view one would expect to find
a fourth correlate; (b) but that phonetic features cannot be defined in terms
of more than two correlates.

(a) In Chomsky and Halle's view phonetic features have two physical correlates: the articulatory correlate which describes the productive aspect of the
speech event by the speaker and the acoustic correlate which describes what
the hearer receives on his eardrums, which we can consider to be the physical
receptive aspect of the speech event. To these two physical correlates
corresponds one mental correlate only: the perceptual correlate, which
describes the **receptive** aspect of the speech event by the hearer. I do not
understand why Chomsky and Halle do not add a second mental correlate which
describes the **productive** aspect of the speech event by the speaker. Mental
correlates which concern the productive aspect of the speech event should
describe what in **SPE** is called the "set of instructions to the physical articulatory system" (p.65). The view one would expect to find in **SPE** is
represented in fig. 2-1. By not adding a second mental correlate to the perceptual correlate, Chomsky and Halle overstress the role of the receptive

aspect of speech, the position of the hearer. However, I think that phonetic
features - being part of a transformational-generative grammar - are to be
viewed as neutral as to production and perception, as required in Chomsky
(1965:9), and that the distinction production-perception in fig. 2-1 should
not be relevant in feature definitions.

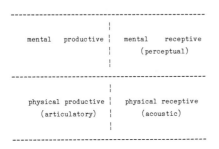

Fig. 2-1. Four correlates of a phonetic feature which describe or refer to
four aspects of the speech event. Three of the four correlates are proposed by
Chomsky and Halle (1968). Only the "mental productive" correlate is absent.

(b) I do not agree with Chomsky and Halle's view that phonetic features can
be defined in terms of a perceptual (i.e. a mental) correlate.

First, phoneticians and phonologists never have provided phonetic features
defined in terms of mental correlates. Though Chomsky and Halle **claim** that
phonetic features have a perceptual correlate, no such correlates are found in
SPE (cf. 1.2.3 above). Phoneticians and phonologists sometimes discuss mental,
especially perceptual aspects of speech, but they never provide examples of
mental correlates of phonetic features, see, for instance, Jakobson et al.
(1952).[1] A phonetician like Ladefoged (1975: Chapter 12) defines phonetic
features, especially those he calls "prime features", in terms of (articulatory or acoustic) physical scales. And phonologists like Kenstowicz and Kisseberth (1979:9) observe that "in an adequate phonetic theory each sound type
would be defined in both acoustic and articulatory terms". The set of parameters used by Anderson (1974:8) is "almost exclusively articulatory in definition", and appears never to be mental.

Second, I think there is a good reason why mental correlates of phonetic
features are never provided. Articulatory properties described by the articulatory correlate can be stated in terms of articulators; and acoustic properties described by the acoustic correlate can be stated in terms of formants.
Both articulators and formants are observable and measurable entities in physical reality. However, mental aspects of speech are not directly observable.
And there is no framework in terms of which we can state the aspects of speech

to be described by mental correlates. It is doubtful whether a perceptual framework can be developed comparable to the articulatory and acoustic frameworks. For the moment, attempts to provide mental correlates are doomed to fail.

Therefore, phonetic features cannot be defined in other terms than those of physical correlates.

In **SPE** (p.299): "Each feature is a physical scale defined by two points, which are designated by antonymous adjectives: high-nonhigh, voiced-nonvoiced (voiceless), tense-nontense (lax)." Since phonetic features have physical correlates, I think that physical scales are to be viewed in relation to these correlates. I take it that Chomsky and Halle mention only one physical scale per feature for practical reasons, since from the discussion earlier in this section it appears that a phonetic feature has two physical correlates - an articulatory and an acoustic correlate - which would correspond to two physical scales: an articulatory scale and an acoustic scale. On the articulatory scales positions of articulators or groups of articulators (like the tongue, the lips, the velum) are stated; on the acoustic scales, we will find formant frequencies. In principle, articulatory scales should be convertible into acoustic scales and v.v., though this may not always be an easy task.

I propose that the scales should be designed in such a way that they need not describe real size measures of acoustic properties of the speech utterances or of the articulatory movements which produce them. Rather I take over the proposal of Ladefoged (1975 chapter 12), which may be viewed as a more sophisticated variant of Jespersen's "analphabetisches Zeichensystem" (1913:9). In Ladefoged's proposal the physical scale of a phonetic feature is determined for each (normal) speaker in a speaker-independent way. Its maximal range for a speaker - whatever the dimensions of his vocal tract - is always 100%. By using percentages we avoid absolute dimensions.

In 2.3 below I will argue that physical scales should include sound properties and that feature definitions may have more than one physical scale. In chapter 6 I will propose a further modification: the substitution of physical scales by physical diagrams.

Phonetic features concern universal and language-specific aspects of the speech process. Chomsky and Halle's view can be inferred from the following quotations (cf. section 1.1 above): "Each feature is a physical scale defined by two points, which are designated by antonymous adjectives: high-nonhigh, voiced- nonvoiced (voiceless), tense-nontense (lax)." (p.299). "The phonetic features ... may ... assume numerous coefficients, as determined by the rules of the phonological component." (p.297).

I infer from these quotations that in Chomsky and Halle's view the physical scale as such is what makes a phonetic feature universal; that the number of coefficients - one, two or more - on the scale is language-specific; and that

the position of these coefficients on the physical scale is language-specific
as well. The universal and language-specific aspects of phonetic features are
represented in fig. 2-2.[2]

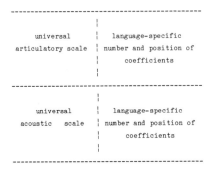

```
-----------------------------------------------
                       |
     universal         | language-specific
  articulatory scale   | number and position of
                       |      coefficients
                       |
-----------------------------------------------
                       |
     universal         | language-specific
   acoustic   scale    | number and position of
                       |      coefficients
                       |
-----------------------------------------------
```

Fig. 2-2. Four aspects of the speech event represented in phonetic features.
The aspects described are two physical correlates , i.e. two physical scales,
which are universal, and the number and position of the coefficients on the
scales, which are language-specific.

As far as phonetic features are universal, they may be said to be the physical reflexes of the FACULTE DE LANGAGE of the speaker-hearers. Consequently,
the list of phonetic features accepted for all languages is universal, but the
number of their coefficients and the position of the coefficients on the physical scales may be different per language. A feature may be either "+" or "-"
in one language, binary in another, multivalued in a third language, cf. **SPE**
p.164, note 1.

I will propose the following condition on feature definitions:

A feature is well-defined when its physical (i.e. articulatory or acoustic)
scales have been chosen in such a way that the relation between any coefficient on the scale and its mental reflex is constant.

For instance, a coefficient expressed as 100 on a physical scale of the
feature NASAL should be perceived as equally nasal under as many different
conditions as possible. This condition is not to be fulfilled entirely, as I
will argue in 2.3 below.

As the number of coefficients on physical scales of phonetic features is
language-specific, we need a convention which serves to convert the "+" and
"-" values at the level of phonological representation (see (2) in 1.1 above)
into the one, two or more coefficients on their physical scales. Chomsky and
Halle (1968) refer to this problem twice, without solving it definitely.
Their observations are paraphrased in (1) and (2):

(1) The "-" of a phonetic feature serves as a "cover symbol" for the coefficient(s) closest to the negative point of the physical scale; the "+" as a "cover symbol" for the remaining coefficient(s) (p.166 note 3).

(2) The "-" of a phonetic feature has the value of only one, viz. the minimal coefficient; the "+" serves as a "cover symbol" for all other coefficients, which are to be expressed as integers (p.66).

Chomsky and Halle (1968:66) introduce (2) as a convention related to one specific feature: STRESS. Observation (1) includes convention (2), since it leaves open all possibilities: it defines rather the possible set of conventions. The number of coefficients closest to the negative point of the physical scale may be one or more, just as the number of the remaining coefficients. In both (1) and (2): a "-" refers to a set of coefficients, the "+" to the complementary set. There is no overlap.

Although Chomsky and Halle (1968:66) recognize the need of conventions such as (2), they say that they have not explored the consequences of convention (2), which is used "merely as a specific one for the present purposes".[3] As Chomsky and Halle mention that the number of coefficients is "determined by the rules of the phonological component" (p.297), and the rules of the phonological components in different languages are not the same, it follows that for every one feature in every one language we may need a different convention.

This is, I think, also the point of view adopted by Anderson (1974:9):

(3) "We will assume that features have binary values, but that underlying these values is a specification of each parameter in more detailed terms, which is given on a continuous real-valued scale which we will arbitrarily assume to vary between 0 and 1. This scale is interpreted in such a way that values below some given point are interpreted as -F, while higher values are interpreted as +F. The dividing point for a given feature may well vary from language to language, and language-particular rules may well affect the detail values as well as the binary values of features."

Since the dividing point for a given feature may well vary from language to language, Anderson proposes, in fact, a general principle as to conventions which convert coefficients ("values") at the binary level into coefficients at less abstract levels. In addition, the "continuous real-valued scale" will be different from feature to feature. Therefore, I infer that in Anderson's opinion conventions may differ from language to language and from feature to feature.

In this section I have proposed that a phonetic feature definition consist of a pair of antonymous adjectives as definiendum and of only two physical correlates: an articulatory and an acoustic, but no perceptual correlate. These correlates should be considered to be neutral as to production and perception. They are related to universal physical (articulatory and acoustic) scales. The number of the coefficients (values) on the scales is language-dependent. Phonologies of specific languages should contain a set of conventions interpreting the coefficients of the features used as "+" or as "-".

2.2 UTTERANCES, PHONETIC TRANSCRIPTIONS AND PHONETIC REPRESENTATIONS

In this section I will suggest some modifications and additions which concern speech utterances, phonetic transcriptions and phonetic representations in **SPE**.

1. Speech utterances.
Not all aspects of speech utterances have to be described or represented in phonetic representations or phonetic transcriptions. We need procedures for data reducing. By means of these procedures we abstract from (accidental and non-accidental) individual speech variations, among which voice pitch and quality, the vocal manifestations of the sex of the speaker, also from loudness of the voice, the movement of most of the facial muscles, the exact density of the transmitting medium, from real time dimensions and utterance rate (cf. Chomsky and Halle 1968:295 and Anderson 1974:5, 7).

Current methods of abstraction are those of taking averages over groups of sounds and/or groups of normal speakers, or considering subjects as prototypical. When speaking of speech utterances, I will often take it for granted that some or all of the above mentioned abstractions have been carried out.

Speech utterances function in phonology in two ways: as phonetic transcriptions and as results of phonetic experiments. Specific physical and mental (especially perceptual) properties of speech utterances are determined by means of phonetic experiments. I will use the expression "speech sound or utterance" as short for "the acoustic reality of a speech sound or utterance" or "the articulatory movements by which the speech sound or utterance is produced".

As the speech level to be described in phonology I would propose the level of careful pronunciation. This level usually comes closer to what speakers know about their language than the more casual levels with their neutralizations and contrast reductions. More casual levels can usually be derived easily from the level of careful pronunciation, but not vice versa, cf. Hooper (1976:111-112). Although Chomsky and Halle do not state it explicitly, the speech level described in **SPE** for American English (AmEng) is that of careful pronunciation as well.

2. Phonetic transcriptions.
Phonetic transcriptions are offered in terms of systems of conventions of which the I.P.A. probably is the best known. They are usually noted between

[...].

The role of phonetic transcriptions is to test phonetic representations. This implies that the transcription system should be convertible into the feature- and coefficient-system used in phonetic representation.

Since the role of phonetic transcriptions is to test phonetic representation, the former and the latter should in many respects satisfy the same requirements. They only differ in the way they are produced: phonetic representations are the output of generative grammar, whereas phonetic transcriptions are the product of the activity of transcribers. I propose that these transcribers need not be native speakers of the languages to be transcribed. This is not in agreement with **SPE** p.26, but in conformity with existing practice.[4] In existing practice, but not in **SPE** (cf. p. 293), phonetic transcriptions are a device for recording facts observed in actual utterances, which does not imply that all facts should be recorded, as we have seen above in 1. In addition, phonetic transcriptions need not contain universal phonetic constraints, since, as we have seen in 1.1 above, phonetic representations do not either.

As phonetic transcription is a device for recording relevant facts observed in actual utterances, it should not include any elements which are not observable in the utterances they describe, and include all the systematically present elements in the utterances they describe, independently of the question whether native speakers are aware of them. Phonetic transcription should reflect, I think, what in Anderson (1974:8) is called: "independent variables in linguistic structures" or in Chomsky and Halle (1968:298): "independently controllable aspects of the speech event". These variables or aspects are, I think, physical in nature and concern both physical and mental properties of speech.

Although phonetic transcriptions serve to test phonetic representations, they are not primary data: they are produced by transcribers by means of an untransparent process. If we could be sure that transcribers never made mistakes and that the system of conventions they use were adequate, we could rely on their transcriptions. Since this is not the case, we need means to test them against the properties of the speech utterances they describe by means of phonetic experiments. These experiments concern physical properties of speech sounds and judgements of speaker-hearers in perceptual tests. It would be attractive to substitute phonetic transcription by results of phonetic experiments. But up till now, phoneticians and phonologists have not succeeded in substituting phonetic transcriptions completely by results of phonetic experiments.

3. Phonetic representations. Almost everything observed with respect to phonetic transcriptions applies to phonetic representations as well. I add two comments which especially concern phonetic representation. The first regards

the question what mental aspects of speech should be included into it. The second the problem that, in fact, two kinds of phonetic representations can be distinguished in phonological studies.

According to Chomsky and Halle (a) Speaker-hearers may be aware of a sound distinction not present in the physical reality of speech utterances of their language. For instance, Chomsky and Halle (1968:44, 294) claim that speaker-hearers of AmEng are aware of differences in stress contours which are not present in the physical signal. (b) Speaker-hearers may not be aware of a sound distinction present in the physical reality of speech utterances of their language. Chomsky and Halle (1968:294) do not provide an example of this case. Labov (1971:431-2) gives a good example, when reporting that speakers of the British English dialect of Norwich are not aware of the sound difference they produce between [tUu̯<] "too" and [tUʋ̯] "toe".

Thus, in **SPE** phonetic representations should contain what the speaker-hearers are aware of, not what is present or absent in the physical signal.

I cannot agree with this decision of Chomsky and Halle, since it makes their position unfalsifiable. I do not understand how speakers could perceive sound differences which are not present in the physical speech signal and which they, consequently, never produce. And I do not understand either why we should ignore in phonetic transcription the fact that speakers have at their disposal a mental speech production rule they use to produce a specific sound difference, only because they are not aware of it. There is no reason to assume that such sound differences are present in the mental reality of the speaker.

In addition, Chomsky and Halle's view is contrary to the usual conception of phonetic transcription in this respect, see 2.1 above and the transcription by Labov above.

Therefore, I see no reason why phonetic representations should contain physically non-existing sound differences which speaker-hearers are aware of, and should not contain physical sound differences, because speaker-hearers are not aware of them.

In some studies in generative phonology we can distinguish in fact two levels of phonetic representation. As we have seen in 1.1 above, features in phonetic representations are, in principle, multivalued. Usually, however, Chomsky and Halle (1968:164, note 1) provide binary phonetic representations: "Often we restrict ourselves to two positions along a phonetic scale, in which case we may use the symbols + and - instead of integers to indicate phonetic values." See also, for instance, Schane (1973:95-6) and Kenstowicz and Kisseberth (1979:253f).

Anderson (1974:10) is the only one who "presume(s) the reality of both sorts of phonetic representation in linguistic description" quite explicitly, i.e. a binary level and a multivalued level of phonetic representation.

Following Anderson, I would suggest that the relation between the two levels be determined by rules. These rules may be called language-specific phonetic constraints, low level phonological rules or "numeric detail rules" (Anderson). The "+" and "-" specifications at the binary level should be interpreted by means of language- and feature-specific interpretation conventions, see 2.1 above. In the present study I am specially interested in the multivalued level of phonetic representation. At this level phonetic representations are comparable across languages, see Anderson (1974:8-10) and Schane (1973:96).[5]

When Chomsky and Halle (1968:297) claim that utterances are comparable across languages at the level of phonetic representation, they refer, I think, to this multivalued level as well. Although the only respect in which sounds cannot be compared concerns, as Chomsky and Halle (p. 298) observe, that of "universal free variation", we will certainly need multivalued specifications to describe all the other aspects. However, if the preceding represents Chomsky and Halle's view indeed, I do not understand why they exclude from phonetic representation properties of speech which concern the articulation base (p. 295, cf. 1.1 above).

In summary, I adopt the following position. As in **SPE,** universal properties of speech utterances should not occur in phonetic representation; they should be captured in universal phonetic constraints. Not in agreement with **SPE,** I propose that **all** language-specific properties of speech utterances should be represented in multivalued phonetic representation to be distinguished from binary phonetic representation. The interpretation of binary phonetic representations in terms of the multivalued phonetic representations and vice versa should be captured in terms of language-specific interpretation conventions and low level phonological rules. These rules should capture properties of speech within and between sounds. Physical scales provide a graphic representation of both universal phonetic constraints and language-specific coefficients referred to in the low level phonological rules. Phonetic transcriptions should be stated in terms which are convertible into multivalued specifications as well.

2.3 INTERFERENCES BETWEEN FEATURE COEFFICIENTS IN SOUNDS

Feature definitions define speech properties which never occur in isolation. These speech properties are part of speech utterances of minimally one sound. The constellations of feature coefficients in the sounds interfere with each other. A vowel which is [+high] cannot be [+low] in the **SPE** framework (p. 305), but more subtle interferences occur which have not been mentioned.

The (successions of) sounds, or speech utterances, are described by means of (sequences of) symbols in phonetic transcription or (sequences of) segments in phonetic representation. Even multivalued phonetic transcriptions and representations do not contain all information on the speech utterance - apart from (accidental and non-accidental) individual speech variations (see 2.2 above) -, since universal phonetic constraints - the function of which it was to smooth succeeding segments in phonetic representation, see 1.1 above - are not included. I would add that they do not contain all information on interferences of feature coefficients in segments either.

I propose that this latter information will be captured by universal phonetic constraints as well. This implies an extension of the function of these constraints. They will function not only between segments but also within them.

In addition, I propose that the information captured in universal phonetic constraints be graphically represented in physical scales. The set of universal physical scales, or the set of universal phonetic constraints, form the universal sound component of generative phonology.

In 2.1 I have proposed a condition on feature definitions:

A feature is well defined, when its physical (articulatory or acoustic) scale has been chosen in such a way that the relation between any coefficient on the scale and its mental reflex is constant.

I have added that this condition cannot be fulfilled entirely. The reason is that coefficients on physical scales may have different mental reflexes depending on the sounds, environments and languages in which they occur; or, conversely, that different coefficients on a physical scale may be needed in order to obtain the same mental reflexes.

Below I will make an inventory of the factors which make it impossible that the condition is entirely fulfilled. These factors can be captured in universal physical scales or universal phonetic constraints. Scales and constraints provide the restrictions on the possible sounds in human language. They form the list of the inevitable interferences within and between sounds. I will distinguish three kinds of interferences to be captured by universal phonetic constraints or universal physical scales.

1. Inconsistencies between physical properties and mental reflexes of coefficients of a feature relatable to the number and position of coefficients on the physical scale of the feature.

2. Inconsistencies between physical properties and mental reflexes of feature coefficients caused by other feature coefficients of the same sound.

3. Inconsistencies between physical properties and mental reflexes of feature coefficients relatable to adjacent sounds.

1. Inconsistencies between physical properties and mental reflexes of coefficients of a feature relatable to the number and position of coefficients on

the physical scale of the feature.

When the same speech sounds are perceived differently with respect to a specific feature by speaker-hearers of various languages, this may be due to the number and position of coefficients on the physical scale which the feature may have. When a feature can have only one coefficient in the vowels of language A and two in the vowels of language B, it is plausible that the perceptual properties of the coefficients in the vowels of the two languages may be different. The functioning of one and not two coefficients in the vowels of language A - and of two and not one coefficient in the vowels of language B - will find a reflex in the perceptual results.

When Russian subjects do not perceive the nasality of French nasal vowels, but French subjects do (cf. Bondarko 1979), this may be due to differences in number and position of the coefficients of the feature NASAL in the two languages. In this way some of the **language-specific** awareness which speakers have of sound differences may be accounted for in **universal** phonetic constraints. The total perceptual potentialities of the physical scale of a phonetic feature as such remain constant, whereas the language-specific perceptual differences would depend on the number and position of the coefficients in that language and the sounds in which they occur. This point will not be developed further in the present study.

2. Inconsistencies between physical properties and mental reflexes of feature coefficients caused by other feature coefficients of the same sound. I think we should distinguish two cases.

(a) We will see that nasal consonants and nasal vowels need in fact different physical scales. Groups of sounds may need different physical scales for one and the same feature. Physical scales capture properties of features as they are realized in various groups of sounds. Correlates of phonetic features may be related to several physical scales. Universal phonetic constraints state the differences between the scales.

(b) For an illustration of this point, I refer to the results of a series of experiments reported in Lindblom et al. (1977). In this study a method is proposed to relate acoustic (physical) properties and perceptual (mental) reflexes of vowel quality differences, which concern the features HIGH, LOW and BACK. The method enables us to predict how quality differences between vowel stimuli will be perceived on the basis of their spectral (= acoustic) characteristics. One of the conclusions we can draw from the results of the experiments is: the more a vowel is nasal, the less well perceived is its vowel quality in terms of the features HIGH, LOW and BACK. If we assume that the physical scales of the features HIGH, LOW and BACK are the same under the different experimental conditions - which is certainly the case in at least one experiment discussed in Lindblom et al. - we have to conclude that physical properties and mental reflexes of the features HIGH, LOW and BACK interfere with the coefficients of the feature NASAL.

Since the coefficients of the features HIGH, LOW, and BACK remain physically constant, it follows that they do not have a constant mental (viz. perceptual) reflex. This perceptual difference would be relatable to a specific context, viz. another feature coefficient of the same sound. Until now I have assumed that physical scale and perceptual (mental) reflex have a constant relation (apart from the case discussed above). Here we see that the same physical scale may correspond with two perceptual scales, the one more limited than the other.

3. Inconsistencies between physical properties and mental reflexes of feature coefficients relatable to adjacent sounds.

Speech utterances have a (quasi-)continuous character. This (quasi-) continuous character can be viewed as the result of a smoothing process. Articulators cannot adopt their positions in the successive sounds without transitions. Therefore, between successive sounds coarticulation or coproduction is inevitable.

As a consequence, a symbol in one context of a phonetic transcription may describe a class of sounds (physical entities) different from the class of sounds (physical entities) described by the same symbol in another context (cf. Chomsky and Halle 1968:164 note). This is the same as saying that the symbols have the same coefficients in the two contexts, which refer to the same physical state of affairs, and that the physical differences left in the speech utterance are accounted for by universal phonetic constraints. The relation between these aspects of successive sounds can be represented again in terms of succeeding physical scales.

Universal phonetic constraints interact with language- specific low level phonological rules (or, as is stated in **SPE**, with phonological rules, see Chomsky and Halle 1968:293). The universal constraints capture the inevitable coarticulation (or coproduction) between sounds. They may be viewed as minimal coarticulation (coproduction) rules. A language-specific low level rule is more or less an "exaggeration" of the corresponding universal phonetic constraint. The complete set of universal phonetic constraints operating between sounds determines the possible set of language-specific coarticulation (or coproduction) rules.

In this section I have discussed the problem of the interference between feature coefficients and sounds.

Low level phonological rules should introduce the number of possible coefficients for a feature in a language.

Since coefficients of phonetic features do not occur in isolation, we need physical scales or universal phonetic constraints in order to capture the interferences between feature coefficients within and between sounds.

Universal phonetic constraints are of three kinds. The same feature may have different numbers and positions on the physical scales of its coefficients in the sounds of a language. The mental reflex (perceptibility) of feature coefficients in a sound may be influenced by other feature coefficients within the same sound or by feature coefficients of adjacent sounds.

The three kinds of universal phonetic constraints or physical scales cannot capture all differences in awareness of sound distinctions. Cases as the one discussed in Labov (1971) (see 2.2 above) will probably always stay exceptional.

2.4. SUMMARY

In the preceding sections I have proposed the outline of a framework of phonology which is more empirical and further articulated than that in Chomsky and Halle (1968). This refinement is far from complete but sufficient to serve as a framework for the rest of this study.[6] In the terms of this framework - as much in line with that of Chomsky and Halle as possible - a research programme can be carried out.

To propose elements for a phonological framework is one thing, to develop its structure quite another. The following chapters - dealing with one feature only - are no more than the beginning of the realisation of this research programme.

In summary, the framework I propose is: Phonetic features have two physical correlates: acoustic and articulatory. They have no perceptual correlate. The physical correlates are stated in terms independent of sounds. The correlates are related to physical scales which incorporate sound properties.

There are two kinds of phonetic representation: binary and multivalued. The number and position of coefficients on a physical scale at the multivalued level of phonetic representation may be different per language and per feature. For any language a convention for the interpretation of the binary coefficients on the physical scales of each of the features is necessary. The number of coefficients may be considerable after the application of the language-specific low level rules to phonetic representations. These low level phonological rules are usually not provided in phonological studies.

The phonological component of a generative grammar should contain a sound component, besides its feature component. The physical scales or the universal phonetic constraints form the sound component of phonology. This sound component is necessary to relate feature definitions, speech utterances, phonetic transcriptions and phonetic representations. In chapter 6 I will argue that the physical scales have to be substituted by physical diagrams.

Phonetic representations should be tested against phonetic transcriptions.

These phonetic transcriptions may be tested against properties of speech utterances determined in phonetic experiments and against judgements of speaker-hearers in perceptual experiments. Before physical properties of speech utterances can be used, we should abstract from their non- linguistic properties.

NOTES TO CHAPTER 2

1. Under the heading "Perception" which Jakobson et al. (1952) provide for each feature, they mention either acoustic properties or results of perceptual experiments, but do not give a description of the perceptual correlate of a phonetic feature.

2. Other distinctions than those in fig. 2-1 and 2-2 can be made of course, such as the one in Jakobson et al. (1952:12) between aural and perceptual. The distinctions made above are the only ones relevant in the present study.

3. Since Chomsky and Halle (1968) do not propose a general convention, I have been obliged to introduce a "?" in diagram (2) of section 1.2 above. Should convention (2) apply in the case of the feature NASAL, the "?" in the diagram could be replaced by a "+".

4. I do not agree with Malécot and Metz (1972:196) when they note between /.../ "the underlying, or 'deep' forms, that is to say, the **intention of the speaker.**" Their view would imply that their transcription of French **maintenant** as "[mɛ̃nã]" on page 198 has not been intended by the speaker, which throws a curious light on what speakers intend to do as compared with what they do.

5. Instead of languages we may read, I think, dialects, sociolects, different stylistic levels of a language and the like.

6. One of the problems I have left out of consideration is the one of the so-called "cover features" (cf. Anderson 1974, Appendix), and "secondary-order features" (cf. Lass 1976:186- 97), i.e "features to be defined ... in terms of other features" (Ladefoged 1974:109). Another is the problem of the relation between phonetic features and prime features (cf. Ladefoged 1975 chapter 12).

CHAPTER 3

The feature NASAL

This chapter introduces the phonetic feature NASAL. Existing definitions of the feature are discussed in 3.1, the number and position of the coefficients on its physical scale in 3.2. In 3.3 a survey of the problems to be dealt with and an outline of the rest of this study is given, while in 3.4 the problems are listed which stay outside its scope.

3.1 DEFINITIONS OF THE FEATURE NASAL

The definitions of the feature NASAL as proposed in phonological and phonetic studies seem to show only superficial variations. This holds not only for the definitions given within the framework of generative phonology but also for the definitions given in earlier studies. Below, six definitions are presented which give some insight into the nature of the variations which occur. The first three definitions come from work in generative phonology.

In **SPE** the feature NASAL is defined as follows:

(1) "Nasal sounds are produced with a lowered velum which allows the air to escape through the nose; nonnasal sounds are produced with raised velum so that the air from the lungs can escape only through the mouth" (Chomsky and Halle 1968:316).

In Anderson (1974:301) a slightly different definition is given:

(2) "Nasal sounds are made with lowered velum, and consequent open passage through the nose. These include the usual nasal sonorants, nasalized glides, spirants and vowels, and prenasalized and postnasalized stops".[1]

Bibeau (1975:37) has a language-specific definition (the language in question is a dialect of French which has three instead of four nasal vowels and three nasal consonants):

(3) "Un abaissement du voile du palais permet à l'air de passer par les voies nasales dans le cas des voyelles ɛ̃, ã, ɔ̃ et des consonnes m, n, ɲ. Elles sont donc [+nas], alors que les autres sont [-nas]."

Going back in time we find in Jespersen (1913:57) that:

(4) "Einen Laut mit geoeffneter Nasenpassage zu sprechen nennt man ihn nasalieren";

in Paris (1898:316, note 1) - a study which has had considerable influence on
publications about the origin of vowel nasality in French - that:
(5) for the production of a nasal sound it is necessary to "abaisser le voile
du palais", so that "l'air passe par les fosses nasales".
Finally a definition from ancient Indian Grammar (quoted from Allen
(1953:39)):
(6) "Nasality is produced by opening the nasal cavity."
Considering these definitions and many others[2], it seems that the parameter
NASAL has not been the subject of revolutionary changes during the last two
millennia.

Before presenting some comments on these definitions, I want to introduce
the terminology I will use in this study in a definition that is as much as
possible in agreement with the preceding ones:
(7) Nasal sounds are produced with nose coupling; oral sounds are produced
without nose coupling.
I define nose coupling as:
(8) The nose coupling N is the opening in mm^2 of the nasal port measured in a
cross-section perpendicular to the airstream at the point of the greatest constriction between the velum and the pharyngeal wall.
Instead of "nasal port" the expressions "velopharyngeal passage", "nasal passage" or "nasopharyngeal passage" are used as well. Instead of "opening of the
nasal port" we find also "velic opening". "Velic" in the present study is
synonym with "of the velum"; "velar" refers to the area of the soft palate:
$[k]$ and $[\eta]$ are velar sounds.

If there is an opening in the nasal port, there is nose coupling. Nose coupling can be expressed either relatively: a sound may be produced with a great
or small degree of nose coupling; or absolutely: a sound may be produced by a
speaker with a specific amount of nose coupling.

Besides "nose coupling" I will use expressions such as "surface of the area
of nose coupling", "area of nose coupling", "amount of nose coupling", "degree
of nose coupling", "cross-section in the nasopharynx", and I will abbreviate
all of them as "N". The expression "nose coupling" is the equivalent of "nasal
coupling" found in House and Stevens (1956). House and Stevens (1956) use nose
coupling as a measure for experiments with their model of the human vocal
tract.

"Nose coupling" replaces the expressions "lowered velum", "abaissement du
voile du palais" or "abaisser le voile du palais" in (1), (2), (3) and (5)
above, as well as "open passage", "mit geoeffneter Nasenpassage", "l'air passe
par les fosses nasales" or "by opening the nasal cavity" in (3), (4), (5) and
(6). The latter series of expressions is slightly more adequate than the
former series: the lowering of the velum does not necessarily imply the opening of the nasal port. In addition, nose coupling may be produced by other
movements than that of the lowering of the velum. This may be the reason why

Anderson and Paris mention the opening of the nasal port and the passage of the air through the nose besides the lowering of the velum. This point will be further discussed in chapter 8.

The use of the term "air" in (1) and (5) may give rise to the wrong interpretations. I assume that what is really meant is "sound waves", "sound pressure", "air vibrant" (cf. (3) above) and the like, expressions which rule out the interpretation that it might be the air as such which makes a sound nasal. This point was made long ago. See for instance Eijkman (1934:27) or McDonald and Baker (1951:12). Moreover, nasal sounds may be produced without air coming out of the nose through the nostrils. The nasal port may be blocked "due to the swelling of the soft tissue during a cold" (Fant 1960:139).[3] Feature definitions must contain only indispensable elements, and references to the vibrating air in the vocal tract in the definition of the feature NASAL do not belong to these.

In definition (2) reference is made to a classification of sounds in terms of "nasal", "nasalized, "prenasalized" and "postnasalized". Prenasalized and postnasalized sounds will not be dealt with in this study (see 3.4 below) and I do not make a terminological distinction between nasal sounds and nasalized sounds.[4]

The majority of the definitions (1) to (6) state what is nasal or oral, and do not explicitly state what is nonnasal. Chomsky and Halle define both. As we have seen in chapter 2, for them (1968:299): "Each feature is a physical scale defined by two points, which are designated by antonymous adjectives", in our case nasal and nonnasal. Chomsky and Halle do not use the term "oral".

The definitions (1) to (6) are articulatory definitions. Acoustic definitions are rarely provided in the literature, Jakobson et al. (1952:39-40) being the only ones who give an acoustic characterization. Yet quite a lot of research has been done as to the acoustic properties of the parameter of nasality. I will not propose an acoustic correlate of the feature NASAL either, because it is not completely clear to me which acoustic properties are relevant for the perception of nasality. Phoneticians present acoustic properties in terms of formants, antiformants, or formant shifts and/or formant reductions. The results they have obtained are not uniform however, although findings often tell us e.g. that for all nasal sounds the sound energy is concentrated in the lower parts of the sound spectrum, and that in the case of nasal vowels the intensity of the first formant is reduced. Yet Debrock (1974) signalizes extreme differences among three French speaking males who produce French nasal vowels. Schwartz (1971) even proposes to reject the term **nasality** (p.803) after a discussion of "four of the primary acoustic features that have been found to be associated with the nasalization of vowels" (p. 798). Fant (1960:149), too, points out a major difficulty of the study of nasal vowels when he observes:

(9) "the acoustic characteristics vary both with speaker and with the particular sound upon which the nasalization is superimposed and with the type and
degree of nasal coupling".

It is, therefore, not surprising that until now no satisfactory answer has
been proposed to the question on what formant properties the hearer bases his
perception of vowel nasality.[5]

Another reason why I will not focus on acoustics is because I think that
the nasality of nasal vowels is often perceived as such not because it is physically present as a class of specific formant configurations, but as a CHANGE
in formant structure from an oral configuration to a configuration in which a
high degree of nose coupling occurs. In other words, it is the contrast
between the part produced with no or a low amount of nose coupling and the
following part produced with more nose coupling which contributes highly to
the perception of a nasal vowel as nasal. This change or contrast, however, is
often overlooked as a possible cue for the perception of nasality.

Summarizing we can say that existing definitions of the phonetic feature
NASAL are usually given in articulatory terms, and that they are not very different from each other. Not surprisingly, therefore, Ladefoged (1979:45, cf.
41-2) considers nasality to be one of the less problematic articulatory parameters: "The degree of velic opening is a well known parameter, and needs no
further comment here".

However, as we will see in chapter 4, there is good reason to modify the
existing definitions of the feature NASAL.

3.2 COEFFICIENTS ON THE PHYSICAL SCALE

All seven definitions of the feature NASAL in 3.1 above are expressed in terms
which can easily be related to physical, viz. articulatory, scales. At one end
of the scale the velum is lowered, the nasal port is open or the amount of
nose coupling is greatest. At the other end the velum is raised, the nasal
port is closed or the amount of nose coupling is zero.

The two extreme coefficients are not the only ones possible on the scale.
Several phonologists and phoneticians mention more than two coefficients on
the articulatory scale of the feature NASAL and some even assign to them a
precise position.

Two phoneticians belong to the latter group: Jespersen and Ladefoged.
Jespersen (1913:55-65) uses a delta followed by the integers 0, 1, 2 or 3 to
indicate the positions of the velum. Delta 0 refers to the position "velum
high" or "nasal port closed"; delta 3 to "velum lowest" or "nasal port far
open". Jespersen's system can easily be converted into the percentage scale
which I have adopted in this study, see 2.1 above. I have reproduced
Jespersen's sound classification below. The delta value is followed by my

corresponding percentage (between parentheses) and by his characterisation of the type of sounds to which it applies.

(10)

0	(0)	Sounds produced with closed nasal port
1	(33)	1. Sometimes [ə] at the end of words
		2. Tendency in the vowel [a]
		3. The sounds of speakers who "speak through the nose"
2	(67)	1. Nasal consonants
		2. Some semivowels in various languages
		3. Nasal vowels in Portuguese and German dialects
3	(100)	Nasal vowels in French

Ladefoged (1975:270-1) has suggested physical scales for sounds of (American?) English. His scale for the feature NASAL has to be interpreted as: the higher the percentage, the lower the soft palate (velum). It looks as follows (left the percentage; right the type of sounds):

(11)

0	[p, t, k, ...], [i, æ , ɔ , o, ...]
5	[ae, h]
100	[m, n]

Ladefoged does not include in his list vowels adjacent to a nasal consonant. So we do not know the percentage he would assign to vowels in that position, though we may guess that it would be higher than 5 and lower than 100. If this guess is right, both Jespersen and Ladefoged would recognize four coefficients on the nasal scale, i.e. four degrees of nasality.

However, scales (10) and (11) do not provide the same classification. The most striking difference is that in (10) the velum is not lowest (or the nasal port is not far open) for nasal consonants, whereas in (11) it is. The [a] in (10) and the [æ] in (11) may not illustrate the same degree of nasalization either. And we may wonder whether Ladefoged would make a distinction between French and Portuguese (or German) nasal vowels. The only clear correspondence between (10) and (11) concerns the nonnasal sounds.

Using a different notational system, viz. "a continuous real-valued scale which we will arbitrarily assume to vary between 0 and 1", Anderson (1974:9-10) discusses the problem of the number of coefficients rather explicitly with

respect to the Breton dialect of Plougrescant: "We ... have at least the following three values (where the precise values, on a hypothetical scale, are
irrelevant; only the relative values matter): [0nasal] (for oral vowels next
to oral consonants); [.3nasal] (say) for oral vowels next to a nasal consonant; and [.7nasal] for distinctively nasal vowels." This gives the following classification (the percentages left are relative values only):

(12)

0	Oral vowels next to oral consonants
30	Oral vowels next to a nasal consonant
70	Distinctively nasal vowels

Thus, according to Anderson the feature NASAL may receive (at least) three
specifications for vowels at the level of phonetic representation. His classification suggests that sounds, viz. nasal consonants, may be more than 70%
nasal. If this is right, Anderson would accept four degrees of nasality within
the same language.[6] This is not sure, however, and his classification may be
viewed as being drawn from that of Jespersen, if vowel nasality in the Breton
of Plougrescant is of the same kind as that of Jespersen's Portuguese and German nasal vowels.

We have seen already (in 1.1 above) that it appears from the examples in
Chomsky and Halle (1968:165) that they assign more than two coefficients to
the feature NASAL in phonetic representations. I quote the relevant part of
their examples:

(13)   (a) inn   (b) algebra
         i n   ae l g e b r ae

nasal   2 +   - - - - - - -

As the degree of nasalization of the [ɛ] is partial (see Chomsky and Halle
1968:165), I take it that the degree of nasalization of the [n] is complete
and that of the [-nas] sounds is zero or less than partial. It follows that
Chomsky and Halle recognize at least three coefficients for the feature
NASAL.[7]

The view that the feature NASAL is multivalued is not generally accepted.
Phonologists often seem to implicitly adopt a binary position. In his "status
report" on phonology, Basbøll (1979:122-3) is more explicit on this point than
many others. Speaking about the inventory and organization of features he

observes: "If the question of binarism is conceived of as an empirical one, the available evidence seems to suggest that some features are binary on the phonological level, e.g. nasality, and others multi-valued (...), e.g. vowel-height". The available evidence he refers to has to be formulated in terms of "surface contrasts" (ibid.), but he does not make clear what kind of surface contrasts he has in mind. We have to assume that they are different from the ones upon which Jespersen, Ladefoged, Anderson, Chomsky and Halle based their views.

To the above inventory I add a few typological remarks concerning languages which are exceptional as to nasality.

In a few languages nasality plays a marginal role, viz. has just one coefficient. Jakobson et al. (1952:40) observe: "The opposition oral vs. nasal is nearly universal in consonant patterns, with isolated exceptions such as Wichita". Ferguson (1975:176) mentions Puget Sound Salish "as a language in which nasality hardly seems to function at all".

A case of three degrees of distinctive vowel nasalization is reported in Ladefoged (1972:34-5): "In Chinantec (Merrifield 1963) there are clear contrasts between oral, lightly nasalized, and heavily nasalized vowels... These contrasts in the phonetic forms have been instrumentally verified (by William Wang and myself)." In (Palantla) Chinantec (Mexico) vowels have a three-way contrast at the level of phonetic representation in exactly the same context. This would imply that at the level of phonological representation - level at which features are specified in binary terms, see 1.1 above - we would need an ad hoc solution - for instance the introduction of a nasal consonant (as Ladefoged ibid. suggests) which never appears in phonetic representation - in order to represent vowel nasality in binary terms. Phonologists who do not accept this type of solution would be obliged to give up the binarity of phonological representation. However, I will not elaborate this point, since it falls outside the scope of this study.[8]

The above inventory of numbers and positions (or relative values) of the coefficients on the physical scale of the feature NASAL does not result in a clear picture. Differences concern both numbers and positions of coefficients, and classifications are rarely complete. Different conceptions of phonetic representation may play a part, see 2.2 above. Therefore, the following summary is tentative.

It looks as if no more than five positions have (so far) been assigned to the coefficients of the feature NASAL on its physical scale. More than three, maybe four, coefficients have never been mentioned explicitly or suggested for any language, and more than three coefficients never occur all in the same context. The number of coefficients per context is never stated to be higher than two, except in one language - Chinantec - which may have three coefficients. The two-way contrast occurs most frequently in nasal and nonnasal consonants, and also in nasal and oral vowels.

This state of affairs would make it possible to apply the following terminology to the great majority of languages:

(14) (a) Nonnasal sounds are produced without any nose coupling.
   (b) Oral sounds are produced with no nose coupling, with a
        a relatively small, or with an accidental amount of
        nose coupling.
   (c) Nasal sounds are produced with a relatively great
        amount of nose coupling.

Nonnasal and oral sounds will usually be represented as [-nas], nasal sounds as [+nas]. Nasal vowels in phonetic transcription will be noted by means of the diacritic sign [~], oral and nonnasal vowels without diacritic. For consonants there is no transcription problem.

The terminology adopted may not be satisfactory in all respects. It has the advantage to be hardly different from its traditional use; and it is sufficient to handle the problems dealt with in the present study.

3.3 SURVEY OF PROBLEMS AND OUTLINE OF CHAPTERS

Having developed the framework in chapter 1 and 2, and having presented a survey of definitions of the feature NASAL earlier in the present chapter, I shall now formulate the problems I will deal with in the rest of this study. These problems are stated as questions:

(15) Is the feature NASAL well defined, i.e. has it been chosen in such a way that the relation between the coefficients on its physical scales and their mental reflex is constant - as far as this is possible -, irrespective of the (succession of) sounds in which these coefficients occur?

(16) Can feature coefficients always be represented on one- dimensional physical scales or do we need two-dimensional physical diagrams?

(17) How many physical scales or diagrams are needed for the feature NASAL?

(18) What is the number and position of the coefficients on the physical scales or in the physical diagrams?

Among these questions, (15) is the most basic one. It will be dealt with in a special chapter: chapter 4.

The other three questions will not be dealt with in special chapters. Before answering them, I shall discuss the relevance (in chapter 5) of data obtained by means of phonetic experiments.

In chapters 6 to 8 I will make an attempt to determine the answers to the questions (16) to (18). They concern the universal phonetic constraints and their relation to the language specific low level phonological rules.

The properties of speech samples I will focus on in these chapters are:
1. The nasality of oral and nasal vowels in their successive physical phases (chapter 6).
2. Differences between oral high and low vowels and between nasal high and low vowels in various languages (chapter 7).
3. The relations between nasal consonants and both nasal and oral vowels, among which coarticulation or coproduction between nasal consonants and vowels (chapter 8).

My choice has been determined by factors such as: the available experimental results, topics frequently dealt with by phoneticians and phonologists and the implications of the problem for fundamental notions in phonology in general.

I conclude the present study with a short retrospect.

3.4 PROBLEMS OUTSIDE THE SCOPE OF THIS STUDY

There are several problems related to the phonetic feature NASAL which will only be touched upon or not be dealt with at all in this study.

A first field of problems that falls outside its scope concerns temporal contrasts and their role in perception, since there is only one experiment, as far as I know, dealing with this subject, see Delattre and Monnot (1968).

A second field which I will not deal with concerns the problem of what feature specifications should occur at levels more abstract than that of phonetic representation. The question whether a positive or negative specification of the feature NASAL in phonetic representation has been introduced by rule or was already present in the underlying forms is not relevant.

A third field concerns the features PRENASAL and POSTNASAL. These features have been proposed in order to account for the correct specifications of prenasalized and postnasalized stops. Anderson (1974 chapter 14; 1975) argues convincingly that postnasalized, prenasalized and also medio-nasalized consonants are better described in terms of the feature NASAL. For references concerning these consonants, see - besides Anderson (1974, 1975) - Chomsky and Halle (1968:316-7), Ladefoged (1974:33-35,105), Goldsmith (1976), Feinstein (1979), and Herbert (1979:19-25).

A fourth field of problems not dealt with here is related to the preceding one. Pre- or postnasalized consonants frequently occur in languages in which the feature NASAL - rather than being a part of a segment in a syllable - is part of the syllable. This problem can be handled within the framework proposed in Anderson (1975). No data are available on the basis of which it can be determined whether the nasality of the vowels in such languages is different from the vowel nasality as it occurs in the languages studied here. Examples of languages in which nasality is a feature of the syllable are Sundanese (cf. Robins 1953, 1957; Anderson 1972; Condax et al. 1974), Desano (cf. Kaye 1971), Terena (cf. Bendor-Samuel 1960), Guarani (cf. Lunt 1973). For other examples see Troubetzkoy (1964:194-6), Anderson (1974:268) and Ruhlen (1975:335).

A fifth field of problems concerns the so-called voiceless nasal consonants. These have a perceptual impact which is quite different from that of the corresponding voiced nasal consonants. Ohala (1975:292) observes that "it is the high air flow through the nostrils that creates audible turbulence" in the case of voiceless nasal consonants. As this turbulence is not created by voiced nasal sounds, I will not propose in this study to characterize voiceless nasal consonants by means of the feature NASAL, such as it is defined here. Nasal sounds in the present study are VOICED. For examples of nonvoiced nasal sounds see Ladefoged (1974:11) and Ohala (1975: 295-6).

A sixth field of problems that lies outside the scope of the present investigation concerns stops, fricatives, frictionless continuants (semivowels), laterals, vibrants, glottal and pharyngeal obstruents: all consonants which are "usually" produced without nose coupling. There are, however, reliable reports that these sounds may be produced with some nose coupling by normal subjects. But the perceptual properties of these various groups seem to be heterogeneous. It may be doubted whether the nose coupling of the voiceless consonants belonging to this group has any perceptual reality in any language, in which case it is not an articulatorily relevant property, cf. Ohala (1975:301). I do not know whether the same applies to voiced stops: there are no reports that there is a perceptual difference between voiced stops produced with nose coupling and voiced stops produced without. As to voiced fricatives Ohala (1975:300) observes that "it is extremely doubtful that voiced fricatives could be produced with a detectable amount of nasalization. Sounds symbolized [v̓], [ð̃] exist (Anderson 1975), but it is unlikely that these are fricatives (and thus obstruents) in the same sense as [v], [ð] are. They might best be considered nasalized frictionless continuants similar to [w̃] and [j̃]." As to these latter sounds, Ladefoged (1974:33) states that "in all languages I have investigated these sounds occur only where one of the adjacent vowels is also nasalized; I do not know of contrasts between nasalized and nonnasalized semivowels in which an adjacent vowel is not similarly specified by the oronasal process. This is, of course, another way of saying that the oro-nasal process often affects a syllable as a whole." I do not know to what extent such semivowels have a perceptual impact different from their counterparts produced without nose coupling. As to the glottal and pharyngeal obstruents produced with nose coupling I refer to Ohala (1975:300-1) for other references. In the present study I will assume that the perceptual impact of the

nose coupling in these consonants is negligible. Such sounds will be considered to be [-nasal]. Some other references besides those already mentioned
are: for stops Charbonneau (1971: 117,139,143,345,352,353), Nihalani (1975)
and references in Ohala (1975:300); for fricatives Durand (1953), Jespersen
(1913:57); for frictionless continuants (semivowels) Jespersen (1913:57),
Ladefoged (1974:33), Ohala (1975:300); for laterals and vibrants Charbonneau
(1971), Condax et al.(1976), Jespersen (1913:57), Ladefoged (1974:33), Ohala
(1975:301).

A last field of problems left aside here concerns syllabic consonants which
are usually produced without nose coupling. In Limbum (see Van Reenen and
Voorhoeve (1980) for details) a nasal syllabic labiodental semivowel occurs
next to a nasal consonant. An example is [ɲʋ̃] 'God' or 'sun' (tone is not
indicated). This nasal syllabic labiodental semivowel corresponds to syllabic
[ʋ] or [fʋ] in nonnasal environment. The [ʋ̃] has a very lax realization,
which confirms Ohala's observation quoted above that nasalized voiced fricatives "might best be considered as nasalized frictionless continuants."

NOTES TO CHAPTER 3

1. Examples of glides are [w, j, h], i.e. sounds which are both [-voc] and
   [-cons]. Cf. Chomsky and Halle (1968:176-7).

2. See for instance Halle (1964: 327), Schane (1973:18), Dell (1973:57-8),
   Francard (1975: 152), Kenstowicz and Kisseberth (1979:10-11). Chomsky and
   Halle's definition actually stems from Jakobson et al. (1952:40) and
   Jakobson and Halle (1956:57), in which a characterization of the acoustic
   correlate is provided as well.

3. Since it is rarely mentioned in reports of phonetic experiments whether
   the subjects who produce the sounds have blocked nose cavities or not,
   and since most subjects do not have blocked nose cavities, it is assumed
   in this study that the sounds examined have always been produced without
   any blocking of the nose cavities other than that by means of the velum
   and that other cases are deviant speech.

4. I have come across six different conceptions of the distinction between
   "nasal" and "nasalized", namely:
   (a) Some phoneticians make a distinction between NASAL CONSONANTS and
   NASALIZED VOWELS. See for instance Ladefoged (1975:205): "Consonants such
   as [m, n, ŋ] are ... nasal, but they are not NASALIZED, since this term
   implies that part of the air goes out through the nose and part through
   the mouth". Jones (1956: §164 and §183, Pike (1968:20,35), Kenstowicz
   and Kisseberth (1979:11) make the same distinction. For Ladefoged the
   point is not very important, as appears from Ladefoged (1974:35).
   (b) For others both consonants and vowels may be either NASAL or

NASALIZED, see the discussion in 4.1 below with respect to Eijkman (1934).

(c) Still others consider the term NASAL as a synonym of "completely nasal", and NASALIZED as a synonym of "slightly nasal". This latter distinction is made by Bondarko (1979:71) and Straka (1955).

(d) A fourth distinction is made by Fant (1960:139): "In this intermediate state of the velum, the opening versus closure within the mouth cavity differentiates NASALIZED VOWELS from the NASAL MURMUR.... So-called NASAL VOWELS, e.g., of the French vowel system, are produced with specific tongue positions in addition to the element of nasalization."

(e) A final distinction, made by Clumeck (1971:29) (cf. Almeida 1976:356) concerns vowels only: "nasal vowels are those which are inherently nasal, that is, they contrast phonemically with oral vowels; nasalized vowels, on the other hand, are oral vowels whose nasalization, if any, is solely a function of the nasal consonant environment."

(f) Jakobson et al. (1952:40) do not seem to make a distinction at all.

5. Further details concerning formant properties of nasal sounds are to be found in Almeida (1971, 1976, 1978), Curtis (1970), Debrock (1974), Delattre (1954, 1965, 1968), Dickson (1962), Fant (1960, chapter 2.4), Fujimura (1962), Hattori et al. (1958), House (1957), House and Stevens (1956), Jensen (1967), Kacprowski (1977), Mrayati (1975), Schwartz (1968b), Stevens et al. (1976), Wright (1975), Zagorska-Brooks (1968).

6. In another publication Anderson (1975:3) observes: "The extent to which varying degrees of nasality may need to be specified is moot."

7. Kenstowicz and Kisseberth (1979:253) mention three coefficients as well: "...many languages which make this contrast (i.e. the two-way distinction [+nasal] versus [-nasal] for this feature in underlying representation, PvR) also have phonological rules that assign vowels a lesser degree of nasality in the context of nasal consonants, giving rise to the three-way phonetic distinction between oral, slightly nasal and heavily nasal vowels."

8. According to Genet (1971), Mo:re (Upper-Volta) might be another language with three degrees of vowel nasalization, but this is not confirmed by the more thorough analysis of the language in Canu (1975). Kenstowicz and Kisseberth (1979:23, cf. 253) make a mistake when they observe that "no language presently known makes an underlying contrast between three degrees of nasality: fully nasal, partially nasal, and oral".

CHAPTER 4

The appropriateness of the definition of the feature NASAL

The question to be dealt with in this chapter is: is the feature NASAL well-defined, i.e. has it been chosen in such a way that the relation between the coefficients on its physical scales and their mental reflex is constant - as far as this is possible -, irrespective of the (succession of) sounds in which these coefficients occur?

Although phoneticians and phonologists generally agree that nose coupling (or equivalent) is a factor relevant to the perception of nasality, there are also phoneticians who consider nose coupling, although a necessary, not a sufficient parameter. These phoneticians are not engaged in feature theory. The disagreement between these phoneticians and the other investigators concerns the nasality of vowels, not consonants. On the basis of their observations and experimental results I will propose a definition of the feature NASAL different from the one used until now.

The core of my proposal is that, besides the nose coupling N, we have to take into account at least one more factor: the amount of constriction in the mouth. This is the same as saying that in the production of a nasal sound there are two regulation mechanisms. When a speaker decreases the sound output of the mouth by making a constriction in the mouth, the sound will be perceived as more nasal though produced with the same amount of nose coupling. When the speaker increases the sound output of the mouth by widening the constriction, the sound will be perceived as less nasal, without any change in the amount of nose coupling. It follows that nasal consonants are inherently more nasal than nasal vowels, because the former are produced with completely constricted mouth cavity, whereas the latter never are.

In 4.1 I will discuss observations in phonetic studies which are related to the question of the appropriateness of the definition of the feature NASAL.

In 4.2 I will extract data from the results of experiments which
(a) prove convincingly that we need a different physical scale from the one referred to in the feature definitions and
(b) can be reanalysed in such a way as to support the physical scale I will propose as a better approximation.

In section 4.3 I present some implications and conclusions.

4.1 TWO OPPOSING VIEWS OF THE PERCEPTION OF VOWEL NASALITY

There are two views of the perception of vowel nasality in phonetic studies.
The first view is: vowel nasality becomes perceptible as soon as the amount of
nose coupling the vowel is produced with exceeds a fixed minimum value, which
is the same for all vowels. The second view is: whether a vowel is perceived
as nasal depends not only on the amount of nose coupling, but also on the
amount of constriction in the mouth.

Explicit proponents of the first view are Straka (1955) and Charbonneau
(1971). Straka (1955) is a study on French nasal vowels. Charbonneau (1971) is
an extremely rich source of X-ray tracings, which will be used abundantly in
this study.

Straka (1955:270) raises the question - central in my opinion -:

(1) "Où est la limite entre la nasalité non perçue et la nasalité pertinente?"

For Straka (ibid.) "nasalite non **perçue**" or "non sentie" is "nasalite impar-
faite". Besides, Straka mentions "nasalité pertinente" or "nasalité complète"
(ibid.). This is the nasality we perceive. Straka's answer to question (1)
runs as follows (id.p.271):

(2) "pour qu'elle (= la nasalisation, PvR) soit perçue, il faut qu'un certain
volume d'air phonatoire passe par le nez." "...pour une voyelle nasalisée dont
la nasalité n'est pas perçue, la dépense d'air nasal n'atteint jamais celle
qu'exige une voyelle réellement nasale."[1]

A "voyelle nasalisée dont la nasalité n'est pas perçue" is for Straka (ibid.)
just an oral vowel, in spite of the fact that the velum does not touch the
pharyngeal wall. Schematically Straka's view is:

> If the nasal port is closed,   nasality is not perceived
> If the nasal port is slightly open, nasality is not perceived
> If the nasal port is further open, nasality is   perceived

Since Straka does not give any further qualifications of the vowels, I conclude that he is speaking of vowels in general, a conclusion confirmed by the
fact that he discusses high and low, front and back vowels indiscriminately
(Straka 1955:269- 71).

It is clear that for Straka the nasality of a vowel depends directly on the
amount of nose coupling or the volume of air passing through the nose. Since
he mentions a specific amount of nose coupling and a specific air volume, it
seems that this amount and this volume have to be the same for all vowels:
different vowels are to be produced with the same amount of nose coupling or
the same volume of air in order to be perceived as nasal.[2]

If his "dépense d'air nasal" is the equivalent of my "amount of nose coupling N" (which I will assume for the sake of the argument), we may conclude
that for Straka the amount of nose coupling is the only factor which determines whether a vowel is perceived as nasal or not.

In Charbonneau (1971:36) - a thesis prepared under the supervision of
Straka - an observation revealing the same view as in (2) above is made:

(3) "la pleine rèsonance nasale... demande un passage de 6 mm de diamètre au
moins..."

The 6 mm refer to measurements of lateral X-ray tracings of the smallest' distance between the posterior side of the velum and the back of the pharyngeal
wall: the velopharyngeal distance VP. Charbonneau (1971:36, note 1a) adds the
following comment to this:

(4) "Lorsque le voile du palais s'èloigne plus ou moins de la paroi phar-
yngeale, on parle, tout au long de ce travail, d'intensité plus ou moins
forte. Il ne s'agit évidemment pas de degrè d'intensité acoustique mais plutôt
de quantité d'air, grande ou petite, évacuèe par les fosses nasales".

We see in (3) and (4) that in Charbonneau (1971) the following notions are
equivalent:

   - a velopharyngeal distance VP of at least 6mm;
   - a full nasal resonance;
   - a rather strong intensity;
   - a rather large quantity of air passing through the nose.

The acoustic intensity is not equivalent to these notions.

If we assume that for Charbonneau (1971) the distance VP is proportional to
the amount of nose coupling N (as I will argue in chapter 5), and a full nasal
resonance is what characterizes a vowel as nasal, we may conclude that,
according to Charbonneau, nasal vowels are produced with a fixed (minimal)
amount of nose coupling. Here, then, we find Straka's view supported.[3]

I think that views such as those of Straka and Charbonneau are essentially
the perceptual counterpart of the feature definitions (1) to (7) in 3.1 above.
They take a coefficient - describing a specific amount of nose coupling - on
the physical scale of the feature NASAL. They listen to any vowel with this
amount of nose coupling whether it sounds nasal. If it does, they have found
the critical amount of nose coupling necessary to the perception of vowel
nasality. Implicitly present in many studies on nasality is the view that all
vowels are equally nasal if produced with a specific amount of nose coupling.

The alternative view would be that for different vowels we need different coefficients on the physical scale of the feature NASAL in order to perceive them as equally nasal. This alternative view of vowel nasality is represented by Eijkman (1926, 1928, 1934), Nusbaum et al. (1935) and Kaltenborn (1948). These phoneticians seem to have arrived at almost the same conclusions independently. Their conclusions can be stated in their most general form as: the moment vowel nasality becomes perceptible depends not only on the amount of nose coupling, but also on the amount of constriction in the **oral** tract.

Eijkman's conception is presented in a terminology at first sight somewhat awkward but not unusual in his time. For Eijkman a sound is "NASAL... when pronounced with open nose" (1934:29) or "with the nose entirely open at the back" (1926:212, 1928:115). The noun corresponding to this adjective "nasal" is "nasalness". Furthermore, according to Eijkman, sounds may also be "nasalized". A sound is "nasalized" when it is pronounced not only with open nose (cf. 1934:29), but also with a back aperture of the mouth which is small in proportion to that of the nose (cf. 1934:28). The nouns corresponding to the adjective "nasalized" are "nasality" and "nasalization" (1926:212, 1928: 115). For Eijkman a sound may be nasal without being nasalized. Conversely, a nasalized sound is always nasal.[4] His expression "nasalized" corresponds, in the case of vowels, to perceived nasality, and his term "nasal" to all vowels produced with nose coupling more than zero.

The following passages contain the core of Eijkman's view of nasality:

(5)(a) "Personal observation has shown that in nasalization the soft palate is less tense than is usual for speech sounds. Also that the nasality becomes less:

1st. when the soft palate is raised with a spatula immediately behind the hard palate; in this case it may even disappear altogether.

2nd. when the uvula is lifted up or pushed backwards;

3rd. when the back of the tongue is pressed down.

In all these cases the aperture at the back of the mouth is made larger. From the fact that with a constant nose-aperture the enlargement of the mouth-aperture causes the nasality to decrease, it is not too bold to conclude that the mouth- aperture is the principal factor for nasality" (1934:29).

(b) "If the mouth-aperture is proportionately too large, there can be no question of nasality" (1934:28, note 1).

(c) "The different vowels cannot be nasalized with equal facility. The greatest chance of success offer ɔ ,..., a, $ɛ$, e, œ , but i, y, u present greater difficulty.

I have not been able to find a satisfactory explanation for this" (1926:218).

Eijkman's view can be schematized as follows:

Term	Definition	Examples
nasal	sounds produced with	all vowels;
nasalness	completely open nose	consonants sometimes
nasalized	sounds produced with	all vowels, but [i,
nasality	completely open nose	y, u] with greater
nasalization	AND with a small back	difficulty;
	aperture (narrowed back	exceptionally [m, n];
	entrance) of the mouth	never [ŋ]

We cannot agree any more with quotation (5c): there is no special difficulty in producing high nasal vowels. And Eijkman's first two observations in
(5a) can be interpreted as a description of the closing of the nasal port,
i.e. as a description of the decrease of the amount of nose coupling. But I
consider the third observation in (5a) and the statement in (5b) very important. With respect to the vowels, Eijkman observes that they are perceived as
nasal, if they are produced
(a) with completely open nose and
(b) with a small aperture at the back of the mouth.
By making this aperture larger the vowel is not perceived as nasal any more,
although it may still be produced with nose coupling. I think that Eijkman has
found something very important, viz. A VOWEL IS PERCEIVED AS NASAL IF THE
CROSS- SECTION OF THE ORAL CAVITY - THE MOUTH OPENING AT THE BACK - IS SUFFI-
CIENTLY SMALL AS COMPARED WITH THE AMOUNT OF NOSE COUPLING THE VOWEL IS PRO-
DUCED WITH. As soon as the small back entrance of the mouth widens, the vowel
is not perceived as nasal any more.

Eijkman based his view upon self-observation and some experiments carried
out with a subject "with a very insensitive throat" (cf. 1934:26, 29). Only
one vowel or kind of vowels was examined: isolated vowels with [a] quality.
Although Eijkman does not give an indication as to the precise amount of nose
coupling N and the size of the back entrance of the oral cavity, his conclusion is highly interesting, since it makes the perception of nasality depen-
dent on different coefficients, and not one (see the views of Straka and Charbonneau above), on the physical scale of the feature NASAL as it has been
defined until now. His approach opens a way to consider the amount of nose
coupling in relation to the opening at the back of the mouth, the area of
mouth constriction MC at this point.[5]

A related view is found in Nusbaum et al. (1935), in which the amount of
mouth constriction is seen in relation to vowel height. Nusbaum et al. found
that the amount of pressure - working from the nose cavities on the upperside

42

of the velum - required to open the nasal port for high oral vowels is greater than for low oral vowels. Nusbaum (p.78) explains this difference in pressure as follows:[6]

(6) "He (Nusbaum, PvR) believes that it may be less important, acoustically, to produce [æ] with a complete closure of the velum, than it is [u]. In both [u] and [i] there is a much greater constriction in the egress of the tone through the oral cavity than there is in the production of the more open vowel [æ]. Hence, for [i] and [u], a proportionally larger volume of tone is shunted through the nose with a slight opening of the velum. Any openness of the nasal passage, then, is more apt to result in an unpleasantly nasal quality during the production of [i] and [u] than during the production of [æ]. Because of this acoustic effect we are more apt to **learn** to close the nasal passage completely, while making the vowels [i] and [u] than in making any of the more "open" vowels, such as [æ]."

Nusbaum's explanation, based upon oral vowels, seems not to have drawn the attention of the specialists. Yet, here again we have a phonetician who states that the amount of nose coupling has to be considered in relation to the amount of mouth constriction. The higher the vowel, the smaller the amount of mouth constriction.

We meet this view again in Kaltenborn (1948), who arrived at the following conclusion (p.20):

(7) "nasality was caused by having too wide an opening into the nasopharynx in comparison with the opening into the oral cavity".

The nasopharynx is the nasal port which may be closed and opened by the velum. We may paraphrase (7) as: nasality is caused when the amount of nose coupling is great in comparison with the amount of constriction in the mouth.

Kaltenborn based his conclusion upon a "superficial comparative study" (p.20) and measurements of X-ray tracings of a group of 6 normal speakers and a group of 5 nasal speakers[7], during the production of the isolated vowel [æ]. In his X-ray tracings it can be observed that the mouth constriction is situated at the back entrance of the mouth. He took his "measurements from the tongue to the anterior surface of the velum at their closest point" (p.20). Therefore, his conclusion is essentially the same as Eijkman's.[8]

Eijkman, Nusbaum and Kaltenborn do not associate their conclusions with definitions of the feature NASAL in phonology. In terms of the definitions quoted in chapter 3, however, their conclusions can be stated as: it is not one specific coefficient on the physical scale of the feature NASAL which causes a vowel to be perceived as nasal, but the amount of nose coupling the coefficient refers to has to be considered in proportion to the constriction in the mouth.

When I consider the views of Eijkman, Nusbaum and Kaltenborn in relation to the definitions of the feature NASAL in 3.1 above, I notice that the result does not satisfy the condition that phonetic features should be well-defined (cf. section 2.3 above). When nasal vowels are not produced with the same amount of nose coupling, it follows that they do not have the same coefficients on the physical scale of the feature NASAL. Therefore, we cannot use a definition in which nose coupling plays the only part. We need a definition in which mouth constriction plays a part as well.

Tentatively I would suggest that the amount of mouth constriction MC is inversely proportional to the amount of nose coupling N and that mathematically this inverse proportion is expressed as follows:

$$N\% = \frac{N}{MC + N}.100 \qquad (I)$$

N% stands for a combination of articulatory states of affairs expressed in terms of the amount of nose coupling N and the amount of mouth constriction MC. In 3.1 above I have defined nose coupling as:

(8) The nose coupling N is the opening in mm^2 of the nasal port measured in a cross-section perpendicular to the airstream at the point of the greatest constriction between the velum and the pharyngeal wall.

Now I add a definition of mouth constriction MC in (9):

(9) The area of mouth constriction MC is the opening in mm^2 of the mouth passage, measured in a cross-section perpendicular to the airstream at the point of greatest constriction in the mouth.

To avoid ambiguities as regards the term "constriction", I will use the expressions "small amount of mouth constriction" as referring to a small quantity of mm^2 and "large amount of mouth constriction" as referring to a great quantity of mm^2. In the above definition it is not stipulated that the area in question is situated at the back entrance of the mouth. This point will be taken up in the next section.

When the nasal port is open (i.e. when the amount of N is great) and when the mouth passage is constricted (i.e. when the amount of MC is low), we have N:(N+MC) = almost 1 or almost 100%. Therefore, I propose to make N% the central concept of the definition of the feature NASAL:

(10) Nasal sounds are produced with N% higher than in oral sounds.

The next section will examine whether (10) is a better definition than (7) in chapter 3: nasal sounds are produced with nose coupling; oral sounds are produced without nose coupling.

4.2 EVIDENCE IN FAVOUR OF A NEW DEFINITION OF THE FEATURE NASAL

We have to make a choice between two definitions of the feature NASAL. In one definition the feature is defined in terms of the amount of nose coupling N. In the other it is defined in terms of N%, i.e in terms of the amounts of nose coupling N and mouth constriction MC, as in equation I:

$$N\% = \frac{N}{MC + N}.100 \tag{I}$$

The great majority of phoneticians and phonologists seem to consider the former definition satisfactory, a small minority has opinions which I have developed into my own definition.

The question which of the two definitions is the better one has to be considered against the background of their appropriateness. We should select the definition in which the relation between physical properties and mental reflexes of the coefficients is the most constant, see 2.3 above. In order to choose the better definition we need evidence on the basis of which we can compare perceptual judgements of nasality and their relation to both N and N%.

Experimental results which can be used as evidence are extremely rare. I have found not more than three experiments with relevant data. They are described in House and Stevens (1956), in Kent (1966) and in Carney and Morris (1971).

The experiment of House and Stevens is by far the most important. As it is based upon artificial vowel stimuli produced by means of an electrical speech model, the articulatory properties of the stimuli, viz. the amount of nose coupling N and the amount of mouth constriction MC, can be calculated with a high degree of precision.

In this experiment House and Stevens examine the relation between vowel stimuli which are perceived as [i, ɛ, a, ɔ, u] and the amount of nose coupling needed for each vowel stimulus in order to be perceived as nasal.[9] They do not give the amount of mouth constriction MC for the different vowels. Since I want to know the N and the N% of these vowels, I will attempt to calculate the MC of the vowels as well.

The electrical analogue of House and Stevens can be represented in physical space as a vocal tract: I will call this the realistic model. However, House and Stevens determine relevant articulatory properties of the realistic model by means of calculations based upon an idealization of this model. In both models the oral cavity is conceived of as circular. The difference between the realistic model and its idealization is that in the latter we have smooth

lines, whereas the former is divided into 35 cascades of 5 mm. The difference
between the two models is illustrated in fig. 4-1.

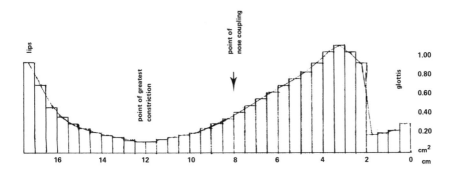

Fig. 4-1. Lateral view of the spatial representation of the electrical speech
model of House and Stevens (1956) and the idealization of the spatial model
used in calculations. The difference concerns the substitution of the segmented cascades of the spatial model by a smooth, parabolic line. The representation above is slightly different from the figure in House and Stevens (1956).

The properties of the idealized model are listed in (11).

(11) (a) The length of the vocal tract tube is 17.5 cm (House and Stevens
1956:219, 220);

(b) The length of the nasal tract is 12 cm; it is connected with the
oro-pharyngeal tract at 8 cm from the glottis (House and Stevens 1956:220);

(c) The degree of nose coupling of each vowel stimulus is known for all
vowels; there are five possibilities: the amount of nose coupling is 0 cm^2,
0.25 cm^2, 0.71 cm^2, 1.7 cm^2 and 3.7 cm^2 (cf. House and Stevens 1956:226, 229
and passim);

(d) The area of greatest constriction in the oro- pharyngeal tract from
glottis to lips (the area with the smallest amount of constriction in the
oro-pharyngeal tract) can be calculated on the basis of the radius at the
point in the oro-pharyngeal tract on which the area is situated (in fig. 4-1,
for instance, the area of greatest constriction is situated at a point at 12
cm from the glottis); the radius at the point of greatest constriction is r_0;
it is given in cm;

(e) The distance d_0 in cm from the point of greatest constriction to the
glottis may vary.

(f) Equation II gives the length in cm of each radius r in the vocal
tract between 3 to 14.5 cm from the glottis, where X is measured from the
point of constriction of radius r to the point of greatest constriction of
radius r_0 (House and Stevens 1956:219).[10]

$$r - r_0 = 0.025(1.2 - r_0) \ X^2 \qquad\qquad II$$

By means of the electrical model vowel-like stimuli of $[i, \varepsilon, a, \jmath, u]$
were produced with the five amounts of nose coupling (11c) and presented to a
group of (AmEng) listeners (House and Stevens 1956:227-8). Results are graphically presented in such a manner that the average amounts of nose coupling for
the five $[i]$'s, the five $[\varepsilon]$'s, the five $[a]$'s etc. are determined at two levels of perception (House and Stevens 1956:228, fig.11):

(12) (a) The level at which listeners judge each of the five
       $[i]$'s, $[\varepsilon]$'s, $[a]$'s etc. nasal in 50% of the cases.
     (b) The level at which listeners judge each of the five
       $[i]$'s, $[\varepsilon]$'s, $[a]$'s etc. nasal in 75% of the cases.

Some results found by House and Stevens (1956) for the vowels $[i, \varepsilon, a]$ are
given in table 4-1 below. I have not mentioned $[\jmath]$ and $[u]$, as these vowels
are produced with a degree of lip rounding which may interfere with the mouth
constriction (see below) and House and Stevens (1956) do not specify the
parameters they have used in the labial area. Column 1 of table 4-1 mentions
the vowels, while in column 2 and 3 the amount of nose coupling in mm^2 is
given for the two levels of response mentioned in (12a) and (12b) above. I
have given a global indication of the influence of lip rounding in column 6. I
assume that it is not relevant in the case of $[i, \varepsilon, a]$.

vowel	N in mm^2 at 50% level	75%	d_0 in cm	r_0 in cm	influence of lip rounding
i	100	140	12	0.4	absent
ε	125	180	7.2	0.4	absent
a	260	340	4.8	0.4	marginal

Table 4-1. Properties of three series of artificial vowel stimuli. Column 1:
vowel stimuli. Columns 2 and 3: average amount of nose coupling N necessary
for the listeners to perceive 50%, respectively 75%, of the vowel stimuli as
nasal. Column 4: the distance d_0 from the glottis to the point of mouth constriction. Column 5: the smallest radius r_0 in the oro-pharyngeal tract
(between glottis and lips). Column 6: estimated influence of lip rounding.
Data adapted from Stevens and House (1955) and House and Stevens (1956).

As I have observed above the amount of mouth constriction MC has not been given in House and Stevens (1956). MC is not easy to determine, especially in the case of $[\varepsilon]$ and $[a]$. The mouth constriction MC can be determined if r_0 and d_0 are known. House and Stevens (1956:219) give these values for $[i]$: r_0 = 0.4 cm and d_0 = 12 cm. For $[i]$ the mouth constriction is situated at 12-8=4 cm from the coupling point to the nasal tract. The surface of the area of mouth constriction at this point is pix0.4^2 = 0.5024 cm^2 or 50.24 mm^2, see column 2 in table 4-3.

I assume that for $[\varepsilon]$ and $[a]$ r_0 is 0.4 cm as well (see table 4-1, column 5), although this is not explicitly stated in House and Stevens (1956). It appears from Stevens and House (1955), however, that a constriction defined by r_0 = 0.4 cm, if it has the right location in the oro-pharyngeal tract, gives satisfactory results for all vowels examined and is indeed used by the authors, at least in the case of $[\varepsilon]$ and $[a]$ (cf. House and Stevens 1955:886-7, fig. 8,9).

I have still to find the distance d_0 from the glottis to the point of greatest constriction for these two vowels in their idealized model. I have made rather precise estimates of the d_0 of $[\varepsilon]$ and $[a]$ with r_0 = 0.4 cm on the basis of Stevens and House (1955:149, especially Fig.7b). In the case of $[\varepsilon]$ and $[a]$ the point of greatest constriction must be located between the glottis and the coupling point of the nasal tract, since it is situated at respectively 7.2 cm and 4.8 cm, i.e. less than 8 cm from the glottis. In the model of House and Stevens the cross-sections in the mouth become bigger the more distant they are from the point of greatest constriction. This implies that in the case of $[\varepsilon]$ and $[a]$ the point of greatest **mouth** constriction - situated in the oro-pharyngeal tract between the coupling point of the nasal tract and the lips - must be located exactly at the back entrance of the mouth, i.e. at the coupling point of the nasal tract, at 8 cm from the glottis. Although it is not self-evident, this point may be considered to be the spot where the back entrance of the mouth is located. It is not self-evident that the coupling point is a **point** and not a **circle**. It is presented as a point and not as a circle because the realistic representation of the electrical analogue is not in all respects a spatial representation. Whereas in the realistic representation and the idealization the amount of nose coupling necessarily would take the form of circles of 0.25 cm^2, 0.71 cm^2, 1.7 cm^2 and 3.7 cm^2 (see above) around the coupling point in the oro- pharyngeal tract, this is not the case in the electrical model, where it takes the form of a point, situated at the back entrance of the mouth at exactly 8 cm from the glottis.[11]

48

vowel	N in mm^2 at 50%	N in mm^2 at 75%	r_m in mm	Distance d_o of r_o from the glottis in cm
ε	125	180	4.2	7.25
a	260	340	6.45	4.75

Table 4-2. Properties of two series of artificial vowels. The point of greatest constriction in the mouth cavity defined by radius r_m is situated at the back entrance of the mouth cavity, at 8.25 cm from the glottis. For further explanation see table 4-1.

vowel	MC in mm^2	N in mm^2 at 50% level	N in mm^2 at 75%	N% at 50% level	N% at 75%
i	50	100		67	
i	50		140		74
ε	55	125		69	
ε	55		180		77
a	131	260		66	
a	131		340		72

Table 4-3. Properties of three kinds of artificial vowels. In the 2nd column estimates of the amount of mouth constriction MC. For further explanation see table 4-1.

   As was pointed out above, there is a difference between the realistic model and its idealization for these vowels. Since the realistic model consists of successive cascades of 5mm (see fig 4-1 above) and since the point of greatest constriction in the oro-pharyngeal tract for [ε] is situated at 7.2 cm from the glottis, it is located in the cascade at 7 to 7.5 cm from the glottis. For calculations in the realistic representation the best approach is to take a distance of 7.25 cm from the glottis, the average distance of the cascade to the glottis. For [a] this gives the value of 4.75 cm, see table 4-2. And the average distance of the cascade at 8 to 8.5 cm from the glottis - the cascade forming the back entrance of the mouth - is 8.25cm from the glottis.

   By means of equation (II) the radii r can be calculated now for these two vowels in the realistic representation. The results are presented in tables 4-2 and 4-3. It appears from table 4-3 that when listeners judge 50% of the vowels nasal N% takes values much more similar than the values of the different N's. The same result appears when listeners judge 75% of the vowels nasal. Therefore, for unrounded vowels N% as defined in equation (I) seems to be reasonably constant, and equation (I) is a satisfactory approximation if we want to convert the various absolute amounts of nose coupling N for the same

degree of nasal perception into an almost constant factor defined in articulatory terms.

As I have mentioned above, there are a few other relevant data apart from
those extracted from the experiment of House and Stevens.[12]

Some data are found in Kent (1966). Kent (1966) has carried out a series of
experiments with six nasal speakers with cleft palates. The speakers produced
the /i/, /u/ and /ɑ/ like vowels with 0, 12, 38 and 113 mm^2 nose coupling.[13]
Each speaker produced the 6x3=18 series of vowels with the four amounts of
nose coupling successively. The nasality of each vowel was judged by a group
of listeners. The listeners did not perceive, or hardly perceived, any difference in nasality for 6 out of the 18 vowel series. Kent analysed X-ray photographs of these vowels and concluded (p.57):

"The results of this analysis tend to support the hypothesis that speakers can
and do compensate for an increase in nasalization due to the introduction of
oral-to-nasal coupling. It appears that the most effective way to offset the
increase in nasality that occurs is to open the oral channel as much as is
compatible with the phonetic integrity of the particular vowel being produced."

This result is important for two reasons: (a) it shows that a definition in
terms of nose coupling N alone cannot account for the fact that the vowels in
question were perceived as almost equally nasal, and (b) it is at least consistent with a definition in which N% plays the central role, as the opening
of the oral channel Kent mentions will result in a greater amount of mouth
constriction MC.

In Carney and Morris (1971) I have found some evidence as well. In the
experiment reported in this study, vowels of nasal speakers with and without
cleft palate are analyzed. The vowels are /i/, /ɛ/, /ɑ/, /ʌ/ and /u/. In their
figure 6 Carney and Morris (1971:316) show, for each of the five vowels and
for both groups of speakers, the relation between the number of vowels produced with open nasal port (i.e. with nose coupling) and the degree of nasality which the groups of vowels were perceived with. Both the speakers with and
those without cleft palate produced lower vowels more frequently with nose
coupling than higher vowels. I assume that the more vowels of a group are produced with nose coupling, the higher the average amount of nose coupling is
for the vowels of the group. If this assumption is correct, we would predict -
on the basis of definition (7) in chapter 3 above, in which the amount of nose
coupling N is the central notion - that the lower vowels are perceived as more
nasal than the higher ones. Indeed, this is what was found in the case of the
nasal speakers without cleft palate. But the vowels of the nasal speakers with
cleft palates are judged differently by the listeners. The /ɑ/'s of this group
of speakers are perceived as less nasal than the higher vowels, though they

were produced with a greater amount of nose coupling than the latter. This result cannot be accounted for by means of a definition in which nose coupling is the central notion.

If N% is the central notion, however, the possibility is left open that the amount of mouth constriction MC neutralizes the effect of the open nasal port. Indeed, in the case of the low vowels we may expect that the mouth is less constricted than in the case of the high vowels.

Although the evidence obtained from Kent (1966) and Carney and Morris (1971) is less precise than the evidence extracted from House and Stevens, it points in the same direction, just as the following observation in Fant (1960:156): "Because of the narrow tongue passage of the vowel [i], ... it is obvious that the nasal sound transmission can be appreciable even at low degrees of nasal coupling."

The results until now suggest that a choice can be made between the two definitions of the feature NASAL. When we take the amount of nose coupling N as the central notion of the definition (and of the physical scale), we see that for the same degree of nasal perception the amount of nose coupling N fluctuates considerably. When we take N% as the central notion of the definition, we see that we have found an almost constant value for a specific level of nasal perception. Therefore, I conclude that a definition of the feature NASAL in which the notion N% takes a central place is more appropriate than a definition in which the nose coupling N is the central notion.

My conclusion could be questioned, however. The results of House and Stevens (1956) may be language-specific. Furthermore, the above argumentation concerns three unrounded vowels only. Consonants and rounded vowels have not, or hardly, been discussed.

As AmEng speakers do not make distinctive use of vowel nasality, they may have provided random answers. Yet, since the results scored are far from random, they are reliable, I think.[14]

With respect to rounded vowels, I have observed above that lip rounding may interfere with mouth constriction at the back entrance of the mouth. This is almost the same as saying that mouth constriction need not necessarily located near the nasal port, and that it may be more fronted, possibility which has been left open in the definition of mouth constriction, see (9) in 4.1 above. Indeed, we have seen already that the mouth constriction MC of the [i] was located at 4 cm from the point of nose coupling. Yet the results in terms of N% for [i] do not seem to deviate from the results found for the other two vowels. This finding is different from the view of Eijkman and Kaltenborn who claimed that the mouth constriction has to be situated at the back entrance of the mouth, see 4.1 above. When the location of the mouth constriction may be at any point in the mouth between the velum and the lips, however, lip rounding may play a part as well. But as we have observed already, data concerning lip rounding of [ɔ] and [u] are not given in House and Stevens (1956) and the point cannot be checked.

For the same amount of nose coupling these two vowel stimuli are perceived as more nasal than the three other vowels dealt with (cf. House and Stevens 1956:228, fig.11). This is probably not due to an extremely narrow mouth constriction at the back entrance of the mouth, since, just as for the other vowels, House and Stevens (1955:886) usually assume r_0 to be 0.4 cm. If equation (I) above applies to mouth constriction in the labial area as well, these vowels may have been produced with amounts of lip rounding of 33 mm^2 for [u], of 40 mm^2 for [ɔ]. It appears from Stevens and House (1955:484, 487, 491 fig.7) that such areas of mouth coupling fall within the range of areas of lip rounding used, but lack of relevant data makes it impossible to check this point.

The choice of a feature definition which has as a central notion N% has implications for consonants. Consider again equation I:

$$N\% = \frac{N}{MC + N} \cdot 100 \qquad (I)$$

MC = 0 for the nasal consonants [m, n, ɲ, ŋ]. If we assume that the mouth constriction may be situated anywhere in the mouth cavity between the velum and the lips, we may conclude that for nasal consonants N% is always 100, which is, I think, a satisfactory conclusion.

For some nonnasal consonants, viz. plosives, there is a problem. As for nonnasal plosives both MC and N are zero, equation (I) cannot be applied, the result being indefinite.[15]

With respect to nonnasal vowels, equation I is quite satisfactory again: for such vowels N = 0 and N% = 0 as well.

Therefore, a definition of the feature NASAL in terms of N% seems to be more appropriate than one in terms of nose coupling. From now on I will use the definition:

(13) Nasal sounds are produced with N% higher than in oral sounds.

4.3 SOME IMPLICATIONS AND CONCLUSIONS

In this chapter I have made a choice between two definitions of the feature NASAL. In the traditional definition the notion of nose coupling N is central; in the definition I propose the notion of N%.

Vowels sound equally nasal, not when they are produced with the same amounts of nose coupling N, but when they are produced with the same N%. N% is defined by the formula

$$N\% = \frac{N}{N + MC} \cdot .100$$

By proposing a definition in which N% is the central notion, I do not want to say that N% is, definitely, the central notion we need in a definition of the feature NASAL. At the moment a definition on the basis of N% accounts for the data better than the traditional one, but it leaves open the possibility that other, more satisfactory, definitions will be proposed. Surely, the best definition will be the one in which the amount of mouth constriction MC is substituted by a parameter in which properties of the mouth cavity as a whole are quantified per sound. The model developed in Kacprowsky (1977) may be a good starting-point for the development of a definition of the feature NASAL based upon such properties. Feature definitions may be more complicated than they have seemed to be up to now.

However, since I have no other purpose than to draw attention to the fact that results of phonetic experiments are relevant to feature definitions in a phonological theory which is claimed to be empirical, I will not attempt to improve upon the definition further. It will still need much experimentation to develop an entirely satisfactory definition of the feature NASAL.

The results of this chapter can be summarized as follows:
- there is not a specific amount of nose coupling per speaker which causes a sound to be perceived as nasal;
- the proportion between the amount of mouth constriction and the amount of nose coupling gives a better indication whether a sound will be perceived as nasal or not;
- for nonnasal vowels N% is zero;
- for nasal consonants N% is 100;
- for nonnasal consonants N% is zero or indefinite.

In this summary oral and nasal vowels are not mentioned. I will analyze the properties of these vowels in chapters 6 and 7 below.

In the following chapters I will use the definition:

Nasal sounds are produced with N% higher than in oral sounds.

NOTES TO CHAPTER 4

1.   For the terms "nasalisée" and "nasale", cf. note 4 of chapter 3 above.

2.   I assume that Straka means something like "for adult speakers", but the point is not explicitly discussed. For the conclusions quoted in (2) he refers to the experiments of the 19th century phonetician Passavant, who expressed his results in terms of mm^2 of nose coupling (although the

expression "nose coupling" is not used).

3. By mentioning explicitly the distance VP of 6mm, Charbonneau (1971) seems to consider the production of the full nasal resonance as a speaker-independent event.

4. For the terms "nasal" etc. and "nasalized", cf. note 4 of chapter 3 above.

5. It is amazing that Eijkman's conception of nasality, just as that of some earlier phoneticians with related points of view he mentions, has not received more attention. Van Gelder (1965, Chapter 28) and Linthorst (1973:14) are the only ones I have found who mention his view.

6. The other authors of the study did apparently not share Nusbaum's view.

7. The difference between these kinds of speakers will be dealt with in chapter 5.

8. Kaltenborn's conclusion is quoted or referred to by McDonald and Baker (1951:11), House and Stevens (1956:218) and Kent (1966:98).

9. The vowel [æ] is excluded by House and Stevens since it sounded nasal even if produced without nose coupling. Apparently, nasality may have other causes than nose coupling, but we do not know what these causes are, cf. also Schwartz (1971).

10. The equation given in Stevens and House (1955:486) apparently contains a misprint: 0.25 should be read as 0.025.

11. I am grateful to G. Bloothooft for his information on the relation between electrical analogues and their spatial representations.

12. Jensen (1969) presents some data in which proportions play a part. His measurements are based upon French nasal vowels produced by French sub-jects. Instead of nose coupling and mouth constriction he measures the quantity of air coming out of the nose and out of the mouth. He finds more nose expiration for [ã] and [õ] than for [ɛ̃] and [œ̃]. Even if we assume that quantities of air coming out of the nose and the mouth can be rendered in terms of an equation such as equation (I), it is questionable whether the results are comparable to N%. In addition, we do not know whether these nasal vowels would be perceived as all equally nasal. Furthermore, Jensen himself observes that (a) the vowels are not constant in structure (p. 63) and (b) the statistical certainty could have been greater (p.59).

13. In the next chapter I will discuss the notions of normal speaker and of nasal speaker with or without cleft palate. In Kent's experiment the speakers used an obturator in which, at the place of the nasal port, a hole was made which simulated an open nasal port to the nose cavity. The surface of the hole was 113 mm^2. It could be made smaller or filled up completely by means of plugs.

14. It appears from Lintz and Sherman (1961), Ali et al. (1971), and Clumeck (1971) that AmEng listeners have no difficulties with the perception of nasality.

15. If MC and N are both very low, equation (I) may concern the consonants briefly mentioned in 3.4 above, where it was observed that consonants of this kind will not be dealt with in this study. For extremely low values of N and MC equation (I) may not apply.

CHAPTER 5

A survey of data on nasality

In this chapter I will provide a survey of data on nasality. Since data on nasality are manifold, and have been produced in various disciplines by inves- tigators who did not publish them with a view to a notion as N%, I had to make a survey of the data and their relation to my linguistic purpose.

In 5.1 I will review the kind of data I will use in an order of roughly decreasing relevance. The survey concerns relevant properties of nasality as they have been determined in phonetic experiments or - rarely - typological studies. I shall discuss one other question in this section: the representa- tiveness of the data on which the phonetic experiments are based.

The most relevant data produced in phonetic experiments concern the amount of nose coupling N and the amount of mouth coupling MC, but data on position and shape of the velum may be relevant as well. It would be useful to have at one's disposal data which concern both articulatory and perceptual properties of speech sounds, as we had in the artificial vowels of House and Stevens (1956) (see 4.2 above), but I have not found many data of this kind.

It is my experience that lateral X-ray tracings - drawn on the basis of X-ray photographs, pictures, films - are by far the most important source of information. The way these tracings can be used to estimate the amount of nose coupling N and the amount of mouth constriction MC will be elaborated in a special section: 5.2.

The results of this chapter will be summarized in 5.3.

5.1 A REVIEW OF DATA ON NASALITY

The data I will discuss here are mainly produced by means of phonetic experi- ments, which bear on nasality in speech sounds. In addition to this review, I will consider the question to what extent the speakers who produced the speech sounds are representative for the language they speak.

The experimental data have been derived from speech samples which were pro- duced by native speakers of various languages. I will shortly discuss the relevance of the data without focusing on the methods by means of which the data have been derived from the speech samples. The following classification of results of phonetic experiments seems to be appropriate:

1. Data in direct relation to nose coupling or mouth constriction.

(a) Data expressible in terms of absolute amounts of nose coupling and mouth constriction;

(b) Data expressible in terms of relative amounts of nose coupling;

(c) Data concerning differences in the amount of nose coupling in successive phases of the same sound.

2. Data indirectly related to nose coupling or mouth constriction.

(a) Articulatory data;

(b) Neurophysical data;

(c) Acoustic data;

(d) Perceptual data;

(e) Typological data.

1. Data in direct relation to nose coupling or mouth constriction.

(a) The best data on absolute amounts of nose coupling and mouth constriction are real size X-ray tracings of the areas of nose coupling and mouth constriction. Such data are very precious but extremely rare. Usually we have at our disposal estimates of the surface of these areas of N and MC on the basis of the velopharyngeal distance VP and the smallest mouth distance SM which can be measured in lateral X-ray tracings. Since these lateral X-ray tracings are important for many purposes, I will deal with the question how the areas of nose coupling and mouth constriction can be estimated in a special section, see 5.2 below.

(b) Data on nose coupling have relative value when the results - although not expressed in absolute amounts - can be compared with each other on an arbitrary scale. Such data may serve to compare vowels in different contexts or of different apertures, or indicate to what extent there is more or less coarticulation or coproduction between successive sounds.[1]

(c) Data concerning differences in the amounts of nose coupling and mouth constriction in successive phases of the same sound are relevant if we want to compare

- the internal structure of different groups of sounds (nasal consonants, oral vowels or nasal vowels) in terms of nose coupling and/or mouth constriction;

- the influence of different adjacent sounds on each other, for instance the shape and position of the velum in sounds which are coproduced or coarticulated.

Such comparisons make it possible to answer questions whether there are differences across languages, among different groups of vowels of a language or among vowels in different environments, as regards the moment at which the amounts of nose coupling or mouth constriction, increases or decreases.[2]

2. By data indirectly related to nose coupling or mouth constriction I understand data which do not concern measurements of the amount of nose coupling itself, but measurements of other properties of the velopharyngeal area or

more global properties of the mouth cavity. The data may be articulatory, acoustic, neurophysical, perceptual, or typological in nature.

(a) Articulatory data concern measurements of velic movement and of velic height. Phoneticians have examined the relation between, on the one hand, velic height or velic movement and, on the other, the velopharyngeal distance VP. They have found that this relation is proportional. However, this is not entirely correct in two respects:

- By measuring velic movement and velic height, phoneticians do not necessarily measure differences in velopharyngeal distance VP, and, consequently, in the amounts of nose coupling N. Beyond the point at which the amount of nose coupling has become zero the velum may still continue to rise somewhat. That this may happen can be seen very clearly in the results of Bzoch (1968:215-7), in which, for various vowels, significant differences in the measure "elevation of the velum" have been found although all the vowels were produced without any nose coupling.[3]

- Even during the lowering of the velum below the level where nose coupling is zero, velic movement and velic height are not always proportional to velopharyngeal distance VP. As we will see in 5.2 below, Mermelstein (1973:1073) uses a measure based upon velic movement in order to estimate the area of nose coupling with which a sound is produced. He assumes that the surface of the area of nose coupling ("velar opening area" in his terminology) is proportional to the squared distance between the tip of the velum in its most elevated position observed and the tip of the velum in the position it actually occupies in the sound in question. Some measurements I have taken reveal that Mermelstein's method does not seem to be very reliable. In the case of the lateral X-ray tracings of the vowels in Charbonneau (1971), velic movement may be considerable for a relatively small velopharyngeal distance VP and v.v.[4] The velum may be made longer or more compact for reasons we do not understand. Indeed, Bzoch (1968:216) reports to have found differences in the length of the velum during rest position as compared to speech.[5]

In summary, it would seem that results presented in terms of velic height and velic movement should be looked at with some caution for at least two reasons: (a) there is the possibility that velic height and velic movement take values independent of the amount of nose coupling, from the moment that the amount of nose coupling is zero, and (b) even when the amount of nose coupling is greater than zero, velic movement and velic height are not strictly proportional to the velopharyngeal distance VP, since there may be changes in the length and the shape of the velum unrelated to the velopharyngeal distance and, consequently, to the amount of nose coupling.[6] Yet these results may contain useful information on relative differences in velic behaviour for various sounds.

(b) Neurophysical data concern measurements of the activity of the muscles

58

in the velopharyngeal passage. Phoneticians have claimed that the activity of
various muscles around this passage is proportional to the degree of opening
of the nasal port, i.e. to the amount of nose coupling. The muscles mainly
involved are the levator palatini - the muscle responsible for the **closing** of
the nasal port - and the palatoglossus - the sphincter responsible for the
opening of the nasal port. There are doubts about the function of the palatoglossus in the process of the lowering of the velum. Bell-Berti (1976:238-9)
observes that in the subjects she examined the "palatoglossus was found to be
active for tongue body movements and pharyngeal narrowing and not for palatal
lowering, as Fritzell reported", although she mentions one subject (id. note
1) showing palatoglossus activity during nasal consonant articulations. By
contrast, Benguerel et al. (1977b:166) report palatoglossus activity for
French nasal vowels but not for French nasal consonants. But as far as the
levator palatini is concerned, both Fritzell (1969) and Lubker (1968) as well
as Bell-Berti and Hirose (1975) have found a linear relationship between muscular activity and velic movement and/or velic height.

As we have seen already, these latter measures should be used with some
caution. This is confirmed by the conclusion of Lubker (1968:12) that "the
linear relationship between force of muscle contraction and the measures of VM
(= velic movement, PvR) and VH (= velic height, PvR) should extend over a
greater range of the correlated variables than is the case for the measure VP
(= velopharyngeal distance, PvR)".

I would like to add another observation. As speakers are not aware of what
muscles they use in order to open or close the nasal port, they may behave
quite differently from a neurophysical point of view. For reasons of anatomical differences some speakers may need to use muscles others never use in
order to produce the same articulatory or acoustic effect. Therefore, neurophysical data can be used only for global conclusions as to the amount of nose
coupling. Comparisons of activities of the levator palatini for the same
speaker may be quite reliable however.

(c) Relevant acoustic data can be found in studies on the nasal sound pressure level measured for different groups of sounds. In these studies the nasal
sound pressure level (measured near the nostrils) is compared either with the
oral sound pressure level (measured near the lips) (in Summers 1958, Von Essen
1961, Hirano et al. 1966, Schwartz 1968a and Clarke and Mackiewicz-Krassowska
1977) or with the highest nasal output level for nasal consonants (in Stevens
et al. 1975, 1976). Results exhibit the same tendencies in both cases.

It would seem that if the nasal sound pressure level were compared with the
oral sound pressure level, we could make up the acoustic correlate of N%. Comparisons, however, cannot be made in a straightforward way. Results found in
the studies quoted suggest the following picture: for high vowels produced by
normal speakers the nasal sound pressure level is usually higher than for low

vowels, other things (environments) being equal. This implies that a low vowel can only be produced with the same level of nasal sound pressure as a high vowel when its amount of nose coupling is greater than that of the high vowel. And differences in the level of nasal sound pressure between vowels of the same aperture will be due to differences in the amount of nose coupling. If interpreted in this way, results concerning nasal sound pressure level are useful (see, for instance, Schwartz 1968a). But as we will see below, data of this kind have not always been correctly interpreted.

(d) Results concerning perceptual properties of sounds may help us to determine the importance of various articulatory aspects. For example, the nasality or nonnasality of vowels interferes with the perceptual scope of the different vowels that listeners have at their disposal, as we have seen in 2.3 above. In this way, perceptual data may help us to formulate universal phonetic constraints.

(e) Typological results are data usually not produced by means of phonetic experimentation. In the preceding I have mentioned high and low vowels. They are high, or low, because they are transcribed as such in any language. High and low vowels are generally considered to be different in terms of tongue height. Differences in terms of tongue height correlate to some extent with differences in the amount of mouth constriction. The higher the vowel the smaller the amount of mouth constriction, the lower the vowel the greater the amount of mouth constriction. In this way, typological data may give rough indications on the amount of mouth constriction.

Data are representative if they are based upon speech samples produced by normal, or prototypical speakers, see 2.2 above. The phonetic transcriptions of the language of the speakers in question usually refer to speech of these normal, or prototypical, speakers. Besides normal speakers, phoneticians distinguish two other groups of speakers: nasal speakers with cleft palates and nasal speakers without cleft palate.[7] Speech samples produced by such speakers are not or not always representative of the language they speak. Perceptual experiments based upon speech samples of speakers of AmEng have shown that vowels produced by normal speakers and the two groups of nasal speakers are different in the following respects: (a) vowels produced by the two groups of nasal speakers are always judged more nasal than those produced by normal speakers; (b) the high vowels of nasal speakers with cleft palates are judged more nasal than their low vowels, whereas for the other two groups of speakers the low vowels are judged more nasal than high ones (other things being equal).

From an articulatory point of view there is confirmation for these findings: nasal speakers with cleft palates produce relatively many high and few low vowels with nose coupling as compared with nasal speakers without cleft palate. And both groups of nasal speakers produce more vowels with nose coupling than nonnasal speakers do.[8] Therefore, we should carefully distinguish between data based upon speech samples produced by normal speakers, by nasal speakers without cleft palate and by nasal speakers with cleft palates.

These data have not always been distinguished, however. Clarke and Mackiewicz-Krassowska (1977) found that, for normal speakers, the nasal sound pressure level (see (2)(c) above) of high vowels is higher than that of low vowels, as appears from the following quotation (p. 202): "The findings in this research indicate an almost direct correlation with the findings of Spriesterbach and Powers (1959) ... Perhaps the most interesting consideration that should be given to the two sets of data is that one set is based upon the utterances of cleft palate speakers whereas the present research is based upon normal subjects. This would appear to suggest that normal speakers operate in much the same way as a cleft palate speaker in that the nasal component for a particular vowel has a direct correlation with the nasal components of all other vowels."

However, the results of Spriesterbach and Powers are perceptual results: listeners had judged the high vowels of nasal speakers with cleft palates as more nasal than their low vowels. If Clarke and Mackiewicz-Krassowska had compared their acoustic results with perceptual results based on the vowels of **normal** speakers, they had found something completely different, viz. - as is correctly pointed out in Spriesterbach and Powers (1959:44) - that, for normal (AmEng) speakers, the **low** vowels would have been perceived as more nasal than the high vowels. Consequently, even if, for normal (AmEng) speakers, the (acoustic) nasal sound pressure level of high vowels is higher than for low vowels, this is not perceived by the hearers. The nasal sound pressure level of high vowels should be much higher than in low vowels in order to become perceptible. This condition is fulfilled in the speech of cleft palate speakers, but not in the speech of normal speakers. Therefore, Clarke and Mackiewicz-Krassowska's suggestion - that normal speakers operate in much the same way as cleft palate speakers do - has no basis at all.

5.2 ESTIMATES OF THE AMOUNTS OF NOSE COUPLING AND MOUTH CONSTRICTION

As I have observed above, for the collection of data on nose coupling N and mouth constriction MC, the most important source of information is X-ray tracings: films, photographs, pictures. The majority of this material consists of lateral X-ray tracings. An example of a lateral X-ray tracing is given in fig. 5-1.

In fig. 5-1, which represents a lateral 70% size view of the vocal tract of an adult male (cf. Charbonneau 1971), several articulators can be distinguished: the upper and lower incisors, the alveolar ridge, the hard palate, the velum (soft palate), the nasal port and the tongue; the lips are not

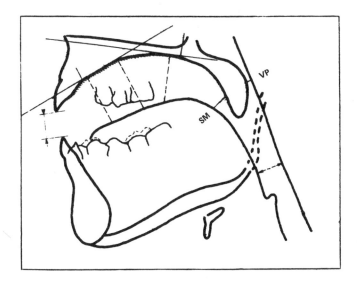

Fig. 5-1. Example of a 70% size lateral X-ray tracing of the vocal tract of an adult male. The line VP gives the shortest distance between the posterior side of the velum and the back of the pharyngeal wall; the line SM the smallest distance between, on the one hand, the velum, the palate, the alveolar ridge and the upper incisors, on the other hand, the tongue and the lower incisors. In the tracing the lips are not visible. Source: Charbonneau (1971:319) (with a few modifications).

visible in the tracing. The borderlines between different regions (the soft palate region, the hard palate region and the region between the alveolar ridge and the incisors) have been roughly indicated by means of lines. The line VP indicates the shortest distance between the posterior side of the velum and the back of the pharyngeal wall.

The line SM indicates the shortest distance in the mouth between velum, hard palate, alveolar ridge and upper incisors on the one hand, and the tongue and lower incisors on the other. The question how SM has to be determined will be answered below. In the tracing SM has not been drawn from the tip of the uvula to the tongue, but from a point about 8mm higher. This has been done because the uvula leaves the pharyngeal cavity open on both sides. As the point where the uvula ends and the velum proper starts is not visible in lateral X-ray pictures, this point has to be guessed. VP and SM have been drawn perpendicular to the air stream.

Now the question is: can we use the lines VP and SM in order to estimate the size of the cross-sections of nose coupling N and mouth constriction MC in cm^2?

First we shall look at SM and its relation to MC. The relation between measurements in X-ray tracings and the corresponding cross-sections has been examined in detail by Mermelstein (1973). Mermelstein divides the vocal tract into four regions: the soft palate, the hard palate, the alveolar ridge and upper incisors, and the labial region. For the four regions he takes the area in cm^2 to be:

$$2g_j{}^{1.5} \qquad \text{(soft palate region)} \qquad \text{(III)}$$

$$1.6g_j{}^{1.5} \qquad \text{(hard palate region)} \qquad \text{(IV)}$$

$$1.5g_j \qquad \text{for } g_j < 0.5 \quad \text{(region between alveolar} \qquad \text{(V)}$$

$$0.75+3(g_j-0.5) \quad \text{for } 0.5 < g_j < 2 \qquad \text{ridge and incisors)} \text{(VI)}$$

$$2+1.5(s_\ell-p_\ell) \qquad \text{(labial region)} \qquad \text{(VII)}$$

where g_j, p_ℓ and s_ℓ are expressed in cm; g_j is the distance between velum, hard palate, alveolar ridge, upper incisors and upper lips on the one hand, and the tongue, lower incisors or lower lips on the other; p_ℓ is the lip protrusion and s_ℓ the vertical lip separation. In the soft palate region Mermelstein has drawn g_j perpendicular to the airstream, in the hard palate region and the region between the alveolar ridge and the incisors g_j has not always been drawn entirely perpendicular to the airstream.

In figures like 5-1 the smallest mouth distance SM may be situated in the soft palate region, the hard palate region, or in the alveolar and incisors region (not in the labial region, since it is not visible). SM should be drawn perpendicular to the airstream (see above), whereas g_j not always is. I have neglected this difference, however. SM can be drawn tentatively in the three regions, its length can be measured - which gives a g_j per region - and equations (III) to (VI) can be applied. The smallest value thus found is the size of the cross-section MC. The SM corresponding with the smallest area of MC is the SM we are interested in. For instance, a smallest mouth distance of 0.5 cm results in amounts of MC of 0.71 cm^2 in the soft palate region (equation III), 0.57 cm^2 in the hard palate region (equation IV), 0.75 cm^2 in the region between the alveolar ridge and the incisors (equation VI). Since g_j is not always perpendicular to the airstream in the two latter regions, whereas SM is, it follows that values in cm^2 found in these regions may be somewhat lower than they should be. However, the influence of this factor will be small, because in the great majority of my measurements (see chapter 6) it turned out that the region in which the smallest amount of mouth constriction was situated was the soft palate region.[9]

The equations of Mermelstein (1973) give results in agreement with data found in Chiba and Kajiyama (1941:112-3, 119-28) and Fant (1960: part II). It should be noted that these equations are approximations and that the size of the cross-sections are estimates. With this proviso X-ray tracings can help us to find the cross-section in which the areas of mouth constriction MC is smallest.

Next we shall look at VP and its relation to N. Here we will not use the method proposed by Mermelstein (1973) for the reason that there is a more direct approach available.

For estimates of the size of the areas of nose coupling N some tracings of **direct** X-ray pictures are available, besides lateral X-ray tracings. I have come across tracings of this type in Bjoerk (1961:40). Bjoerk presents X-ray tracings of the largest possible areas of nose coupling for 10 normal Swedish speaking adults. These X-ray tracings were based on photographs taken from a position above the heads of the subjects by means of a special scanner. Bjoerk has made photographs of the cross-section with the velum in rest position. When the velum is in rest position, i.e. completely lowered, the area of nose coupling is at its largest. I have reproduced Bjoerk's tracings in fig. 5-2.

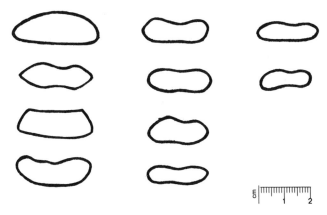

Fig. 5-2. Tracings (70 % size) of areas of nose coupling of 10 normal adult speakers. The velum is in rest position and the amount of nose coupling is at its largest. Source: Bjoerk (1961:40).

As Bjoerk's tracings of the largest areas of nose coupling are real size, I have measured their surfaces by means of a mm^2 grid. The number of mm^2 included within the circumferences of the different cross-sections are presented in table 5-1. In table 5-1 the difference between the smallest area

64

of nose coupling and the largest is as much as 190 mm^2. The data in table 5-4
concern adult speakers (Bjoerk does not mention details about sex). For children maximal areas of nose coupling even smaller than 120 mm^2 will be found.
Bjoerk's data prove that the maximal amounts of nose coupling vary considerably among adult speakers. This implies that the degree of nose coupling with
which speakers produce nasal sounds may vary considerably as well. This may be
a source of differences among speakers for the production of nasal sounds.

| 310 | 260 | 220 | 200 | 200 | 200 | 200 | 150 | 140 | 120 |

Table 5-1. Maximal areas of nose coupling in mm^2 of 10 normal Swedish speaking
adults. Data extracted from real size tracings in Bjoerk (1961:40).

Thanks to the real size representation of Bjoerk's areas of nose coupling,
his tracings can also be measured in terms of velopharyngeal distance VP. The
distances vary between about 4 mm for the subjects with the narrowest and
about 12 mm for the subject with the largest area of nose coupling.[10] Bjoerk
(1961:41) has not only taken photographs of the area of nose coupling with the
velum in rest position but also during the production of nasal sounds. He has
measured in each of 35 photographs both the distance VP and the size of the
cross- section of nose coupling N. He has presented his results in the form of
a diagram which I reproduce as figure 5-3.

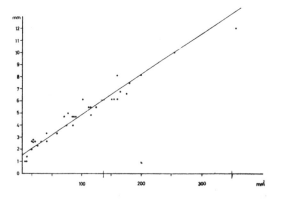

Fig. 5-3. Diagram showing the relationship between velopharyngeal distance in
mm and the corresponding size of the cross-section of nose coupling in mm^2 in
10 normal Swedish speaking subjects. Source: Bjoerk (1961:41, fig.23).

According to Bjoerk (1961:41) it can be seen in this diagram that "there is a linear relationship between the sagittal minor axis of the cross-section and its area", i.e. the relationship between the distance VP in mm (Bjoerks "sagittal minor axis of the cross-section") and the cross-section of nose coupling N in mm^2 ("its area") is rectilinear. This is, however, not entirely correct. As Warren and DuBois (1964:66) have observed, Bjoerk's data "suggest a possible quadratic relation between the two parameters at small orifice sizes". Indeed, below about 2 mm the relation seems to be curvilinear rather than rectilinear.

Taking as a starting point the straight line drawn by Bjoerk corrected for the values below 2 mm, I propose the following equations:

$$N = 15 + (VP - 2)30 \qquad \text{for } 2 \leqslant VP \qquad\qquad (IX)$$

$$N = 4VP^2 \qquad\qquad \text{for } VP < 2 \qquad\qquad (X)$$

where N is the area of nose coupling in mm^2 and VP is the velopharyngeal distance in mm.

Equations (IX) and (X) are approximations. Application of equation (IX) for a VP of 2.6 to 2.8 mm, for instance, results in an area of nose coupling of 33 to 39 mm^2. Consulting fig. 5-3, we see that for such values of VP the corresponding amount of nose coupling will be about 15-50 mm^2. For a velopharyngeal distance of about 8 mm equation (IX) gives 195mm^2, whereas according to fig. 5-3 the amount of nose coupling will be situated between 165-225 mm^2. Bjoerk does not mention whether the deviations could be corrected - at least partly - by taking into account individual properties of the subjects. Anyhow, even if individual anatomical properties of the subjects might explain the deviations to a certain extent, this would be of no help since these properties will usually not be known. Values for a VP between 2 mm and 10 mm correspond to amounts of nose coupling which may be 20 to 30 mm^2 smaller or greater.

The findings of Bjoerk are supported by information found in Fant (1960). This information is obtained from the vocal tract of one Russian speaking male subject. I have extracted the relevant details from X-ray tracings and corresponding area functions of Russian [m, n] ("normal") and [m, n] ("palatalized") in Fant (1960:140, 142). Some of Fant's area functions (two-dimensional representations of the vocal tract) are reproduced in fig. 5-4.

I estimate Fant's tracings to be at a scale of 1:3.33. For the velopharyngeal distance of palatalized [m] and [n] I measure 3 1/3 x 2.5 = 8.3 mm, of normal [m] 3 1/3 x 4.05 = 13.5 mm and of normal [n] 3 1/3 x 4.8 = 16.0 mm. Application of equation (IX) above gives an estimated area of nose coupling of 204 mm^2 for palatalized [m] and [n], of 360 mm^2 for normal [m], of 435 mm^2 for normal [n]. These areas are estimates: the real areas may be 30 to 40 mm^2 larger or smaller. I estimate that the values Fant (1960:142) presents in his

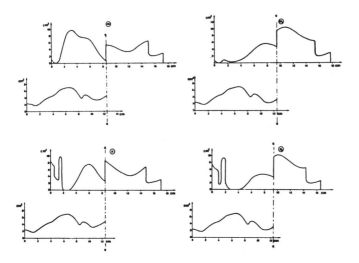

Fig. 5-4. Two-dimensional representations or area functions of nasal consonants: "normal" [m] and [n], and "palatalized" [m] and [n]. The oral and
nasal parts of the vocal tract are shown separately. The places of intercon-
nection are indicated by the lines o-o. Source: Fant (1960:142).

area functions are 210 mm^2 nose coupling for palatalized [m] and [n], and 340
mm^2 for normal [m] and [n]. This result is quite satisfactory for the two
[m]'s and for palatalized [n], but not for normal [n]. Comparison of the tracings of normal [n] and [m] with their respective area functions in Fant shows
that the deviation of normal [n] may be due to a slight inaccuracy in the
tracing of the X-ray photograph. Another possibility is that the deviation is
due to the area function of this consonant, since the velopharyngeal distances
VP in the tracings of normal [m] and [n] are different, whereas their respective area functions N are about the same.

I conclude that the equations proposed by Mermelstein (1973) and the equations extracted from the data in Bjoerk (1961), supplemented with some data
from Fant (1960)[11], make it possible to estimate the smallest amount of mouth
constriction MC and the amount of nose coupling N on the basis of the velopharyngeal distance VP and the smallest mouth distance SM measured in X-ray
pictures. Since the equations are approximations, reliable conclusions had
best be based upon the averages of series of estimates.

In the following chapters these equations will be used in order to estimate
the values of nose coupling N and of mouth constriction MC, which together
determine the N% for a given sound.

5.3 SUMMARY

1. A survey has been given of various kinds of data - mainly results of phonetic experiments but also some typological data - which concern nasality. Some indications have been given as to their reliability and their relevance to the notions nose coupling and N%. A few observations have been added as to their representativeness.

Results of phonetic experiments which concern the amount of mouth constriction MC are rare. Data may be directly related to the notion of nose coupling N, or indirectly related to the notions of nose coupling or mouth constriction MC. Data concern articulatory, neurophysical, acoustic, perceptual or typological aspects of speech sounds. They may be based upon speech samples produced by representative speakers of a language or by more or less defective speakers.

2. A method has been proposed to convert measurements taken in lateral X-ray tracings of productions of sounds into estimates of the amounts of nose coupling N and mouth constriction MC with which the sounds have been produced.

NOTES TO CHAPTER 5

1. Data of this kind are produced by means of instruments such as the nasograph of Ohala (1971), the wide angle fiberscope of Benguerel et al. (1977a), and the photo-electric nasal probe of Condax et al. (1976).

2. Data of this kind are produced by means of the nasograph (see Ohala 1971, Clumeck 1975), and can be obtained from successive X-ray tracings of the same vowel, as we will do in chapter 6 below on the basis of Charbonneau (1971) and Brichler-Labaeye (1970).

3. The same point is made in Lubker (1968:11-2).

4. I have measured some tracings in Charbonneau (1971, plates 8, 35 and 53).

5. We might express a third objection against measures of velic movement and velic height as compared with velopharyngeal distance VP. The former measures do not take into account any movements of the posterior pharyngeal wall. However, as Fritzell (1969:10) reports, the contribution of these movements to speech may be insignificant.

6. For additional data on velic movement or velic height, see for instance Fritzell (1969), Benguerel et al. (1977a and 1977b), Kuenzel (1978).

7. Speakers were chosen out of subjects who were "clinically diagnosed as functionally nasal", i.e. not "free from unpleasant nasality" (Lintz and Sherman 1961:382) or they were subjects who were judged "by three

certified speech pathologists as having clinically significant nasality during the reading of a connected speech passage" (Carney and Morris 1971, Carney and Sherman 1971).

8.   Cf. Carney and Morris (1971) and Moll (1962).

9.   Mermelstein (1973:1074) adds one other equation for g_j greater than 2 in the alveolar and incisors region. As I have not found in X-ray tracings any lines SM longer than 2 cm, situated in this region, we do not need this equation.

10. These findings show that the observation of Charbonneau (1971) concerning the "pleine nasalisation" which would need at least 6mm of velopharyngeal distance (cf. 4.1 above) cannot be taken seriously.

11. The tracings reproduced in Skolnick (1970) and Skolnick et al. (1973) cannot be used, since their scale is not stated.

CHAPTER 6

The internal structure of oral and nasal vowels in various environments

The purpose of this chapter is to determine, in various languages, the relations between the feature NASAL, phonetic representation, phonetic transcription and speech utterances in terms of internal vowel properties. I shall
examine the modifications in the value of N% in the successive phases of oral
and nasal vowels in different environments. As one of the results of the
investigation I shall propose a change in my theoretical framework: the substitution of one- dimensional physical scales by two-dimensional physical
diagrams.

I will restrict myself to oral vowels - noted as [V] - and nasal vowels -
noted as [Ṽ] - only, since phonologists and phoneticians do not usually make
more distinctions than these two in phonetic transcriptions, and I prefer to
discuss the few exceptions in due time.

I will distinguish three environments: vowels in nonnasal environment ([C-
C]), vowels preceded by a nasal consonant ([N- C]), and vowels followed by a
nasal consonant ([C-N]). [C] stands for "nonnasal consonant", [N] for "nasal
consonant". Instead of the nonnasal consonant [C] I will also examine
"utterance-final position" ([-#]), "utterance-initial position" ([#-]) and
even vowels in isolation. Other possible environments: vowels both preceded
and followed by a nasal consonant [N-N], or vowels preceded or followed by
other vowels [V-] or [-V] will not be dealt with, apart from a few exceptions,
not for lack of phonetic transcriptions of relevant speech utterances, but for
lack of experimental data concerning these utterances.

Phonologists or phoneticians do not always use the same phonetic transcription for the same speech sample. For instance, Kenyon and Knott (1944) note
inn as [In] and Chomsky and Halle would note this word with a partially nasal
vowel, as appears from their phonetic representation of it, cf. 3.1 above.
The reason is, I think, that they have different presuppositions as regards
the relation between a vowel and its environment.

Investigators who note [VN] apparently consider the nasality in the vowel
as part of the nasal consonant and do not transcribe it in the vowel. In their
view the vowel and the nasal consonant partly overlap. The point in time where
the vowel ends and the nasal consonant starts is not exactly the same: the

opening of the nasal port starts before the end of the vowel, that is at the moment that the obstruction in the mouth cavity is formed.

Investigators who note [ṼN] take it that the nasal consonant starts where the vowel ends - namely the moment when the mouth cavity is obstructed - so that they indicate the nasality in the vowel, even if the nasality apparently is caused by the nasal consonant. Thus, the point in time where the vowel ends and the nasal consonant starts are the same. In their view the nasal consonant apparently has a kind of anticipation in the vowel, manifesting itself in the opening of the nasal port. But the anticipation does not belong to the consonant as such, and has to be indicated in the vowel.

I think that the former view is more frequently (not exclusively) held by phonologists. They will state that it is not possible to isolate speech sounds out of speech utterances for experimental purposes. The latter view is somewhat more typical for experimental phoneticians. This has a practical reason: it enables them to select and isolate speech sounds out of speech utterances without problems.

The mutual influence of the sounds on each other is usually referred to as coproduction, coarticulation (sometimes assimilation).

The existence of different views on segmentation has repercussions on the way investigators view coarticulation and coproduction between sounds. This causes phonetic transcriptions to be ambiguous. If we want to solve the problem, we have to determine where, in the physical reality corresponding to the phonetic transcription, a vowel ends and its environment starts and v.v. In chapter 8 I will give my view on the segmentation problem. But it cannot be avoided here completely.

In sections 6.1, 6.2 and 6.3 I will make an inventory of the properties of oral and nasal vowels in respectively nonnasal environment, when preceded by nasal consonant and when followed by nasal consonant.

In section 6.4 I will attempt to relate the results of the inventorization to my theoretical framework.

In the course of this chapter I will refer to several appendices. In appendix 1 I discuss two studies on the basis of which I have produced data and the method by which I have produced them. In appendices 2, 3 and 4 I have presented tables from various sources with data about the nasality of vowels.

6.1 VOWELS IN NONNASAL ENVIRONMENTS

Vowels in nonnasal environments are generally[1] transcribed as either oral or nasal: as [V] or as [Ṽ]. I will examine the value of N% in the successive phases of these vowels in sets of data from various languages. In 6.1.1 I will focus on the oral vowels, in 6.1.2 on the nasal vowels. In these subsections I word, first, what we expect to find in terms of nose coupling and/or N%;

second, what I have found in phonetic experiments; and, third, what are the consequences of the findings for the transcriptions. In 6.1.3 the results will be summarized.

6.1.1 ORAL VOWELS

It seems that phonologists and phoneticians generally consider the [V] occurring in nonnasal environments to be a vowel produced without nose coupling. Indeed, as the vowel is both preceded and followed by nonnasal sounds, we would not expect the nasal port to be open.

This is exactly what I have found in the X-ray tracings - published in Brichler-Labaeye (1970) (for more details see Appendix 1) - of a European French (EurFr) speaking subject. The 25 oral vowels of this subject in [C-C] (or once [V-C]) environments are produced without nose coupling, with one exception: the [a] of PATE (id. fig.43). The eleventh and last tracing of that [a] - the phase of the vowel preceding the [t] - has been produced, I estimate, with about 45 mm^2 nose coupling and N% is about 26. But on the whole the [V] in [CVC] sequences refers to vowels produced without any nose coupling, i.e. N% is zero, see equation (I) in 4.1 above. According to other reports this finding is not exceptional. Bzoch (1968) does not find any opening of the nasal port in AmEng vowels either.

However, in the X-ray tracings of the oral vowels of a Canadian French (CanFr) subject - published in Charbonneau (1971) (for more details see Appendix 1) - the situation is quite different. I have found that phases of all the five vowels published were produced with some N% at least, and values of N% from 10 to 30 are not extreme during the central phases of the vowels (see Appendix 2, table A2-1). According to other reports this is not an exceptional finding. Condax et al. (1976) found some nose coupling in North African French vowels, though the method they used does not make it possible to determine the value of N% and the phase of the vowel in which it occurs. Moreover, there is evidence that vowels of AmEng are often produced with N% greater than zero, as appears from a series of X-ray tracings in Delattre (1965), from the measurements of velopharyngeal distance reported in Schwartz (1968a) and Lubker (1968), and from the nasograph measurements in Clumeck (1975:138).

That oral vowels are produced without any nose coupling, as in EurFr and in (at least one dialect of) AmEng, is just what we expected to find. By contrast, we did not expect to find that oral vowels are produced quite frequently with a value of N% greater than zero during their central phase. In chapter 7 I will return to this finding.

In Brichler-Labaeye (1970) and, maybe, Charbonneau (1971) oral vowels in [C-#] environment show another pattern. During their final phase oral vowels in utterance-final position are produced more often with nose coupling than without. Ten out of the twelve oral vowels of the EurFr subject in Brichler-Labaeye, and one of the three oral vowels of the CanFr subject, in Charbonneau illustrate this. For the vowels of the CanFr subject see Appendix 2 table A2-5. In the case of the EurFr subject the results are not completely reliable, since according to Brichler-Labaeye (1970:17-19) the end of the vowels occurring in utterance-final position could not always be determined with certainty, see also Appendix 1. Yet, the results found have been confirmed by many other studies.

Allen (1953:40) reports that in Sanskrit:"The nasalized vowels are not of frequent occurrence. They appear in certain types of junction (...) and as a feature of finality in the sentence or breath-group." Zagorska-Brooks (1968:22, cf.45) seems to make the same point in Polish: "It is a fact that even with oral vowels the velum can be lowered... especially in case of vowels in word-final position", though "word-final position" is not always the same as "utterance-final position". Something even more extreme seems to occur in Palauan (a Micronesian language). In Palauan a "rule adds a [ŋ] to a word ending in [a] or [o] at the major constituent breaks" (Ruhlen 1975:226). Since major constituent breaks frequently occur in utterance- final position, I think that the same tendency underlies the Palauan rule. The way in which foreign words ending in a vowel are converted into Palauan words may be another manifestation of the same tendency. In such words either the final vowel drops or [ŋ] is added, cf. Ruhlen ibid.

I think that the tendency is also present in a finding reported in Ferguson (1974:9-10; cf. 1975:187). Ferguson observes that "words for 'yes' tend to acquire nasal vowels" in many languages. As words for 'yes' will often be used as one word utterances and as these words end in a vowel in the languages which Ferguson mentions, these vowels frequently occur in utterance-final position.[2]

This tendency can easily be explained. In utterance-final position the velum may leave its raised and closed position before the end of the vowel in anticipation of its rest position during silence. As a consequence the vowel is produced with a certain amount of nose coupling and N%.

However, the vowel does not always occur in utterance-final position. In other positions it will simply be nonnasal. Since words for 'yes' may frequently occur as one word sentences - i.e. in utterance-final position -, their vowels occur more frequently in utterance-final position than vowels in other words. Consequently, they will be pronounced quite often with a nasal vowel.

It may also be that their nasality - and that of vowels in other words occurring in utterance-final position - is due to lax and careless pronunciation. In that case, it would fall outside the scope of this study, since we are interested in the level of careful pronunciation only, see 2.2 above. The tendency may be more integrated in the system of some languages than in that of others.

We expected to find that [V] in nonnasal environment concerns vowels produced without any nose coupling. However, I have found that it may describe vowels which are produced with some nose coupling: not only when the vowel occurs in utterance- final position, but even when it is followed by nonnasal consonant. N% in these vowels is generally low. Apparently, vowels transcribed as [V] are produced with N% zero or low.

6.1.2 NASAL VOWELS

It is generally assumed that vowels transcribed as [Ṽ] are produced with a considerable amount of nose coupling. It is also generally assumed, I think, that in [CṼC] sequences there are two transitional phases between the [Ṽ] and its nonnasal environment - one in which the amount of nose coupling increases (after the initial [C]) and one in which the amount of nose coupling decreases (before the final [C]). But opinions as to the exact distribution of the nose coupling over the vowel are rarely made explicit and as far as they are, they are not uniform.

Some phoneticians seem to have the point of view that, apart from these transitions, the amount of nose coupling has a constant value during the vowel as they had in the artificial speech stimuli of House and Stevens (1956) dealt with in chapter 4. See Mrayati (1975:18) and Simon (1967:72), which concern EurFr.

Others observe that a nasal vowel is characterized by a change in the amount of nose coupling from low to high. The existence of the change in French nasal vowels has been observed in Hattori et al. (1958:274), in Jensen (1967:59, 62- 4, as far as nasal vowels in context are concerned), in Benguerel et al. (1977a:152), in Borel-Maisonny (1967:11) and in Linthorst (1973:74). The observations on French nasal vowels have been supplemented by observations made by various phonologists on nasal vowels in Portuguese quoted in Almeida (1976:355), but Almeida (1971:32) mentions that in one of his two subjects "der fuer verantwortlich fuer die Nasalitaet gehaltene Fn1 um ca. 750-800 Hz sowohl erst ab der Mitte als auch ab Anfang des Vokals vorhanden sein kann", i.e. there was not always a (sharp) change in the amount of nose coupling. Linthorst (1973:76) has found a change in nasal vowels in Portuguese and in Afrikaans, though it was less outspoken than in his French data.

A third opinion I have come across is that the amount of nose coupling can be measured independently of their distribution over the various phases of the vowel. At least that is how I understand the view of Straka (1955:271, note 1) and Durand (1953:34), who consider the total quantity of air leaving the nose during the production of a vowel as a valid indication of its degree of nasal-ity.

I have not found opinions in which the exact distribution of N% over the nasal vowel plays a part.

Experimental results can give an answer to the questions what is the amount of nose coupling N, and what the value of N%, in the successive phases of a nasal vowel in [cṼc] sequences. Especially the X-ray tracings of the nasal vowels in Brichler- Labaeye (1970) and Charbonneau (1971) of the EurFr and CanFr sub-jects mentioned above contain a wealth of data.

In one respect these two subjects produce their vowels in the same way. Their average nasal vowel is characterized by a change in N%, which is essen-tially the same, viz. N% increases from (almost) zero to about 75. This has been expressed in graphic form in fig. 6-1, in which I have represented time in cs (centiseconds) on the x-axis and the average articulatory structure of the nasal vowels in terms of N% on the y-axis. The average value of N% of the 12 nasal vowels of the EurFr subject has been indicated by means of *-----*; the 31 nasal vowels of the CanFr subject by means of +-----+.

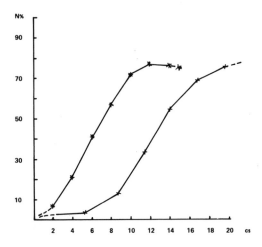

Fig. 6-1. Graphic representation of averages of 12 EurFr (*-----*) and 31 CanFr (+-----+) nasal vowels in nonnasal environment. On the x-axis the time in cs, on the y-axis the value for N%. I have taken measurements from tracings in Charbonneau (1971) and Brichler-Labaeye (1970). They have been extracted from table 6-1 below.

There is also a difference between the N%'s of the nasal vowels of the two subjects. Though the nasal vowels start with N% (almost) zero and end with N% about 75, the increase in N% starts earlier in the vowels of the EurFr sub-ject.[3] As a consequence N% in the second half of the EurFr vowels is almost constantly about 75, whereas the nasal vowels of the CanFr subject do not have such an almost constant phase, but their N% gradually increases. It takes the EurFr subject about 70 ms to arrive at a level of N% = 50, the CanFr subject about 135 ms to arrive at the same level.[4]

Taking into account both the nose coupling N and N%, see table 6-1, two other conclusions can be drawn.

	Canadian French							European French			
	17 utterance-final vowels				14 other vowels							
	N	SD	N%	SD	N	SD	N%	SD	N	SD	N%	SD
1	0	0	0	0	0	1.34	5	18.94	8	20.58	7	16.86
2	1	3.19	2	4.62	1	2.06	4	7.81	31	41.07	21	26.27
3	12	19.54	14	18.15	9	16.60	12	18.14	63	50.61	41	27.94
4	32	28.00	36	25.50	26	28.35	30	25.69	97	43.17	57	19.13
5	56	33.94	54	26.23	53	29.58	54	23.38	144	42.22	72	11.19
6	76	36.78	66	20.35	73	27.93	72	22.47	(150)	38.02	(77)	10.96
7	(79)	30.78	(76)	19.48	75	25.32	76	13.97	(151)	31.02	(76)	11.34
8					(78)	18.46	(84)	7.86	(144)	36.64	(77)	12.95
9									(152)	24.72	(82)	13.05

Table 6-1. Averages in terms of N and N%, and standard deviations (SD), of the articulatory structure of nasal vowels produced by a CanFr subject and by a EurFr subject. Numbers in the 1st column refer to the number of the tracing in which the measurements have been taken. Between the successive tracings about 28 ms have elapsed in the case of the CanFr subject, about 20 ms in the case of the EurFr subject. Values between parentheses do not concern all vowels: of the shortest vowels only 5 tracings could be made. Data have been obtained from Appendix 2, tables 2-2, 2-3 and 2-4.

A comparison of the amount of nose coupling N and N% reveals that on an average an increase in nose coupling N involves an increase in N% although the relationship is not simply rectilinear. This conclusion is valid for the two speakers.

The second conclusion concerns a difference in size of the nasal port, cf. 5.2 above. When we compare averages of the amount of nose coupling N in table 6-1, we see that the greatest amount of nose coupling of the EurFr subject is about twice as great as that of the CanFr subject, whereas the highest N% of both subjects is the same. I think it plausible that this difference in the amount of nose coupling is not an essential property of nasal vowels, but is due to anatomical differences between the two speakers: the EurFr subject can open his nasal port considerably more than the CanFr subject.

In fig. 6-1 and table 6-1 I have presented the nasal vowels of each speaker as a group. The question may be raised whether this is justified.

The differences between the two kinds of nasal vowels of the CanFr subject - 17 utterance-final and 14 followed by a nonnasal consonant - are small, except in one respect: vowel length, as can be observed in Appendix 2, tables A2-2 and A2-3. The duration of the utterance-final nasal vowels is 6 to 7 tracings, i.e. about (6 to 7x28ms=) 168 to 196 ms; of the other vowels 12 to 15 tracings, i.e. about (12 to 15x28ms=) 336 to 420 ms. However, if we examine what happens in the extra final phase of these latter vowels, it is no longer possible to detect a systematic pattern. In terms of N% this vowel portion may even range from 0 to 100. This is the same as saying that the structure of the extra phase may range from that of a nonnasal vowel to that of a nasal consonant. As the phase is absent in utterance-final vowels and has no typical structure in the other vowels, it cannot be a characteristic part of the articulatory structure of nasal vowels (although it may have some language-specific function in making the vowel longer in [-C] environments). Therefore I do not consider this portion of the vowels to be an inherent part of nasal vowels and I feel justified to take the two kinds of vowels of this subject together in table 6-1 and fig. 6-1.

The tendencies observed for the vowels of the CanFr speaker are also present in the vowels of the EurFr speaker, though less outspoken and not related to context. See Appendix 2 table A2-4. For the EurFr speaker the length is unpredictable and ranges from about (5x20 ms=) 100 ms to about (12x20 ms=) 240 ms. But Brichler-Labaeye (1970:69-70, 82) observes that the differences of length in the vowels are a consequence of a particular speech habit of her subject. Therefore, there is no reason to split up the vowels of the EurFr subject either.

A last observation concerns the nonnasal sound - usually a consonant - which precedes the nasal vowel. Both the vowels of the Canadian subject (Appendix 2, tables A2-2 and A2-3) and those of the European subject (Appendix 2, table A2-4) are preceded by either a [-continuant] sound or a [+continuant] sound. Whenever the vowels are preceded by a [+continuant] sound, the EurFr subject seems to start the lowering of the velum earlier, where the CanFr subject does not.

Having compared the nasal vowels in nonnasal environment of the two subjects, we see that

(a) they have in common that the value of N% increases from (almost) zero to about 75;

(b) when N% increases, the amount of nose coupling N increases as well, though not rectilinearly;

(c) the only linguistically systematic difference concerns the fact that in the EurFr nasal vowels N% increases earlier than in the CanFr nasal vowels;

(d) the other differences - concerning the amount of nose coupling, vowel length and the transition to the next consonant - are either individual or language-specific but not linguistically systematic.

Though it is risky to base conclusions on the nasal vowels of two speakers only - I assume that they are representative speakers of their language -, the findings suggest that the increase in N% from (almost) zero to about 75 or an increase in the amount of nose coupling N are characteristic for a nasal vowel and that investigators who have this view are right. Transcriptions [ṽ] do not present problems, though a nasal vowel in EurFr is slightly different from a nasal vowel in CanFr. I will come back to this difference in 6.4 below.

6.1.3. SUMMARY

Oral vowels ([v]) in nonnasal environment (mainly [C-C]) are not always produced with N% zero. In CanFr, N% in the central phase of such vowels may be as high as 30. In EurFr, oral vowels are usually nonnasal, i.e. N% is zero.

Oral vowels in utterance-final position ([C-#]) are usually produced with N% greater than zero at the end of the vowels. The exact value of N% may differ from language to language.

Nasal vowels ([ṽ]) in nonnasal environment are produced with an increase in N% from (almost) zero to about 75 in their successive phases. Taking the beginning, the centre and the end of the average nasal vowel, the change can be described as increasing from almost 0 via 50 to 75 (almost 0-50-75) in EurFr, as increasing from almost 0-20-75 in CanFr.

The distinction in terms of N% between oral and nasal vowels in EurFr is greater than that in CanFr. Between the oral and nasal vowels of the EurFr subject there is always a considerable difference, whereas specific oral and nasal vowels of the CanFr subject cannot always be distinguished.

Transcriptions of oral and nasal vowels are correct, but some further qualifications should account for small differences among oral vowels and among nasal vowels.

6.2 VOWELS PRECEDED BY A NASAL CONSONANT

Vowels preceded by a nasal consonant are generally noted as [v] or [ṽ]. I will examine the value of N% in the successive phases of these vowels in sets of data from various languages. In 6.2.1 I will focus on the oral vowels, in 6.2.2 on the nasal vowels. In the subsections I will state, first, what we

expect to find in terms of nose coupling and/or N%; second, what I have found
in phonetic experiments; and third, what are the consequences of the findings
for the transcriptions. In 6.2.3 the results will be summarized.

6.2.1 ORAL VOWELS

Though the notation [NVC] is quite commonly used to describe speech utterances
in many languages, I think that phoneticians and phonologists will agree that
the [V] in such sequences stands for an oral vowel produced with a slight or
accidental amount of nose coupling in its initial phase. The nasal port is
open during the nasal consonant and it takes some time to close it during the
beginning of the vowel. During the initial part of the vowel we expect to find
a decrease in the amount of nose coupling N. Investigators will view the fact
that the amount of nose coupling N is greater than zero in the beginning of
such vowels as a property of the nasal consonant which need not be indicated:
a more or less inevitable consequence of the coarticulation (coproduction)
between the nasal consonant and the subsequent oral vowel.

For example, Hyman (1972:169f) observes that "in all languages a vowel that
is adjacent to a nasal consonant must become at least slightly (perhaps imper-
ceptibly) nasalized". And he uses the convention that "nasalization will be
marked ... only when the nasalization represents a **phonological** property of a
given language... In order for nasalization to become phonologized, it is only
necessary that the process exceed the degree that can be said to characterize
all languages".

Balasubramanian (1980:372-3) - writing on vowel nasality in Tamil - goes
even further than Hyman: "The I.P.A. nasalisation diacritic ([~], PvR) has not
been used in the transcriptions ..., except when phonemic nasalisation is
indicated. This is ... because it is felt that this diacritic should be used
only to indicate distinctive nasalisation in a language in which both accidental and distinctive nasalisation are possible."[5] This implies for Balasubramanian that he never notes nasality in Tamil vowels next to nasal consonant.

Straka (1955:270) takes a deviant position, it seems. He proposes to use a
special symbol for incomplete and imperceptible nasality in vowels next to
nasal consonants. Although this is a logical step for those investigators who
have the opinion that the nasal consonant ends and the vowel begins at the
same point in time, I think that the majority of investigators does not indicate slight or accidental or (perhaps) imperceptible nasalisation in vowels
next to a nasal consonant.

As to N% I expect that during the beginning of the oral vowel N% will be
greater than zero, since during the preceding nasal consonant N% is 100. But
N% will decrease early in the vowel, because the vowel is an oral vowel, i.e.
produced with N% zero or low. As we have seen in 6.1.2 above, the typical

structure of a nasal vowel in nonnasal environment is an increase in N% from (almost) zero to about 75. The typical structure of an oral vowel preceded by a nasal consonant will be a rapid decrease in N% from 100 (the end of the nasal consonant) to zero. This decrease parallels the decrease in the amount of nose coupling N described above.

Indeed, I have come across data which show that N% and N decrease during the oral vowel. As far as N and N% are concerned a few data have been found in Brichler-Labaeye (1970), in Charbonneau (1971) and in Lubker and Moll (1965:266, fig. 6). These data are presented in Appendix 3, tables A3-1 to A3-3. I observe the same tendency in data about nose coupling only, see Clumeck (1975:136), Fritzell (1969:56-7), Kuehn (1976:97), Ohala (1974a:363; 1975:304), Ohala (M.) (1975:322) and Perkell (1969:72-3). Here again the nose coupling decreases during the vowel. Except for Ohala (M.) (1975), a study of Hindi, these data concern AmEng.

Yet, it would be misleading to conclude that all the data confirm the expectation that N% and N decrease to zero during the initial phase of the oral vowel.

In the data of Brichler-Labaeye (1970), and of Charbonneau (1971), we see that several vowels are produced with a greater amount of nose coupling N than the preceding nasal consonant during its final phase, or that during the first phase of the vowel the amount of N increases and does not decrease. Of the 16 (Canadian and European) French vowels in tables A3-1 and A3- 2 (Appendix 3) as much as 10 show such irregularities.

Other data - about nose coupling only - are not in agreement with the expectation either: they show that the amount of nose coupling N is not greatest during the nasal consonant, but during (part of) the oral vowel: see Kuehn (1976:98,100,101), Weatherly-White et al. (1966:295) and Clumeck (1975:136 [mæ]) for some very clear cases, and Fritzell (1969:57) and Moll (1960:235, 237) for some less clear cases.[6]

There is another peculiarity. When I look at the moment at which the nasal port is closed, I observe that this moment often occurs late in the vowel. Of the six vowels in the (Canadian and European) French data (tables A3-1 and A3-2) in which the amount of nose coupling decreases, four are produced with closure of the nasal port in the second half of the vowel. This is also the case in Clumeck (1975:147, cf. Clumeck 1976:347) which contains data on the moment at which the nasal port is closed after vowel onset from an AmEng, a Hindi and a Swedish subject. These latter data do not contain information about the increase or the decrease of the amount of nose coupling during the time the nasal port is open.

I conclude that
- I have not come across any examples of oral vowels in [NVC] (sometimes [NV#]) sequences produced without any nose coupling, i.e. N% and N at the

beginning of these vowels is always greater than zero;
- in various languages vowels may be produced with a greater amount of nose coupling N than the (final phase of the) preceding nasal consonant;
- the velum tends to close the nasal port later in the vowel than we had expected.

These results suggest that the notation [NVC] may not always be correct. In several examples discussed above the nasality in the "oral" vowel cannot be simply attributed to the nasal consonant. I will take up this point again in 6.2.2 below.

6.2.2 NASAL VOWELS

Phoneticians and phonologists quite frequently indicate vowel nasality in vowels preceded by a nasal consonant. See Hyman (1972), Ternes (1973) and Bothorel (1977), to mention some studies which do not concern French. Sequences of the type [NṼC] contain fully, or phonological, nasal vowels in their notation.

As we have seen (in 6.1.2) that the typical structure of a nasal vowel in nonnasal environment consists of an increase in N% from (almost) zero to about 75, the next question is what is the N% of nasal vowels preceded by a nasal consonant. If the increase in N% from (almost) zero to about 75 - or at least an increase in N% - is typical for nasal vowels in other environments than [C-C], we may expect that it will be present in nasal vowels preceded by a nasal consonant as well, and that the [Ṽ] in an [NṼC] sequence will refer to almost the same physical state of affairs as the [Ṽ] in [CṼC].

However, taking into account coarticulation (coproduction), we may not find an increase in N% from (almost) zero to about 75 in nasal vowels preceded by a nasal consonant. The nasal port is open during the production of the nasal consonant, and it may simply remain open during the initial and central phases of the following nasal vowel. In other words, the amount of nose coupling N at the end of the nasal consonant may be the same in the nasal vowel (and decrease at the end of the nasal vowel during the transition to the nonnasal sound). Consequently, coarticulation (coproduction) would rather predict no increase in the amount of nose coupling N from low (or zero) to high (rather, at the end of the nasal vowel, a decrease from high to zero). As we have seen in 6.1.2 - with respect to the EurFr and CanFr subjects - an increase in the amount of nose coupling N corresponds to an increase in N% (although not rectilinearly). The influence of coarticulation (coproduction) on N% is not clear, but - since N will decrease during the vowel - an increase in N% is not to be expected.

If both the increase in N% is linguistically relevant and coarticulation (coproduction) is physically inevitable, we may find as a result a kind of compromise. Instead of an increase from (almost) zero to about 75, we will find an increase from a higher value to about 75, i.e. a relatively small increase in N%. The amount of nose coupling N, which is already greater than zero at the start, will slightly increase as well.

It would be interesting to see whether we find this compromise reflected in the data. However, very few relevant data have been published. Some information on velic movement can be found in Clumeck (1976) (to be supplemented by Clumeck unpublished - a slightly more complete version of Clumeck 1976), Benguerel et al. (1977a) and Ohala (M.) (1975). In addition, I analyzed two unpublished X-ray films at the INSTITUT DE PHONETIQUE of the UNIVERSITE DES SCIENCES HUMAINES at Strasbourg.[7] The evidence I have found concerns French, Breton, Amoy (a Chinese language) and Hindi.

In the French data of Clumeck (unpublished) we find some nasograph graphics of three speakers, representing relative differences in amount of nose coupling in sequences of nasal consonant and nasal vowel in a frame sentence (cf. Clumeck 1976:5). The speakers mentioned by Clumeck generally produced nasal vowels with increase in N from rather low to high. In order to realize this change they used two different strategies. One was to open the nasal port - already open during the nasal consonant - even further during the succeeding nasal vowel. The other was to close the nasal port to some extent during the final phase of the nasal consonant and to open it further again during the succeeding nasal vowel.[8]

In Benguerel et al. (1977a) there is a difference between a sequence of a nasal vowel preceded by a nasal consonant in isolation and in a frame sentence. In a frame sentence, a slight movement of the velum towards closure of the nasal port can be observed during the vowel. The difference between [a] and [ã] in this environment (ibid. fig. 1) - and between [v] and [ṽ] (ibid. fig. 5b) - consists of more and longer nose coupling of the nasal vowel. This finding is more or less in correspondence with what we expected (see above) on the basis of coarticulation (or coproduction). In isolation, however, sequences of [Nṽ] were produced with the amount of nose coupling increasing during the nasal consonant and the nasal vowel (ibid. fig. 4 and 5b). This finding is more in correspondence with the kind of compromise we expected to find.

The best evidence comes from X-ray films. I have examined (1) [Nṽc], (2) [Nṽn] and (3) [Nṽ] sequences in an X-ray film analyzed for other purposes in Simon (1968).

    (1) Les **mon**tagnes rocheuses
    (2) **Mon** opinion sur les oignons
    (3) L'enseigne**ment**, l'éloigne**ment**

In the four relevant nasal vowels - occurring in the syllables in bold type- N%

increased. The increase was most clearly present in both [ã]'s which have an almost identical structure, somewhat less clearly in the [õ] of **montagne**, and least clearly, but still present in the [õ] of **mon**. In all examples the velum continued the lowering started during the nasal consonant.

It appears from the above data that French nasal vowels following a nasal consonant usually exhibit an increase in N or in N%.[9]

The same conclusion can be drawn from the analysis of the relevant nasal vowels in an X-ray film of a Breton speaker (of Argol, a village in Finistère-Sud). The movement of the velum could be followed in the film without too much difficulty, but whether the nasal port was open or closed was hardly ever visible. Therefore, my observations can be expressed in terms of velic movement only. Nasal vowels or diphthongs preceded by a nasal consonant (and in some cases even followed by it) occur in nine utterances, which have been reproduced from Bothorel (1978) in Appendix 3, table A3-4A below. The utterances have been given in three forms: (a) in one of the more or less standard Breton orthographies; (b) in narrow phonetic transcription (IPA);[10] (c) in English translation. The majority of data concerns nose coupling N. I found that the nasal vowels had a structure in which the amount of nose coupling N usually increased and in which N% always seemed to increase, see Appendix 3, table A3-4B.

Besides the French and Breton data there are reports which concern Amoy and Hindi. Clumeck (1976, fig.2,p.345-6) presents the relative difference in nose coupling between the vowels in [mĩ] and [mã] of an Amoy speaker. During [mĩ] the nose coupling decreased, although slightly, from the beginning to the end of the nasal vowel, whereas during [mã] the nose coupling - which slightly decreased during the last part of the [m] - increased. Probably the [ĩ] does not contain an increase in N%, but the [ã] - again - does.[11]

As far as Hindi is concerned, Ohala (M.) (1975:321) observes with respect to minimal pairs like [mas] "month" and [mãs] "meat", [mɛ] "wine" and [mɛ̃] "I": "Such minimal pairs are rare... and in fact, may be homophonous for most speakers. When the contrast is made, nasograph data revealed that both the vowels have the same amount of nasalization immediately after the initial nasal, but the distinctively nasalized one has much greater nasalization towards the end of the vowel." Indeed, it appears from her fig.1 (p.322) that the amount of nose coupling at the end of the distinctive nasal vowel in [mãs] is much greater than the amounts of nose coupling in (a) the beginning of this vowel; (b) the preceding [m]; (c) the vowel in [mas].

Though there are exceptions, the general pattern in French, Breton, Amoy and Hindi is that nasal vowels preceded by a nasal consonant tend to be produced with an increasing amount of nose coupling N and a small increase in N%. I consider this to be evidence in favour of the prediction that both coarticulation (coproduction) and the increase in N% play a part in the formation of these nasal vowels. Since the increase in N% is usually present - as it was in nasal vowels in nonnasal environment -, it follows that the increase in N% characterizes a nasal vowel rather independently of the environment in which it occurs, although it may be overruled to some extent by the nose coupling of a preceding nasal consonant.

In 6.2.1 above I have found that the [V] in many [NVC] sequences had the same structure as the [Ṽ] in [NṼC]. Apparently, phonetic transcriptions [NVC] should often be substituted by [NṼC]. Speech utterances transcribed as [NṼC], however, usually have been noted correctly.

6.2.3 SUMMARY

Oral vowels in [NVC] (or [NV#]) sequences are always produced with some nose coupling in their initial phase.

Many of these vowels are produced with an increase in the amount of nose coupling N and in N% or with nose coupling during a more considerable part of the vowel than we would have expected on the basis of coarticulation (coproduction). As a consequence, [NVC] transcriptions should often be substituted by [NṼC].

Nasal vowels in [NṼC] ([NṼ#] or [NṼN]) sequences are usually produced with an increase in the amount of nose coupling and in N%. Coarticulation (coproduction) between the nasal consonant and the nasal vowel makes the increase in N% smaller than that in a nasal vowel in nonnasal environment.

6.3 VOWELS FOLLOWED BY A NASAL CONSONANT

Vowels followed by a nasal consonant are generally noted as [V] or as [Ṽ]. I will examine the value of N% in the successive phases of these vowels in sets of data from various languages. In 6.3.1 I will focus on the oral vowels, in 6.3.2 on the nasal vowels. In these subsections I will state, first, what we expect to find in terms of nose coupling and/or N%; second, what I have found in phonetic experiments; and, third, what are the consequences of the findings for the transcriptions. In 6.3.3 the results will be summarized.

6.3.1 ORAL VOWELS

Phoneticians and phonologists will agree that the [V] in [CVN] sequences is produced with a slight or accidental amount of nose coupling. Many of them will view the fact that the amount of nose coupling is greater than zero at the end of the vowel as a property of the nasal consonant, which needs not be indicated: a more or less inevitable consequence of the coarticulation (coproduction) between the oral vowel and the following nasal consonant. Schourup (1973:203) states: "a certain amount of nasalization is inevitable on any prenasal vowel; otherwise the nasal would have to be released by means of velic plosion."

However, some investigators feel the need for a special symbol. A special symbol for partial vowel nasality is urgent for those investigators who are of the opinion that the vowel ends and the nasal consonant begins at the same point in time. Besides nonnasal ([VN]) and completely nasal sequences ([ṼN]), Straka (1955:270) recognizes as many as three other possible degrees of partial vowel nasality. And as we have seen in chapter 3, Chomsky and Halle (1968) provide a phonetic representation of **inn** in which the vowel is partially nasal, which suggests a corresponding phonetic transcription in which the vowel is partially nasal as well.

In terms of N% I expect an increase from zero to 100. N% will be 100 the moment at which the mouth cavity is obstructed for the production of the nasal consonant. Thus, I would predict that
- the amount of nose coupling N and, consequently, N% will start to be greater than zero already during the vowel;
- the amount of nose coupling N will never become greater in the vowel than in the beginning of the nasal consonant (this is self-evident for N%, see equation (I) in chapter 4);
- the moment at which the amount of nose coupling N or N% will start to be greater than zero will be rather late in the vowel, if we want to view it as an inevitable property of the nasal consonant.

For those investigators who segment the vowel and the nasal consonant at one and the same moment in time, the vowel is characterized by an increase in N and N%, similar to - but not the same as - what I have found for nasal vowels in [CṼC] sequences, see 6.1.2 above. The differences from nasal vowels in [C-C] environment will be that
- N and N% start to be greater than zero later in the vowel in [C-N] environment;
- N does not need to become as high;
- N% increases from zero to 100, not from (almost) zero to 75;

I have been able to examine two points in the experimental data:
1. The moment at which the nose coupling N and, consequently, N% starts to be greater than zero during the vowel;
2. The question whether or not the amount of nose coupling N during the (last part of the) vowel is smaller than the amount of nose coupling N (at the beginning) of the nasal consonant.

1. The moment at which the nose coupling N and, consequently, N% starts to be greater than zero during the vowel.

I have found data on six languages in Clumeck (1976). Clumeck examined the moment at which the nasal port opened in vowels preceding a nasal consonant. His results answer the question what percentage of the duration of a vowel followed by a nasal consonant is produced with nose coupling (in his terms: velic opening) greater than zero. These results are presented in Appendix 4, table A4-1.

Apparently, there is a considerable difference between Amoy and EurFr on the one hand, in which the nose coupling starts rather late in the vowels, and Portuguese and AmEng on the other hand, in which it starts early or even before the vowel, i.e. more than twice as early in the vowel as in Amoy. Languages such as Hindi and Swedish are situated in between.

The EurFr, AmEng and Swedish data of Clumeck (1976) can be supplemented by some other data from these languages. Since these data have not been obtained by the same methods, comparisons must, of course, be made with caution.

The X-ray tracings in Charbonneau (1971) of the vowels of the CanFr subject allow estimates of the moment at which the nasal port has opened. The CanFr data have been presented in Appendix 4, table A4-2: four times [ɛ] and three times [a]. A few simple calculations reveal that, on an average, the CanFr vowels were produced with nose coupling for about 75% of their duration. However, this kind of result was not obtained by Delattre (1965:103) for the vowel [a] in EurFr [blam] "(he) blames" - representative of three EurFr subjects. In one out of four X-ray tracings of the vowel the nasal port is open, which means that the vowel was produced with nose coupling for about 13% to 37% of its duration, which is an extremely short time in comparison with the EurFr vowels mentioned in Clumeck. The EurFr speakers in Delattre (1965) start nose coupling much later than those in Clumeck (1976). The CanFr speaker behaves more like Clumeck's EurFr speakers than Delattre's EurFr speakers do. But in any case nose coupling in French vowels starts relatively late in the vowel, probably later in EurFr than in CanFr.

It appears that in AmEng nose coupling, as a rule, starts relatively early in the vowels.[12] From various publications on (measurements based upon) X-ray tracings of AmEng vowels I have obtained some data on the moment at which the nasal port opens, and put them together in Appendix 4, table A4-3. As can be seen in this table, it is almost a rule that vowels in [C-N] in AmEng are produced with nose coupling and N% greater than zero for two thirds or more of their total length.[13]

Clumeck's results on Swedish can be compared with a set of Swedish data published in Bjoerk (1961), in which vowels preceding a nasal consonant have been classified in the following terms: (a) the vowel was produced with the nasal port open from beginning to end; (b) the vowel was produced with the nasal port closed; (c) the nasal port opened during the vowel. For these data see Appendix 4, table A4-4. As the great majority of Swedish subjects examined by Bjoerk produced vowels before nasal consonant with the nasal port open right from the beginning, we find the kind of result we have found for AmEng vowels, and this is different from what has been found by Clumeck, see above.[14]   Therefore, there are at least two trends in Swedish: one group of speakers produces oral vowels before a nasal consonant with nose coupling starting early, as in AmEng (the great majority of the subjects of Bjoerk and one speaker of Clumeck, see note 4). The other group produces oral vowels before a nasal consonant either without any nose coupling or with the nasal port starting to be open after the onset of the vowel. This latter group behaves more like the EurFr subjects.

Therefore, the moment at which nose coupling starts in a vowel preceding a nasal consonant is not the same in different languages. In languages like AmEng, Portuguese, some Swedish dialects it starts early in the oral vowel, in languages like EurFr, Amoy it starts late. In Hindi, CanFr and other Swedish dialects the nose coupling starts neither early nor late. The oral vowels preceding nasal consonant in AmEng and Portuguese have in fact the structure of a nasal vowel in nonnasal environment, see 6.1.2 above. This has been explicitly stated for Hindi as well, see Ohala (M.) (1975:323):[15] "Velic open-ing is about the same for "distinctive" nasalization and "non- distinctive" nasalization, e.g., [sãs], [mãs] vs. [kan] and [nam] show a similar degree of nasalization."[16]

So far I have compared vowels from different languages without taking into account language-intrinsic factors such as differences in vowel height, vowel length, the nature of the preceding sound. In chapter 7 I will return to vowel height. Vowel length and the nature of the preceding sound can be illustrated here.

Concerning vowel length, it appears from the data in Clumeck (1976) that in Swedish nose coupling starts earlier in short vowels than it does in the long ones.

As to the preceding sound, Moll en Daniloff (1971:682) report that, when the preceding [C] is a stop or fricative, the nasal port opens (or nose cou-pling starts) later than when it is not. This difference is hardly ever indi-cated in AmEng transcriptions. Balasubramanian (1980:364-7) finds in Tamil that [CVN...] sequences are produced with nasality but [#VN...] sequences are not.

In these cases we see that, within the same language, vowels noted as [V] preceding a nasal consonant are different with respect to nasality depending on vowel length and nature of the preceding sound. These differences should be indicated in phonetic transcriptions.

2. The amount of nose coupling in the last part of the vowel and the amount of nose coupling at the beginning of the nasal consonant.

I have compared the amount of nose coupling in AmEng vowels with the amount of nose coupling in the following nasal consonant, wherever this was possible. I have found quite a number of such vowel tokens. The results have been presented in Appendix 5, table A5-6.[17] In about one half of the tokens the amount of nose coupling during the vowel is not greater than that during the nasal consonant. This is the result we expected.

However, in about the other half of the tokens the amount of nose coupling in part of the vowels is greater than the amount of nose coupling during the beginning of the nasal consonant. The same phenomenon occurs in the CanFr data (see Appendix 4, table A4-2) for 4 out of 7 vowels, but not in the EurFr vowel of [blam] in Delattre (1965). (No other data of this kind are available.)

The finding that the amount of nose coupling N in (part of) the vowel is frequently greater than that in the beginning of the nasal consonant is unexpected, since it cannot really be accounted for by considering it a consequence of coarticulation (coproduction) between vowel and nasal consonant. Yet I will not deal with it here, as the data upon which the finding is based show systematic differences in terms of vowel height, which will be further analyzed in chapter 7.

Vowels - transcribed as [V] - preceding a nasal consonant refer to a wide variety of structures in terms of nose coupling and N% in various languages and even sometimes within the same language. Especially in AmEng these vowels have the structure of nasal vowels and should be noted as [Ṽ]. Below in 6.3.2 I will come back to this problem.

6.3.2 NASAL VOWELS

Sequences [cṼN] or [#ṼN] do often occur, although Balasubramanian does not use them (see 6.2.1 above): they occur (besides [CVN]) in the Breton examples of Bothorel (1978), see Appendix 3, table A3-4; in the French examples of Jespersen (1913:60) (for instance [ã ndã] en dedans); in the Scottish Gaelic transcriptions of Ternes (1973); and in the AmEng transcriptions of Malècot (1960) and Lovins (1978). I expect that these vowels have the same structure as nasal vowels in nonnasal environment. The increase in N% will be from (almost) zero to about 75, followed by a transitional phase to the nasal consonant during which N% increases from about 75 to 100 (the moment of obstruction of the mouth cavity during the nasal consonant). The amount of nose coupling during the vowel may be greater than it is during the nasal consonant, since the vowel is nasal in its own right.

I have not found experimental data published on the articulatory properties of [Ṽ] in [cṼN] sequences, apart from those mentioned in 6.3.1 above on AmEng. As I have observed there, AmEng vowels before a nasal consonant have the structure of nasal vowels and should be transcribed as such. I have found this conclusion confirmed by comparing two experiments on perceptual qualities of AmEng and EurFr vowels followed by a nasal consonant: Ali et al. (1971) and

Clumeck (1971) (in chapter 7 I will come back to these experiments). Although we do not know the articulatory properties of the vowels used in these experiments, we may expect that in the AmEng vowels, nose coupling and N% start earlier than in the EurFr.

In the two experiments listeners were AmEng. In the speech samples the nasal or nonnasal consonant following the vowels was removed. Thus, two groups of vowels could be distinguished: vowels which had been followed by nasal consonant, and vowels which had been followed by nonnasal consonant. In the French data a third group of vowels was added: nasal vowels. The listeners perceived a clear difference in nasality between the two groups of AmEng vowels, whereas they did not perceive any difference between the two groups of EurFr vowels. The only vowels they perceived as nasal were the nasal vowels. For the detailed results concerning the EurFr vowels, see Appendix 4, table A4-5. This finding would confirm that vowels before a nasal consonant in EurFr are oral, whereas those in AmEng are nasal.

That AmEng vowels before a nasal consonant are nasal can also be derived from the conclusions in Malècot (1960). On the basis of perceptual experiments with words of the structure CVNC' (V = oral or nasal vowel, N = nasal consonant homorganic with C', C'= voiceless stop) Malècot finds confirmed his hypothesis that "vowel nasality is by itself a sufficient cue to convey the impression of a following nasal" (p.224) The same result was found, though slightly less convincing, for the only word ending in a voiced stop (p.225): **canned** [kæ̃d] of which "the nasal consonant resonances were removed", but not the voicing of this consonant.[18]

Sequences transcribed as [CṼN] in AmEng seem to be correct. They may not be different, in terms of N%, from such sequences in EurFr, for instance [ãndã̃] **en dedans**, mentioned in Jespersen. In chapter 8 I will discuss these transcriptions further.

6.3.3 SUMMARY

Oral vowels in [CVN] ([#VN]) sequences are usually produced with at least some nose coupling during their final phase.

Many of these vowels are produced with more nose coupling, or nose coupling during a longer portion of the vowel, than might be expected on the basis of coarticulation (coproduction) between the oral vowel and the nasal consonant.

The moment at which nose coupling starts, and the amount of nose coupling in the vowel differ in different languages. For instance, in EurFr it is late, but in AmEng it is early in the vowel. This moment may even be different for vowels before a nasal consonant occurring in different environments within the same language, as in Tamil and Swedish.

Apart from AmEng, no experimental data are available concerning the articulatory properties of nasal vowels in [CṼN] sequences. Both articulatory and perceptual data point out that in AmEng these vowels are nasal vowels.

Many vowels in [CVN] sequences and probably all vowels in [CṼN] sequences have the same structure, in terms of N%, as nasal vowels in nonnasal environment [CṼC]. This implies that many transcriptions of the type [CVN] are not correct.

6.4 THEORETICAL IMPLICATIONS

In the preceding sections I have attempted to determine what are the physical properties - in terms of N% and N - of oral vowels [V] and nasal vowels [Ṽ] in three environments - [(C)- (C)], [N-(C)], [(C)-N] - in various languages. In this section I shall discuss some theoretical implications.

In 6.4.1 I will focus on the necessity to substitute one- dimensional physical scales by two-dimensional physical diagrams, substitution which enables me to take into account relative time properties of sounds.

In 6.4.2 I will deal with relations between universal physical diagrams (universal phonetic constraints), language- specific physical diagrams (low level phonological rules and the language-specific interpretation conventions of the feature NASAL) and phonetic transcription.

Other results obtained in the preceding sections have to be analyzed further in later chapters before I will attempt to relate them to my theory. Especially problems related to the segmentation of vowels and consonants will hardly be dealt with below.

6.4.1 THE INCREASE IN N% AND THE PHYSICAL SCALE

Nasal vowels [Ṽ] in nonnasal environment or followed by a nasal consonant are characterized by an increase in N% from (almost) zero to about 75, see 6.1.2 and 6.3.2. Nasal vowels preceded by a nasal consonant are usually characterized by a smaller increase in N%, which starts at a higher value, as a consequence of the coarticulation (coproduction) between the nasal consonant and the nasal vowel, see 6.2.2.

According to my definition of the feature NASAL (its articulatory correlate), nasal sounds are produced with N% higher than in oral sounds, see 4.2 above. On each physical scale related to the articulatory correlate there is a point - which may be different per language - indicating the borderline between nasal and oral sounds of a certain kind.

In the preceding sections I have found that the **higher** value of N% in nasal vowels as compared to that of oral vowels, appears to be **a gradual increase to** this higher value. This increase cannot be expressed on a one-dimensional physical scale, we need a two-dimensional physical diagram. A two- dimensional physical diagram will enable us to present the increase in N% from (almost) zero to about 75 in relative time, see fig. 6-2.

90

N%

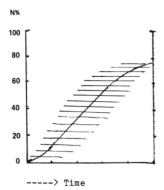

-----> Time

Fig 6-2. Physical diagram related to the feature NASAL. The line indicates
nasal vowels.

The x-axis in fig. 6-2 represents time, the y-axis the value of N%. Nonnasal vowels are situated on the x-axis (N% is zero). Oral vowels will be
dealt with later. The physical diagram represents graphically the following
universal phonetic constraint:

In vowels the feature coefficient [+nas] refers to an increase in N% from
(almost) zero to about 75; [-nas] does not refer to such an increase.

The increase in N% has been drawn in a broad area. Nasal vowels may be called
nasal as long as they occur in this area. This area should be specified in
the universal constraint as well. Parts of the diagram will not be used. For
instance, for vowels N% will never be as high as 100. Of course, on the basis
of further experimental research we may want to adapt the diagram and the constraint slightly.

My proposal to introduce the factor "relative time" is something new, at
least for nasal vowels, and I should consider the possibility whether I can do
without it. For instance, I could view the (almost) zero value of N% in the
beginning of the increase in the vowel as the consequence of coarticulation
(coproduction) between the nasal vowel and the preceding nonnasal environment.
This would make the increase in N% an accidental property of nasal vowels preceded by a nonnasal consonant.

However, I think that such views have to be rejected and that the introduction of the factor "relative time" is well justified.
1. As we have seen in 6.-1.2, in CanFr the increase in N% starts rather late in
the vowel and the nature of the preceding nonnasal consonant ([+cont] or
[-cont]) does not seem to influence the moment at which nose coupling starts.
Therefore, it is not likely that the increase in N% has something to do with
the preceding nonnasal consonant. (This cannot be said of the nasal vowels
produced by the EurFr subject, however.)

2. If the increase in N% in $[c\check{v}c]$ sequences were the consequence of coarticulation (coproduction) between the nasal vowel and the preceding nonnasal
sound, we would expect it to be lacking when the preceding sound is a nasal
consonant as in $[N\check{v}c]$. However, as we have seen in 6.2.2, nasal vowels in
$[N\check{v}c]$ sequences are usually produced with a small increase in N% as well. Consequently, the increase in N% is a property of the nasal vowel, and the relatively high N% in its initial phase has to be attributed to coarticulation
(coproduction) between the nasal vowel and the preceding nasal consonant. For
more details on this subject, see chapter 8.

3. Something of the same kind can be extracted from the X-ray film analysed in
Simon (1968). Simon proves that there is no difference in (a dialect of)
French between the last syllable of, on the one hand, words of the type **gnon,**
oignons, and on the other hand, words of the type **opinion.** She found that the
relevant parts of both types of words have to be transcribed as $[nj]$ and never
as $[\text{ɲ}]$, as has usually been claimed in phonetic transcriptions. During the
production of the $[n]$ the nasal port is open; during that of the $[j]$, however,
it is completely closed, to open again for the production of the $[\tilde{\text{ɔ}}]$. I
inspected the relevant sequences in the film of one of Simon's two subjects,
and found that the $[j]$ is followed by a typical nasal vowel, as they occur in
nonnasal environment, see 6.1.2 above, viz. a vowel characterized by an
increase in N% from (almost) zero to about 75 (I did not measure it). As the
$[j]$ was surrounded by two nasal sounds, we would not have been surprised if it
had been produced with some nose coupling as well. However, as part of the
strategy to realize the nasal vowel with an increase in N% from (almost) zero
to about 75, the speaker made the preceding $[j]$ nonnasal, even in this
unfavourable environment in which the $[j]$ was preceded by a nasal consonant.

4. The nature of the preceding evidence is articulatory. There is also perceptual evidence that the increase in N% makes nasal vowels better perceived as
nasal. In an experiment, Linthorst (1973:88-9) used several combinations of
the vowels occurring in the French words **même, dais** and **baie** produced by a
French subject. I will refer to the vowel of **même** as $[V1]$, to the vowels of
dais and **baie** as $[V2]$. Though Linthorst did not examine the articulatory properties of $[V1]$ and $[V2]$, we may guess that in $[V1]$ - obtained from an
environment of nasal consonants - N% was high and the amount of nose coupling
considerable, whereas in $[V2]$ - occurring in a nonnasal environment - N% and
nose coupling were zero.

Linthorst cut off the second $[m]$ of **même** and added to the remaining speech
sample either nothing or $[V1]$ again. In addition, to the $[V2]$ of **baie** and **dais**
Linthorst added $[V1]$, and to the $[V2]$ of **baie** $[V2]$ again. Thus, 5 speech samples were formed (see table 6-2) which (except no 4 in the table) were
presented twice to 9 French speaking listeners. They had to make a choice
between the interpretations **main** "hand" or **mais/mets** "but/dish", see nos 1 and

2 in the table, and between **daim/bain** "fallow-deer/bath" or **dais/baie** "canopy/bay", see nos 3 to 5. The results found by Linthorst are presented in table 6-2.

	Total number of occurrences	Number of nasal scores	
		absolute	percentage
1. mV1	18	1	6
2. mV1V1	18	0	0
3. dV2V1	18	15	83
	}27	}21	}78
4. bV2V1	9	6	67
5. bV2V2	18	4	22

Table 6-2. Perception of nasality for different types of vowels. N% is probably high in [V1]; N% is probably zero in [V2]. Data slightly adapted from Linthorst (1973:88-9).

These results can be summarized as:
- the items with vowels [V1] or [V1V1] in which N% was high were perceived as nonnasal;
- the items with vowels [V2V2] in which N% was zero were perceived as slightly nasal;
- the items [V2V1] with vowels in the first half of which N% was zero and in the second half of which N% was high were perceived as nasal.

The result that [V1V1] - with twice as much N% as [V2V1] - was perceived as much more nasal than [V2V1] is at first sight surprising. Linthorst concludes from this experiment (and also another one, see Linthorst 1973:83) that the increase in N% during the [V2V1] is sufficient for the listeners to perceive the vowel as nasal. I fully agree with his conclusion, but it does not explain why [V1] and [V1V1] were not heard as nasal. I do not believe that the absence of the increase in N% in [V1V1] and [V1] necessarily makes the nasality of these vowels unperceived. The presence of the [m] preceding [V1] and [V1V1] made the listeners believe, I think, that part of the nasality of the vowels [V1] or [V1V1] was in fact a portion of this [m]. In other words, it is both the absence of any increase in N% and the presence of the preceding [m] which together explain the paradoxical result found by Linthorst, that [V1] and

[V1V1] with their high N% were perceived as nonnasal. A sequence such as
[mV1V1] is not unlike many of the speech samples [NV] discussed in 6.2.1
above. I will come back to this subject in 8.3.2 below.

I consider the preceding four points as evidence in favour of the claim that
the increase in N% in a nasal vowel is an inalienable property of the nasal
vowel and not a consequence of the coarticulation (coproduction) with a
preceding nonnasal sound. If my claim is granted, it follows that relative
time plays a part in vowel nasality and that, instead of a ⟋one- dimensional
physical scale, we need a two-dimensional physical diagram to relate the
definition of the feature NASAL to nasal vowels.

6.4.2 UNIVERSAL AND LANGUAGE-SPECIFIC PHYSICAL DIAGRAMS

The physical diagram in fig. 6-2 is a universal diagram. In this diagram nasal
vowels may cover a broad area. The physical diagrams for specific languages
will contain lines, based upon average values.

When we select the beginning, the centre and the end of the nasal vowels of
the EurFr and the CanFr speakers (see 6.1.2), we can characterize these vowels
in terms of N% as 0-20-75 for the CanFr subject, as 0-50-75 for the EurFr subject, see fig. 6-3. Such series of percentages may be characteristic of nasal
vowels in specific languages.

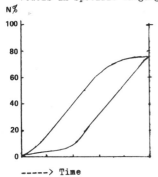

----> Time

Fig 6-3. Language-specific physical diagram related to the feature NASAL. The
lines indicate nasal vowels in EurFr and in CanFr.

The language-specific part of the increase in N% will be specified in multivalued phonetic representations by means of the language-specific low level
phonological rules. These rules should contain information stated in the physical diagrams of the language. The exact content of these rules has to be
determined by means of phonetic experiments. Examples of such rules are:

$$[\text{+nas}] \dashrightarrow [\text{0-20-75 nas}] / \begin{bmatrix} --- \\ -\text{cons} \\ +\text{voc} \end{bmatrix} \quad \text{Nasal vowels in CanFr}$$

$$[\text{+nas}] \dashrightarrow [\text{0-50-75 nas}] / \begin{bmatrix} --- \\ -\text{cons} \\ +\text{voc} \end{bmatrix} \quad \text{Nasal vowels in EurFr}$$

The language-specific interpretation convention interprets the "-" and "+" of the binary phonetic representations of the feature NASAL. Examples will be given in chapter 8.

We can characterize the oral vowels of the CanFr subject in the same way by a series of percentages of about 0-20-0. For the EurFr subject the series is 0-0-0 (cf. 6.1.1 above). This kind of differences can be made visible in physical diagrams and stated in low level phonological rules again. I will return to this point in chapter 7.

The fact that oral vowels in utterance-final position tend to be produced with some N% at their final stage (see 6.1.1 above) can easily be captured in a physical diagram as well. If the tendency is not the same in various languages, language- specific differences can be stated in language-specific physical diagrams and low level phonological rules.

Systems of conventions for phonetic transcriptions should refer to physical diagrams of the kind represented in fig. 6-2. As long as vowels of a language are situated in the broad area in which N% increases from (almost) zero to about 75, they may be described as nasal vowels. Vowels of different languages may have different values. The $[\tilde{\mathbf{V}}]$ in EurFr is different from the $[\tilde{\mathbf{V}}]$ in CanFr, as we have seen above. Phonetic transcriptions should be relatable to such universal and language-specific physical diagrams, and the question whether they are correct or not can be answered in the light of these diagrams.

NOTES TO CHAPTER 6

1. As we have seen already in 3.2 above, Palantla Chinantec is an exception. The phonetic representation in **SPE** of **inn** with a vowel which is [2 nasal], i.e. partial nasal (see 3.1 above), corresponds with an exceptional phonetic transcription as well. Though Chomsky and Halle (1968:ix-x) state that they follow the phonetic transcriptions of Kenyon and Knott (1944) unless otherwise indicated, the latter transcribe **inn** phonetically as [In], i.e. without partial nasality, whereas the former

do not indicate their deviating from it. Another group of exceptions may be found in transcriptions of dialects. See for instance Oftedal (1956:41) and Lahti (1953:4). The latter, following Bruneau, seems to recognize, besides nasal vowels, the existence of both nasalized vowels and incompletely nasalized vowels. The difference between these latter vowels seems to concern the distribution of the nose coupling or N% (or a similar notion) over the vowel. But Lahti does not propose a specific convention to differentiate between the various cases of vowel nasality.

2. There are other reports and/or data showing that utterance- final vowels tend to be produced with nose coupling. For AmEng Warren & DuBois (1964:63), Fritzell (1969:32-3, 40, 48, 56-7), Moll & Daniloff (1971:679, 681-2), For French Chlumsky et al. (1938:75-6, 157), Straka (1955:269 note 2), Lanher (1972:346- 7), Benguerel et al. (1977:153-4,157). For German Von Essen (1961:272) and, maybe, Jespersen (1913:58). For Spanish (of rural Panama) Schourup (1973:214).

3. In Rochette (1973: vol. II passim) it can be seen that his Parisian French speaker behaves the same as the EurFr speaker in Brichler-Labaeye.

4. Ohala (1975:302) observes with respect to the velum: "It might take about 50 ms. to move from a closed to an open position large enough to create noticeable nasalization." At this moment N% is about 5 for the CanFr speaker and about 30 for the EurFr speaker.

5. Balasubramanian goes on: "A further reason for not marking accidental nasalisation in transcription is that this kind of nasalisation is present in varying degrees (...) and it is not possible to indicate this kind of variation by the simple use of [~]." This further reason is not valid, I think, since (a) the linguist is free to propose supplementary symbols to the I.P.A., and (b) whether distinctive or not, vowel nasality will always be present in varying degrees, cf. 6.1.2 and the relevant tables in Appendix 2.

6. In Moll (1960) the high degree of nose coupling may be due to the fact that the vowels in question occur in utterance- final position.

7. Thanks to the hospitality and the help of Mme Simon and M. Bothorel of the INSTITUT DE PHONETIQUE (Strasbourg), I have had an opportunity to inspect these films (January 1979). The films mentioned in Simon et al. (1979) were not accessible. The only X-ray tracings published are to be found in Simon (1967) and in Brichler-Labaeye (1970), but I have not used them, since they either concern only part of the vowel (cf. Simon 1967:150-4) or are not reliable (cf. Brichler-Labaeye 1970: pp.13-4 and fig. 52). See on this latter point Appendix 1.

8. In one case the closing movement of the velum goes on during the beginning of the nasal vowel and the nasal port is opened further again during the rest of the nasal vowel.

9. The increase in N in the $[\tilde{a}]$ in **-ment** is too outspoken to be (completely) attributable to the fact that it occurs in utterance-final position.

10. Standard orthography and phonetic transcriptions may be quite different, since several dialects use it.

11. The difference may be related to a difference between high and low vowels. Since this point is the subject of the next chapter, I will not discuss it here.

12. By AmEng I do not understand special dialects such as the one described in Rueter (1975).

13. In one case only nose coupling starts at the end of the vowel. This case is a real exception as appears not only from the other data in tables A4-3 and A4-1, but also from data in Moll and Daniloff (1971:682, figures 6 and 7): data on velic movement in 69 vowels or vowel sequences. Even if, as Moll and Daniloff observe (p.580), the movement of the velum by which the nasal port opens starts slightly earlier than the actual opening of the nasal port, it is clear that nose coupling usually starts either before the vowel onset or quite early in the vowel or vowel sequence. From evidence in Warren and DuBois (1964:62-5), Wheatherly-White et al. (1966:296-7), Fritzell (1969:56-7), Perkell (1969:73), Ohala (1974a, cf. also Ohala 1972), Ohala (1975, cf. also Ohala 1971), Clumeck (1975:137) and Kuehn (1976), no precise conclusions can be drawn, although the general trend is that vowels followed by a nasal consonant are produced with nose coupling early in the vowel.

14. It is, however, interesting to observe that Clumeck (1976:339) has not included all the information on Swedish in the figures reproduced in table A4-1: "Data of one Swedish speaker are not grouped with those of the other Swedes because the velic behaviour exhibited by this subject is much more like that of the American English speakers than of the Swedish subjects." In other words, the vowels of the speaker excluded by Clumeck seem to be more in accordance with the findings of Bjoerk (1961). Clumeck (1975:141) adds with respect to this speaker that he produces utterances "with heavy nasalisation during the vowels before nasal consonant".

15. In her transcriptions Ohala (M.) has apparently adopted the same practice
    as Balasubramanian, see the quotation in 6.2.1 above.

16. Almeida (1976:356) quotes a conclusion (which he apparently agrees with)
    from Lacerda/Head which points in a direction different from Clumeck's
    Portuguese data: "An oral vowel before nasal consonant does not always
    manifest nasalisation: its course is frequently oral throughout. When
    there is nasalization it appears almost always only in a brief final sub-
    section." In Petursson (1974), X-ray tracings are presented which give
    some idea of the properties of [VN] sequences in Icelandic. Petursson's
    presentation does not concern the whole vowel: the beginning of the vowel
    seems to be absent sometimes (cf. p.57,58), and a comparison of different
    figures (e.g. fig.75 and 138) reveals that the same may hold for the end
    of the vowel. The general impression emerging from the data is that
    Petursson's subject is late in opening the nasal port in vowels before a
    nasal consonant. See his fig. 6, 11, 14, 19, 21, 27, 28, 29, 30, 37, 42,
    74, 75.

17. They do not include those of Moll and Daniloff (1971:680), since the
    presentation in that study does not make it entirely clear what is the
    nose coupling in the four vowel tokens as compared with that in the fol-
    lowing nasal consonant.

18. At least, this has to be concluded, I think, since according to Malècot
    (p.224) the nasal consonant could not be substituted by silence.
    Malècot's result obtained with **canned** seems to have been overlooked by
    Chomsky (1964:96), Ruhlen (1973:13; 1978:226) and Lovins (1978:14). In a
    perceptual experiment with Dutch vowels, Noske (1979) found that Dutch
    listeners perceive vowels from nasal environments [N-C], [C-N] or [N-N]
    as more nasal than vowels from [C-C] environment. This result may imply
    that vowels before a nasal consonant in Dutch have the structure of a
    nasal vowel, just as the Dutch vowels in the other nasal environments.

CHAPTER 7

Height in oral and nasal vowels

This chapter concerns the relation between vowel height and nasality. The choice of the subject "vowel height" does not follow directly from my definition of the feature NASAL or from other aspects of my theoretical framework. It has been chosen because many phonologists and phoneticians have claimed that high and low vowels do not behave the same with respect to nasality.

Vowel height is usually described as high, mid and low. Instead of "high" and "low" I will use also "higher" and "lower". By using these latter terms I deliberately create an ambiguity. "Higher" and "lower" cover the complete range of possible vowel height, so that I need neither mention mid vowels nor specify whether mid vowels behave as high or as low vowels. High(er) and low(er) vowels will sometimes be abbreviated as [HV] and [LV] respectively.

The difference with respect to nasality which investigators claim to have observed between higher and lower vowels falls into two categories. It is stated either in terms of intrinsic properties of the vowels or in relation to the following nasal consonant.

As we have already seen in chapter 4, for Eijkman (1926:218) the difference is an intrinsic property of the vowel:

(1) "The different vowels cannot be nasalized with equal facility. The greatest chance of success offer ɔ, ..., a, ɛ, e, œ, but i, y, u present greater difficulty."

I paraphrase this statement as: it is more difficult to make high nasal vowels ([HṼ]) out of high oral vowels ([HV]) than it is to make lower nasal vowels ([LṼ]) out of other oral vowels ([LV]).[1]

The statements that refer to the presence of the nasal consonant following the vowel usually place the matter in a diachronic perspective. A representative statement is presented in Schourup (1973:192; cf. 1972:540):

(2) "Low vowels are more likely to be regressively nasalized than high ones" (i.e. by a nasal consonant, PvR).

I paraphrase this statement as: when followed by a nasal consonant, lower oral vowels ([LVN]) are more likely to become nasal ([LṼN]) than higher oral vowels

([HVN]), or, in diachronic terms, vowel nasality tends to begin in lower vowels.[2]

The main difference between statements such as (1) and (2) is that the latter is restricted to a specific environment. Whatever aspect is stressed, either facility or probability of nasalisation of lower vowels, the question is whether these tendencies are reflected in real speech, how they are perceived, how they can be explained and how they are to be integrated into my phonological framework.

In order to examine what we find in real speech I will review the results of phonetic experiments and some typological data. In 7.1 these results concern articulatory properties of higher and lower vowels, in 7.2 perceptual properties of these vowels. The results will be discussed in 7.3; in 7.4 they will be integrated into my theoretical framework.

In the course of this chapter I will examine and discuss two other properties of lower and higher nasal vowels as compared with oral vowels. The first property concerns restrictions upon the possible amount of mouth constriction in the production of low nasal vowels. The second concerns restrictions upon the perceptibility of nasal vowels in the perceptual vowel space.

7.1 ARTICULATORY DATA

The purpose of this section is a review of data in terms of nose coupling and N% and their relation to vowel height. Many data have been produced on the position of the velum. These data provide us with information on the amount of nose coupling N. I will review them in 7.1.1. In 7.1.2 I will show that, in nonnasal environment, N% in lower oral vowels may be higher than in higher oral vowels; and that there is a difference in the amount of mouth constriction MC between low oral vowels and low nasal vowels.

7.1.1 NOSE COUPLING AND VELIC BEHAVIOUR

During silence the velum of a speaker is typically in rest position: it is lowered and rests against the back of the tongue. It blocks the mouth cavity, the nasal port is wide open and breathing takes place through the nose. During speech the velum is typically in a raised position and the nasal port is usually blocked. When it is blocked, the obstruction may be firm or feeble, and the velic raising may still vary somewhat. When, during speech, the obstruction of the nasal port is not complete, the port may be open to different degrees although the velum is seldom lowered to rest position. The degree of obstruction depends on the nature of the sound to be produced.

There are many data concerning the degree of obstruction of the nasal port. Phoneticians do not always express the data they have obtained in their experiments in terms of the notions "opening- and obstruction of the nasal port", terms which I shall use. Therefore I give a list of expressions they use in connection with these notions:

(3) The more firmly the nasal port is obstructed
the smaller the amount of nose coupling;
the smaller the velopharyngeal distance;
the shorter the time of velar opening;
the higher the velar height;
the more velar (muscular closing) activity;
the more velar movement from rest position;
the lower the velopharyngeal orifice airflow and
the higher the oropharyngeal pressure.

The evidence from phonetic experiments has been presented per environment in Appendix 5, tables A5-1 to A5-8. The evidence in these tables concerns oral vowels in nonnasal environment, oral or nasal vowels preceded by nasal consonant, oral or nasal vowels followed by nasal consonant, and nasal vowels. For all these environments the high and the low vowels have been compared, and for vowels next to nasal consonant the degree of opening of the nasal port of the high and low vowels has been compared with that of the adjacent nasal consonant (tables A5-4 and A5-6). These latter tables concern AmEng.[3]
These experiments reveal that:

(4) In any language higher vowels tend to be produced with the nasal port more obstructed than lower vowels, other things being equal.

With hardly any exception, the higher vowels are produced with more obstruction of the nasal port than the lower ones in Amoy, Czech, Dutch, (American, Australian, European) English, (Canadian and European) French, German, Hindi, Icelandic, Italian, Japanese, (Brazilian) Portuguese, Russian and Swedish. This holds for oral vowels in nonnasal environment, oral or nasal vowels preceded by a nasal consonant, oral or nasal vowels followed by a nasal consonant, and nasal vowels in nonnasal environment.
As to oral vowels in nonnasal environment and nasal vowels, some additional observations can be made.

1. Oral vowels in nonnasal environment.
Although there is much evidence in favour of (4) and almost none against, low oral vowels in nonnasal environment may differ greatly with respect to the amount of nose coupling. The data in table A5-1 give information on the relative degree of obstruction of the nasal port, but do not tell us whether the amount of nose coupling is zero or (slightly) more than zero. The reason is, as we have seen in section 5.1 above, that velic movement, velic height, and

velic muscular activity are usually defined in such a way that they may vary
to some extent in high and low vowels without necessarily resulting in a
change in the amount of nose coupling. This makes the trend stated in (4) a
rather vague one as far as the amount of nose coupling is concerned.

From some more precise data on AmEng - presented in Appendix 5, table A5-2
- it appears that, as a rule, higher oral vowels are produced with complete
obstruction of the nasal port, i.e. without nose coupling.[4] Exceptions to
this rule can be found in data sets 7 and 8. In data set 7, 13% of the high
vowels are produced with an open nasal port and in data set 8 even 25%. But
in this latter case the vowels have been produced by subjects that are non-
typical, viz. the nasal speakers without cleft palate mentioned in section 5.1
above. And, since in the other data sets of table A5-2 high vowels are produced with a closed nasal port, it is quite plausible that even in the 13%
high vowels with open nasal port in data set 7 the amount of nose coupling N
will be extremely low.[5]

For low oral vowels in AmEng the situation is different. Here the amount
of nose coupling N[7] in the results of different experiments varies considerably. Just as for high vowels, nose coupling may be absent. But amounts of
nose coupling of 40 to 45 mm^2 are also frequently found.[6] An amount of nose
coupling greater than zero is more often present than not. On an average,
about 20 mm^2 nose coupling for low oral vowels seems to be a realistic estimate. Phoneticians have suggested three explanations for this variation, viz.
(a) speech rate, (b) the sex of the subject or (c) the nature of the environment:

(a) The higher the speech rate, the lower the degree of nose coupling.
(b) Some of the American female speakers produce low vowels without nose coupling, male and the other female speakers produce them with nose coupling.
(c) The more tense the environment, the smaller the amount of nose coupling.[7]
These factors are not independent of each other and may all be present in the
data mentioned in tables A5-2 and A5-1.

If these explanations are correct, the differences among low oral vowels in
AmEng are not only determined by linguistic differences in the nonnasal
environment, but they are also sociolinguistic or stylistic in nature.
Apparently, systematic linguistic differences in the amount of nose coupling
may occur in the low oral vowels in nonnasal environment of one and the same
language.

We have already seen that in other languages, too, just as in AmEng, higher
oral vowels are produced with the nasal port considerably obstructed, i.e.
probably without nose coupling (see Appendix 5, table A5-1). As regards lower
oral vowels, the variation in the amount of nose coupling in AmEng seems to be
rather exceptional, since data on EurFr, Portuguese, Amoy, Hindi and Swedish
show that in these languages, as a rule, the low oral vowels in nonnasal

environment are produced without nose coupling, as appears from Clumeck (1975:139), Brichler- Labaeye (1970) and Bjoerk (1961). CanFr, however, seems to be more like AmEng in this respect (cf. Appendix 2, table A2-1). For low oral vowels, differences between languages seem to vary, from no nose coupling to substantial variation in the amount of nose coupling. At one end of the scale we find EurFr, Hindi, Amoy, Portuguese and Swedish, at the other end AmEng and CanFr.

2. Nasal vowels.

The question I will examine is: what is the amount of nose coupling in high nasal vowels as compared with that in low nasal vowels?

Nasal vowels occur in Appendix 5 in nonnasal environment (table A5-7); followed by a nasal consonant (tables A5-5 and A5-6); and preceded by a nasal consonant (tables A5-3, A5-4). Very few of these data sets have been presented in such a way that I have been able to estimate the amount of nose coupling.

The most important exception is the set of AmEng nasal vowels in Moll (1962). In this study the velopharyngeal distance VP has been measured in vowels preceded by a nasal consonant and in vowels followed by a nasal consonant. As we have seen in chapter 6, vowels preceded by a nasal consonant are irregular in structure. They may be nasal or oral in an unpredictable way. I will note them as $[N\tilde{V}(?)C]$. When they are followed by a nasal consonant, they are nasal vowels $[\tilde{V}]$. Moll has measured the velopharyngeal distance VP in these vowels, and obtained the following results:

    (a) In $[C\tilde{V}N]$ syllables the average VP = 4.45 mm
    (b) In $[N\tilde{V}(?)C]$ syllables the average VP = 2.15 mm
    (c) In $[C\tilde{I}N]$ and $[N\tilde{I}(?)C]$ the average VP = 2.45 mm
    (d) In $[C\tilde{u}N]$ and $[N\tilde{u}(?)C]$ the average VP = 2.03 mm
    (e) In $[C\tilde{æ}N]$ and $[N\tilde{æ}(?)C]$ the average VP = 4.62 mm
    (f) In $[C\tilde{a}N]$ and $[N\tilde{a}(?)C]$ the average VP = 4.00 mm

As the question which I am interested in concerns the comparison of the amounts of nose coupling in high and low nasal vowels, I have elaborated these data in the following ways.

First, I have taken the average velopharyngeal distance VP of the high vowels ((c) and (d) above), and that of the low vowels ((e) and (f) above), see table 7-1, first column.

Second, I have estimated the proportion of the VP's of the high vowels in the two environments and of the low vowels in the two environments. I take it that this proportion is the same as that between the averages of all the

104

	VOWEL NEXT TO NASAL CONSONANT	VOWEL PRECEDED BY NASAL CONSONANT		VOWEL FOLLOWED BY NASAL CONSONANT	
	1	2	3	4	5
	VP	VP	N	VP	N
HIGH	2.24	1.49	9	2.98	45
LOW	4.31	2.87	41	5.75	128

Table 7-1. Velopharyngeal distance VP and the corresponding amounts of nose coupling N in high and low vowels in AmEng. I have made estimates on the basis of data extracted from Moll (1962). The values in columns 3 and 5 have been obtained after the application of equations (IX) and (X) in chapter 5.

vowels together in these respective environments, viz. 2.15 : 4.45, see (a) and (b) above. The resulting VP's are presented in table 7-1, columns 2 and 4.

Third, I have applied equations (IX) and (X) of chapter 5 to the VP's found for the high and the low vowels in the two environments, see table 7-1, columns 3 and 5.

As a result we see that Moll's low nasal vowels (before a nasal consonant) were produced with almost three times as much nose coupling as the high nasal vowels: 45 as against 128 mm^2 respectively.[8]

That the results in table 7-1 may be quite reliable estimates appears from a few comparisons with other data.

First, as we have seen in Appendix 3, table A3-3, the central phase of the high vowel in $[n \mid p]$ is produced with 15mm^2 nose coupling. This value is of the same order as the 9 mm^2 I have estimated for Moll's high vowels preceded by nasal consonant.

Secondly, the $[\dots N\tilde{V}N\tilde{V}N\tilde{V}\dots]$ syllables in Lubker (1968) were produced with an average velopharyngeal distance:

VP = 2.0mm for the $[\tilde{\imath}]$ (standard deviation 0.82); VP = 6.9mm for the $[\tilde{æ}]$ (standard deviation 2.16).

Application of equation IX of chapter 5 results in:

15 mm^2 nose coupling for the $[\tilde{\imath}]$

162 mm^2 nose coupling for the $[\tilde{æ}]$.

The difference from Moll's data in table 7-1 is that Lubker's vowels are both preceded and followed by a nasal consonant. This does not seem to influence the VP of the $[\tilde{\imath}]$ but may have influenced the VP of the $[\tilde{æ}]$ since it is much greater than in Moll's data.[9]

Thirdly, Moll's nasal vowels can be compared with two Swedish nasal vowels produced in isolation (Bjoerk 1961:40). For the Swedish speaker, I estimate the amount of nose coupling N in $[\tilde{\imath}]$ and $[\tilde{\mathrm{\ddot{o}}}]$ about 30 mm^2 and 60 mm^2 respectively. The fact that the mid nasal vowel $[\tilde{\mathrm{\ddot{o}}}]$ is produced with twice as much nose coupling as the high nasal vowel $[\tilde{\imath}]$, is consistent with the results in table 7-1.

We may summarize the results of this subsection as follows:

1. In all languages examined, lower vowels are produced with less obstruction of the nasal port than higher vowels, other things being equal (see (4) above).

2. With respect to oral vowels in nonnasal environment, the higher vowels are usually produced without any nose coupling, but the lower vowels may display considerable variation, from no nose coupling to more than 40 mm^2 This variation - which is mainly language-specific - may be due to stylistic or (socio-) linguistic factors such as speech rate, the sex of the subjects or the tenseness of the adjacent sounds.

3. The difference in amount of nose coupling N between high and low nasal vowels in AmEng is considerable. It is considerably more than that between high and low oral vowels in nonnasal environment in AmEng.

7.1.2 N% AND MOUTH COUPLING

In this subsection I will establish how much N% may be higher in lower oral vowels than in higher oral vowels when these vowels occur in nonnasal environment. In addition I will show that there is a fallacy in the term "low" in low oral and low nasal vowels, because the latter vowels are produced with a smaller amount of mouth constriction than the former.

1. N% in oral vowels in nonnasal environment.
It is easier to determine whether for a particular vowel N% is zero than whether N% has specific values greater than zero, for if the amount of nose coupling N is zero, N% is zero as well, so we need not determine the amount of mouth constriction. One of the conclusions of 7.1.1 was that higher vowels in nonnasal environment are usually produced without any nose coupling, i.e. their N% is zero.

As regards the lower vowels, I have concluded (in 7.1.1) that in the majority of languages the amount of nose coupling is usually zero as well, but that the lower oral vowels in AmEng and in CanFr are exceptions. In the data of these languages the lower vowels in nonnasal environment are, on an average, produced with an amount of nose coupling N greater than zero in their central phase. So for these vowels, we need to determine the amount of mouth constriction, in order to determine N%.

In the CanFr data presented in chapter 6 and Appendix 2, table A2-1, N% tends to be more than 15 on an average in the central phase of the lower vowels. For AmEng we do not know the amount of mouth constriction in low vowels. Therefore, I have based myself on the amounts of mouth constriction in general. Some data are presented in table 7-2 below.[10] Since the average amount of nose coupling in low vowels for AmEng speakers (male and female) is about 20 mm^2, and the average amount of mouth constriction is about 275 $mm.^2$, it follows that the average value for N% in low oral vowels is about 7. This is a very rough estimation, however. For speakers who produce lower oral vowels with an amount of nose coupling of about 40 mm^2, N% is about 15, maybe even higher.

AMOUNT OF MOUTH CONSTRICTION IN ORAL VOWELS

	i	u/ɯ	æ	a	ɑ	subjects
1	80	120L		500V		Japanese
2	75	10L			160V	Russian
3	75	40L	400	300L	350V	Arabic (Egyptian)
4	65	75VL	200	200V	120V	English (British)

Average of high vowels	Average of low vowels
74	279

Table 7-2. Amount of mouth constriction MC in mm^2 in high and low oral vowels of four adult subjects and averages. The numbers in the first column refer to diagrams of area functions in the following sources:
1 Chiba and Kajiyama 1958:120-8
2 Fánt 1960:108
3 Wood 1979:27
4 Wood 1979:26
A value followed by L has been measured near the lips; by V near the velum. If no letter follows I have measured the value in between the lips and the velum in the diagrams of the area functions of the sources.

2. Low oral and low nasal vowels.
The expressions "low oral vowel" and "low nasal vowel" refer to vowels which

differ not only in nasality, but also in vowel height. Nasal low vowels are less low than oral low vowels. This appears from a comparison of data on the amount of mouth constriction MC in oral low vowels with those in nasal low vowels. There we find that, for the same speaker, the nasal ones tend to be produced with a lower amount of mouth constriction MC than the oral ones, see table 7-3.[11] Since in low nasal vowels the tongue body is higher than in low nasal vowels, it follows that low nasal vowels are less low than low oral vowels.

AMOUNT OF MOUTH CONSTRICTION IN ORAL AND NASAL VOWELS

	EUROPEAN FRENCH			CANADIAN FRENCH	
	i	ε	a/ɑ	ε	a/ɑ
Oral	34	124	104	53	59
Nasal	–	78	40	25	13 ([ṼC])
	–	–	–	48	48 ([Ṽ#])

Table 7-3. The values in mm^2 are averages. They have been determined by means of the equations mentioned in chapter 5. For the nasal vowels the area of mouth constriction MC is situated always in the soft palate region, for the oral vowels of the EurFr subject in the soft or hard palate region or in the incisor/alveolar region. The data are taken from Appendix 2, tables A2-1 (CanFr oral vowels), A2-2 (CanFr nasal vowels in utterance final position), A2-3 (other CanFr nasal vowels), A2- 4 (EurFr nasal vowels) and from measurements in Brichler- Labaeye (1970) and Charbonneau (1971). There is one tracing selected per vowel: the first tracing situated in the second part of the vowel.

It should be added that especially the low oral vowels can be produced with considerable differences in the amount of mouth constriction. One of the more striking differences in this respect is the one between the [ɑ]'s of the Egyptian Arabic and the Southern British English subjects of Wood: 350 and 120 mm^2, see table 7-2.[12] The variability in the amount of mouth constriction is considerably reduced in the case of the nasal vowels (this is not visible in table 7-3).

The decrease in the amount of mouth constriction is brought about by means of two complementary movements. The first is the raising of the back of the tongue towards the velum, the second the lowering of the velum towards the back of the tongue.

For many investigators, the expression "to lower the velum" is synonymous with the expression "to open the nasal port". However, it is doubtful if the velum always has to be **lowered** in order to **open** the nasal port. In X-ray tracings it can be observed that the nasal port may be opened not only by a **lowering** movement but also by a **fronting** movement of the velum in the direction of the hard palate. The fronting movement is often visible in nasal consonants, see chapter 8. However, during the central phase of lower nasal vowels the velum lowers and takes the shape of an arch parallel to that of the back of the tongue.[13] This lowering movement makes the amount of mouth constriction smaller than in the corresponding oral vowel.

This subsection can be summarized as follows:

1. In several languages, but not all, we find that low oral vowels are produced with N% somewhat higher than zero, i.e. somewhat higher than in high oral vowels.

2. Low nasal vowels and low oral vowels are low in different ways. "Low" in oral vowels refers to greater amounts of mouth constriction and greater standard deviations than low in nasal vowels does.

We can represent the difference between high and low oral vowels and high and low nasal vowels as in fig. 7-2, in which the main points of the above discussion have been graphically represented:

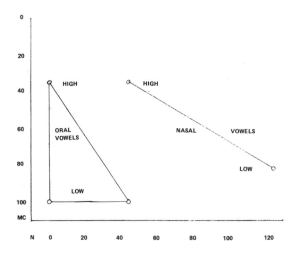

Fig. 7-1. Relation between the amount of nose coupling N and the amount of mouth constriction MC in oral and nasal low and high vowels. On the x-axis N, on the y-axis MC. Several elements in the figure are tentative.

7.2 PERCEPTUAL AND TYPOLOGICAL DATA

Some articulatory results found in the preceding section can be compared with corresponding perceptual data. These perceptual data confirm or are consistent with what we would expect on the basis of the articulatory findings in the preceding. The articulatory properties of vowels which are judged in perceptual experiments have usually not been determined, and I will make inferences on the basis of the conclusions arrived at in the preceding section. I have classified the data to be reviewed in five subsections. The last subsection concerns a perceptual aspect of nasal vowels which could not be derived from their articulatory properties.

1. We expect to find that in languages like AmEng lower oral vowels will be perceived as more nasal than higher oral vowels, whereas lower and higher oral vowels in languages like EurFr will be perceived as equally nasal. This expectation follows from the finding in 7.1 above that in AmEng lower oral vowels in nonnasal environment are produced with N% greater than zero, whereas AmEng higher oral vowels and EurFr oral vowels are produced with N% zero.[14]

The experimental results in Lintz and Sherman (1961) - which concern oral vowels of 10 male speakers - confirm this. Lintz and Sherman (1961:391) conclude: "Results in this study indicate that severity of nasality, in general, increases progressively from the high vowels to the low vowels."

The results in Ali et al. (1971:540) - which concern oral and nasal vowels of one speaker - probably confirms our expectation as well. Ali et al. cut off the last consonant (plus transition) in [CVC] or [CṼN] syllables and presented them to listeners.[15] They found that the low back oral vowel /a/ was perceived as nasal with a significant greater frequency than the vowels /u/, /eI/ and /i/. From other findings in this study I infer that they found more frequently (relatively and absolutely) nonnasal vowels perceived as nasal than nasal vowels perceived as nonnasal, though they do not indicate exact scores. It follows, I think, that listeners scored vowels more frequently nasal than expected, especially when the oral vowel was the low vowel /a/. This is the kind of result we expect to find in AmEng.

Clumeck (1971) is a repetition of the experiment of Ali et al. with EurFr vowels. We have already seen in Appendix 4, table A4-5, that there is no significant difference between the nasality of lower and higher oral vowels.

When AmEng speakers produce high and low oral vowels without nose coupling, we find no significant difference in nasality between these vowels. This appears from an experiment by Massengill and Bryson (1967) with the vowels [i, u, æ, a]. Judgements whether these vowels were nasal or not were expressed by means of the numbers 0 and 1, where 0 stands for "nasal" and 1 stands for "normal". The results are reproduced in table 7-4 below. The values in the second column represent the mean number of judgements for each vowel produced with velopharyngeal opening of 0 mm^2 (cf. Massengill & Bryson 1967:49).[16]

	mean score	number of vowels
i	7.25	4 or 8
u	8.75	4 or 8
æ	7.25	4 or 8
a	8	1 to 10

Table 7-4. Perceptual judgements based upon isolated oral vowels without nose coupling. The mean score in the second column may range from 0 to 10 (10 included). The higher the mean score the less nasal the vowel. Data extracted and adapted from Massengill & Bryson (1967: Table I, first row).

Table 7-4 shows that the high oral vowels were perceived as slightly less nasal than the low vowels (8 versus 7.125), but this difference is statistically far from significant within the possible limits of the data, and this is what we expected to find.[17]

Therefore, the perceptual results are what we expect them to be. Vowels produced with N% zero are perceived as equally (non)nasal, while vowels with N% somewhat more than zero are perceived as more nasal than vowels produced with N% zero.

2. When lower vowels followed by nasal consonant are produced with the same increase in N% as higher vowels, lower and higher vowels will be perceived as equally (non)nasal, in spite of the fact that the amount of nose coupling N is greater in the lower vowels than it is with the higher ones.

In the EurFr data from Clumeck (1971) in appendix 4, table A4-5, we see that high and low vowels followed by (removed) nasal consonant were perceived as about equally nonnasal, i.e. about as nonnasal as oral vowels in nonnasal environment. (As we have seen in chapter 6, we may assume that these vowels are rather oral.)

I think that we may interpret the results of the experiment in Ali et al. (1971) in the same way. For all vowels Ali et al. conclude that "... nasal consonants were correctly perceived better than chance", without adding any comments as to low vowels. In their conclusion on vowel height they seem to consider nonnasal and nasal consonants together. As I have argued above, I think that the conclusion concerns the oral vowel /a/. If this is right, it follows that the low nasal vowel [ã] and the higher nasal vowels were perceived as equally nasal.

3. When lower oral vowels in nonnasal environment are produced with N% somewhat greater than zero and higher oral vowels are produced with N% is zero,
and when higher and lower nasal vowels are produced with the same increase in
N%, listeners will confuse lower oral and nasal vowels more frequently than
they do higher oral and nasal vowels.

As we have seen above, Ali et al. (1971:540) found that the low back vowel
/a/ was perceived as nasal with a significant greater frequency than the
vowels /u/, /eI/, and /i/. I interpret this finding as follows: since the /a/
- but not the other vowels - in nonnasal environment was produced with a value
for N% greater than zero, it was more frequently perceived as nasal than the
higher vowels in nonnasal environments. Hence the oral /a/ and the nasal /a/
were more frequently confused than higher oral and nasal vowels.

4. As lower nasal vowels are produced with a smaller amount of mouth constriction than lower oral vowels (see 7.1.2), I expect that height in lower and
higher nasal vowels will be less clearly perceptible than in lower and higher
oral vowels.

This expectation is contrary to the alleged language- universal according
to which there is, in the words of Chen (1973:235), a "tendency... of nasalized vowels to fall", i.e. to become lower (for some other references see
Ruhlen 1974:273 note 2).

I have found two relevant perceptual experiments: Mohr and Wang (1968,
tables V, VI, VII) and Wright (1975). Their results can be interpreted as evidence in favour of my prediction. Some typological data point in the same
direction.

Mohr and Wang (1968, tables V, VI, VII) have examined the perceptual distance between vowel pairs in the set [i, a, u, ĩ, ã, ũ].[18] In table VI of
their study (p.37; cf. also table VIII, p.38) we observe that [ĩ, ã, ũ] were
judged to be more similar than [i, a, u]. This is the same as saying that in
the nasal vowels the listeners did not perceive the high/low and front/back
distinctions very well.

Wright (1975) has carried out an experiment with more vowels. His "test
stimuli were articulated as steady state oral vowels during the course of
which the velum was lowered" and "500 msec segments were spliced from the oral
and nasal portions of the recorded utterances" (p.376). Speakers (one male and
one female) produced in this way the vowels [i, e, ɛ , æ , y, œ, u, o, ɔ , a,
ɑ] (and the male speaker produced a few others (p.376-8)). Listeners made
judgements by locating the vowels in the traditional vowel space (p.375).[19]

Wright (1975:382) concludes: "The general findings of this investigation
have been that vowel nasalization is accompanied by an auditory lowering of
the vowel except for the low vowel [æ], which rises, [ɑ] which changes very
little in quality and [ɔ] which also rises." It appears from his figures 1 and
2 that the change in the [ɑ] is a small rise as well.[20] Thus, a general

lowering tendency is not present in these data, rather a centralizing tendency.

It is not either in typological data. The alleged language universal that vowels tend to lower when nasalized, is no language universal at all, but "an idiosyncratic characteristic of FRENCH",as Ruhlen (1978:230, passim) argues convincingly.[21] After having compared the systems of nasal vowels in 155 languages, Ruhlen (1978:222) states: "While information on positional differences between NV's (nasal vowels, PvR) and OV's (oral vowels, PvR) is quite sparse, I would hypothesize that high and mid NV's tend to be somewhat LOWER than their oral equivalents, whereas low NV's tend to be somewhat HIGHER than their oral partners." Brito (1975:60) provides some specific information on Brazilian Portuguese: "The nasal low vowel /ã/ in comparison to the oral vowel /a/ is raised and centralized, assuming a quality conventionally transcribed as [ɜ̃]." And in his IPA diagram (quoted in Almeida 1978:357) Stevens (1954) writes nasal /a/ in European Portuguese as [ʌ̃].

Thus, the finding that lower nasal vowels are produced with a smaller amount of mouth coupling MC and, consequently, with less tongue lowering than their oral counterparts (see 7.1.2) finds a parallel in perceptual and typological data: height is less well perceived in nasal vowels than it is in oral vowels.

5. That the features LOW and HIGH, and also BACK, are influenced by the coefficient of the feature NASAL has been illustrated in chapter 2 already. There it was argued that the perceptual scale of these features in terms of HIGH and LOW decreases when they occur together with a positive nasal coefficient, as appeared from the experiments in Lindblom et al. (1977).

This appears from other perceptual and typological data as well. Not only lower nasal vowels are perceived as somewhat higher than their oral counterparts, but also higher nasal vowels are perceived as somewhat lower than their oral counterparts; and the same applies to the distinction front/back. What we observe here is a centralizing tendency of nasal vowels in general as compared with oral vowels. This centralizing tendency cannot be attributed only to the fact that lower nasal vowels are somewhat higher than their oral counterparts.

In the experiments of Mohr and Wang (1968) and of Wright (1975) nasal vowels were judged to be more similar or to occupy a more central position in the perceptual vowel space than oral vowels. In a third experiment - reported in Meinhold (1970) (Cf. also Klingholz and Meinhold 1975:81-2) - we see that nasal vowels are sooner confounded with each other.

Meinhold compared vowels of two speakers: "Normale Vokale [a,e,i,o,u] und ihnen entsprechende, im Sinne einer Rhinolalia aperta nasalierte"(p.641). The perceptual results were based upon judgements by German "phonetisch vorgebildeten Hoerern" (p.641-2). These listeners did not confound any of the vowels of the normal speaker and they perceived the [a] of the speaker with rhinolalia aperta always as "a". With respect to the other vowels of the latter speaker they confused them with many other vowels. If we consult "Tabelle 2, Konfusionsmatrix" (Meinhold 1970:643), we can calculate that, on an average, as much as 83% of these vowels were not correctly identified. I have classified the incorrect "identifications" of the [e, i, o, u] produced by this speaker into four groups:

(a) 48% is perceived as "ə";
(b) 14% is perceived as "œ";
(c) 10% is perceived as "m";
(d) 28% is perceived as "a, ɛ, y, u" or "e".

We see that there was a rather strong tendency to perceive the vowels as more centralized than they were meant by the speaker.

Before we leave these three experiments, it may be relevant to signalize a difference between the vowels that were used. In the case of Mohr and Wang, and of Whright we may assume that the speakers consciously produced either nasal or nonnasal vowels. Meinhold's speakers behaved differently. They attempted to produce vowels which are as nonnasal as possible. The attempts of the speaker with rhinolalia aperta apparently were not very successful, except in the case of [a]. The reason why the [a] of this speaker is well perceived may well be that he attempted to produce his vowels with a relatively great amount of mouth constriction in order to compensate for the great amount of nose coupling he was forced to produce them with, just as cleft palate speakers produce low "oral" vowels which are perceived as relatively oral as compared with their high vowels (cf. section 5.2 above and the results in Carney and Morris 1971 and Carney and Sherman 1971). As we have seen in 7.1.2, low vowels can be produced with considerable amounts of mouth constriction, high vowels cannot. Consequently, the higher vowels of this speaker were confused, whereas the low [a] was not.

I add a few typological observations. The results of Ruhlen (1978:218-23) show that nasal vowels merge quite easily into each other: languages never have more nasal vowels than nonnasal ones, and quite often fewer. He found that for 83 of the 155 languages the number of nasal vowels was equal to the number of oral vowels. The remaining 72 languages had fewer nasal vowels than oral vowels. (cf. also Ferguson 1963:58, universal 12). Ruhlen (ibid.) observed that mid nasal vowels tend to be lost more frequently than high or low nasal vowels. In another study (Ruhlen 1973:273) we see that in 55 languages with nasal vowels, 49 have high nasal vowels and 49 low nasal vowels (and 45 have both).

A merger of [ɛ̃] with [ĩ] in sequences like **pen** and **pin** is apparently going on in AmEng (see Labov 1972:118). A merger of **eN** with **aN** has occurred in Old French dialects (see Van Reenen to appear). When merging, mid nasal vowels may become either higher or lower.

Thus, perceptual and typological data suggest that nasality tends to supersede vowel qualities along the high/low and front/back dimensions.

The results of this section can be summarized as follows:
1. Low oral vowels in nonnasal environment in AmEng are perceived as more nasal than high oral vowels in AmEng; low and high oral vowels in EurFr are perceived as equally (non)nasal.
2. EurFr high and low vowels before nasal consonant are perceived as equally nasal. Probably the same holds for AmEng high and low vowels before nasal consonant.
3. AmEng lower oral vowels in nonnasal environment are more easily confused with lower nasal vowels than higher oral vowels are with higher nasal vowels.
4. Since nasal low vowels are produced with a smaller amount of mouth constriction than oral low vowels, they are perceived as more central in the vowel space than low oral vowels.
5. Nasality tends to supersede vowel qualities along the high/low and front/back dimensions, i.e. nasal vowels tend to be perceived as central vowels.

7.3 DISCUSSION

This section will deal with several matters touched upon in the above. First, in 7.3.1, I will discuss the statements (1) and (2) - which concern the probability or ease of low oral vowels to become nasal - in the light of the articulatory, perceptual an typological results reviewed in sections 7.1 and 7.2. Secondly, in 7.3.2, I will propose an explanation why the amount of mouth constriction with which lower nasal vowels are produced is smaller than that with which lower oral vowels are produced. Thirdly, in 7.3.3, the influence of nasality on other vowels qualities will be briefly discussed.

7.3.1 THE SLIGHT NASALITY OF ORAL LOWER VOWELS

For those investigators who consider the amount of nose coupling N as directly proportional to the degree of perceived nasality, the articulatory, perceptual and typological results in 7.1 and 7.2 can be summarized as follows:
1. In some languages, for instance AmEng, lower oral vowels in nonnasal environment tend to be produced with an amount of nose coupling greater than zero, whereas higher oral vowels do not.
2. In all languages, lower vowels followed by nasal consonant are produced with more nose coupling than higher vowels in the same position.
These results would be sustaining evidence in favour of statements (1) and

(2): there is a greater amount of nose coupling in the case of lower vowels as compared with higher vowels, at least in languages such as AmEng.

However, other results do not fit into this pattern, for instance:

1. Low oral vowels in AmEng may be produced with as much nose coupling as high nasal vowels, but the high nasal vowels are perceived and transcribed as nasal, whereas the low oral vowels are hardly perceived as nasal and transcribed as oral.

2. Low nasal vowels followed by nasal consonant in AmEng are produced with about three times as much nose coupling as high nasal vowels in that environment and yet they seem to be perceived as equally nasal.

3. Even in AmEng the difference in amount of nose coupling between oral and nasal low vowels is greater than the difference between oral and nasal high vowels. Yet in AmEng oral and nasal low vowels are perceived as more similar than oral and nasal high vowels.

For investigators who take the amount of nose coupling as the central notion in the definition of nasality, these problems cannot be solved.

The problems disappear when I take N% as the notion which is directly proportional to the degree of perceived nasality:

1. Low oral vowels are produced with N% zero or tend to be produced with N% somewhat greater than zero, high oral vowels are produced with N% zero. Low oral vowels produced with N% somewhat greater than zero are perceived as slightly less nonnasal than high or low oral vowels produced with N% zero.

2. Low nasal vowels are produced with the same change in N% as high nasal vowels. Consequently, the amount of nose coupling in the low vowels should be much greater than that in the high nasal vowels.

From the point of view of N%, the articulatory, perceptual, and typological results in the preceding sections suggest that statements (1) and (2) are not correct, though it is true that in some languages low oral vowels tend to be produced with N% greater than zero and that they may be perceived as more nasal than high oral vowels are. However, these low vowels are still **oral** vowels.

In (1) and (2) above it is stated that it is (a) more difficult or (b) less probable for high oral vowels to become nasal than it is for low oral vowels. Both (a) and (b) are incorrect.

(a) It is not more difficult, since the articulatory movements necessary to make a high oral vowel nasal are simpler than those necessary to make a low vowel nasal. A small opening of the nasal port makes a high oral vowel nasal, whereas a considerable opening of the nasal port is necessary to make a low oral vowel nasal. In addition, the low oral vowel has to be made less low, see also 7.3.2 below.

(b) It is not less probable, since just as lower nasal vowels, higher nasal vowels occur frequently, as we have seen in 7.2 above. I think that historical evidence points in the same direction. Nasal vowels usually develop from oral vowels followed by nasal consonant, sometimes from oral vowels preceded by nasal consonant, exceptionally otherwise, cf. Ferguson (1975:180-1). Though low (and not high) oral vowels in nonnasal environment tend to be **slightly nasal**, there is no historical evidence that they become **nasal** more frequently than high oral vowels in nonnasal environment do.

Consequently, attempts to explain why it is more difficult or less probable for high oral vowels than it is for low oral vowels to become nasal have been idle. What they have tried to explain is a nonexistent state of affairs.[22]

An attempt to explain why it would be difficult to make high vowels nasal which probably has had much influence is given in Jespersen (1913:59). Jespersen argued that, as these vowels should be produced with the nasal port VERY OPEN (see 3.2 above) - i.e open to such an extent that the lowering of the velum necessary to create the opening only allows of the production of lower vowels - the raised back of the tongue would prevent the necessary lowering of the velum for the high vowels. However, this explanation was based upon the assumption that the amount of nose coupling, not N%, is directly proportional to the degree of perceived nasality. As such it concerned a nonexisting state of affairs.[23]

Jespersen's explanation seems to have been implicitly adopted by later studies, though apparently not by Eijkman (1926). Eijkman believed, just as Jespersen did, that it is more difficult to nasalize high vowels than it is low vowels, but he could not accept a reasoning based upon the assumption that the amount of nose coupling should be directly proportional to the degree of perceived nasality. Seeing no alternative, he concluded honestly (as we have seen above in chapter 4.1 quotation (5c)) that he had not been able to find a satisfactory explanation for this, i.e. for what now appears to be a nonexistent state of affairs.

What needs to be explained is why lower oral vowels in nonnasal environment tend to be **slightly nasal** (without becoming **nasal**), i.e. in my terminology tend to be produced with N% somewhat greater than zero or, conversely, why high oral vowels do not become slightly nasal.

I think that two strategies are at work, which are both manifestations of the general principle to keep linguistic distinctions intact.

(1) For the change of a low oral vowel into a low nasal one, the velum would have to move a rather long distance, since a small movement would hardly make a low oral vowel nasal. In addition, the position of the tongue should be adapted. Consequently, there is no reason for speakers to keep their nasal port as obstructed as possible.

For the change of a high oral vowel into a high nasal one, the velum has to move only a short distance. As a small movement would already make a high oral vowel nasal, speakers keep their nasal port as obstructed as possible.

However, cleft palate speakers are unable to follow this strategy. Consequently, their high vowels sound nasal, but not their low vowels. These low
vowels can be produced with an amount of mouth constriction great enough to
supersede the amount of nose coupling with which they are obliged to produce
their vowels, see section 5.2 above.

(2) The second strategy concerns low vowels only. It is described in Fant
(1960:161): "...nasalization may compensate for too neutral a position of the
tongue when the vowel [a] is to be articulated; that is, a widening of the
pharynx or an increase of the volume behind the point of minimum cross- sec-
tional area may be compensated for by nasalization. Without this compensation
the vowel quality comes too close to the schwa. Systematic reconstructions of
speech spectra ... support in part this observation." If Fant is right, the
passage may be paraphrased as follows: in producing low vowels, speakers may
have a more urgent problem than keeping the nasal port completely obstructed:
they need make perceived their low vowels low enough. If the amount of mouth
constriction is too small, they have a way to compensate for it by coupling
the nasal cavity somewhat to the pharyngeal cavity. Now their low vowels sound
low enough, but they sound slightly nasal as well. This is no problem as we
have seen above.

7.3.2 MOUTH CONSTRICTION IN LOW NASAL VOWELS

In 7.1.2 I have shown that low nasal vowels are produced somewhat higher than
their oral counterparts. Here I will discuss the question why low nasal vowels
are produced with a smaller amount of mouth coupling than low oral vowels.

I will argue that for many speakers it is difficult, if not impossible, to
produce low nasal vowels in the literal sense of the word, because they cannot
open their nasal port sufficiently.

The average area of nose coupling maximally possible for ten adult Swedish
speakers was 200 mm^2, as we have seen in chapter 5 above (table 5-1). It follows that the maximal amount of nose coupling of which speakers make use in
producing vowels is lower than their maximal amount of mouth constriction: an
amount of mouth constriction MC of 500 mm^2 is quite possible, whereas an
amount of nose coupling N of 500 mm^2 will be quite exceptional, if not completely impossible for any normal human speaker, the highest value in Bjoerk
being 310 mm^2.

If we assume that the average area of nose coupling maximally possible for
adult speakers is 200 mm^2, we may assume that the average area of nose coupling for the ten AmEng speakers of table 7-2 above is about 200 mm^2 as well.
It follows that, on an average, these speakers do not use more than about 2/3
of their possible area of nose coupling, viz. 128 mm^2, during the production
of their low nasal vowels.

If we assume that for their low nasal vowels average adult speakers maximally use an amount of nose coupling N between 75 and 175 mm^2 - as do the CanFr and EurFr subjects and the group of the AmEng subjects of Moll (1962) -, we can calculate the maximal amount of mouth constriction with which we expect a low nasal vowel to be produced. In fig. 7-2 the relation between the values for N% and mouth constriction MC has been presented for seven amounts of nose coupling N. Two examples may serve to explain how to read this figure:

1. The curve, N = 75 mm^2 indicates the relation between MC and N% for an amount of nose coupling of 75 mm^2. It shows that in the area in which N% = 75, MC is about 25 mm^2.

2. In the area in which N% = 75, MC is about 55 mm^2 for N being 175 mm^2.

As regards the oral vowels we arrive at surprising conclusions. As we have seen above in table 7-2, low oral vowels are produced with an average MC of about 275mm^2. In order to make these vowels nasal, i.e produced with an increase in N% from (almost) zero to about 75, we would need an amount of nose coupling of about 825 mm^2 for N% to be 75. When the average value of the EurFr oral low vowels is 0.5x(124+104)= 114 mm^2 (see table 7-3), it follows that N would be about 342 mm^2; for the CanFr subject the average MC is 0.5x(53+59)= 56 mm^2, and N will be 168 mm^2 for N% to be 75. Except maybe for the CanFr speaker, the calculated values for the amount of nose coupling N are too high to be anatomically possible.

It may be objected that a value for N% of 75 is too high because values of mouth constriction MC found on the basis of the equations of Mermelstein in chapter 5 are too low. But figure 7-2 tells us that even if the N% of a nasal vowel should be between 60 to 70, it would make vowels with an amount of mouth constriction MC greater than 100 mm^2 insufficiently nasal in terms of N% for a speaker whose maximally possible amount of nose coupling N during speech is 150 mm^2. It also tells us that for a speaker whose maximal amount of nose coupling N during speech is 75 mm^2, the maximal amount of mouth constriction cannot be higher than 40 mm^2.

I think that the upshot of these considerations and calculations is that low oral vowels produced with a high amount of mouth constriction can only be made nasal if **the amount of mouth constriction decreases.**

We can now return to the statement earlier in this subsection that it is often impossible to produce lower nasal vowels in the literal sense of the word. If the amount of mouth constriction is too great in relation to the maximal amount of nose coupling possible, a speaker will never succeed in making the vowel sufficiently nasal. But the problem can be avoided by producing the vowels with a smaller amount of mouth constriction.

In order to produce low nasal vowels with a smaller amount of mouth constriction, speakers use two strategies: they lower the velum to put it in an arched position parallel to the tongue and they raise the back of the tongue.

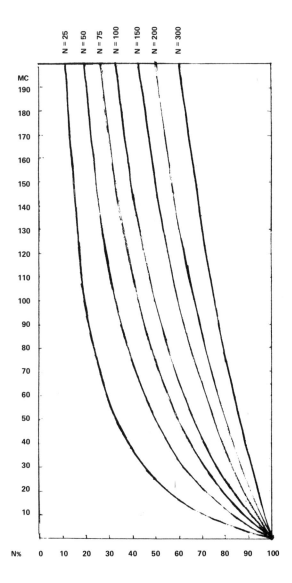

Fig. 7-2 Relations between values for N% and mouth constriction MC for seven amounts of nose coupling N.

The velum has to make the lowering movement in order to adopt not only the optimal position for the considerable amount of nose coupling necessary but also the optimal position for the right amount of mouth constriction. The latter movement has to be coordinated with that of the back of the tongue. By raising the back of the tongue speakers will raise the body of the tongue as well. As a consequence the low nasal vowels will be produced somewhat higher than the low oral vowels.

For high nasal vowels the situation may be different. In the case of high front nasal vowels, and maybe also high back vowels, the velum does not regulate the access to the mouth cavity and the amount of mouth constriction. As has been observed in chapter 4, for high front vowels the smallest mouth passage is located near the hard palate, for high back vowels it may be located either near the velum or near the lips. Therefore, I do not expect that the velum is necessarily always arched and lowered during the production of the central phase of high nasal vowels.

The strategy of making low nasal vowels less low than low oral vowels has not been applied in the speech analogue of House and Stevens (see chapter 4). Although the $[a]$ in their model is produced with an amount of mouth constriction of 131 mm^2 (not an extremely high value in the light of the data in table 7-2 above), an extremely great amount of nose coupling - 340 mm^2, probably greater than any real speaker would be able to make - would be needed in order to make the value of N% high enough.[24]

We may summarize the results of this subsection as follows:

In terms of N% we have explained that high oral vowels are less nasal than low oral vowels.

Since vowel nasality in terms of N% is an increase from (almost) zero to about 75, we have to conclude that the velum has to move a short distance in order to make a high oral vowel nasal, a longer distance in order to make a low oral vowel nasal. This distance may be so long that the nasal port cannot be opened sufficiently. In order to solve this problem the amount of mouth constriction of the low oral vowel has to decrease, and the low oral vowel will become somewhat or much higher. Therefore, to make low oral vowels nasal, more movements are necessary than to make high vowels nasal.

7.3.3 THE INFLUENCE OF NASALITY ON OTHER VOWEL PROPERTIES

I will terminate this subsection with a short discussion of the influence of nasality on vowels and their relations to other sounds.

The perceptual space of nasal vowels is smaller than that of the oral vowels. One reason is articulatory in nature. Since the amount of mouth constriction for low nasal vowels is smaller than for low oral vowels, the low nasal vowels are somewhat higher than the low oral vowels (cf. 7.1.2 and 7.2).

The other reason is perceptual in nature. Making a vowel nasal implies that other properties become perceptually less dominant (cf. 7.2). But in this case it is only the perceptual, and not the articulatory vowel space which becomes smaller than that of oral vowels. The properties of vowels represented in the vowel space can be described by means of the features HIGH, LOW and BACK. That the perceptual vowel space of nasal vowels is smaller than that of oral vowels implies that perceptually the features HIGH, LOW and BACK are superseded by the nasality. In articulatory terms the HIGH, LOW and BACK or FRONT position does not change.

Nasal vowels have to be perceptible as nasal sounds and as vowels of specific qualities. They have been characterized by an increase in N% from (almost) zero to about 75. If N% becomes too high the vowel would be perceived as a indistinctive sound: a kind of murmur or a central vowel. The **increase** in N% makes it possible that

(a) the nasality of the vowel is made perceptible because of the contrast between its central nasal phase and its preceding, more oral phase;

(b) the specific vowel quality of the vowel is relatively well perceived by means of the first, still oral phase of the vowel.

Speakers may increase the perceptibility of their nasal vowels by

(a) making them longer than their oral counterparts;[25]

(b) giving the nasal vowels a position in the vowel space slightly different from their nonnasal counterparts.[26]

Increasing the perceptibility of one property may decrease that of another. Hence, nasal vowels may become either too nasal or too oral. The fact that they are nasal already makes them tend to merge with each other (as we have seen in 7.2 above). They may also change into a succession of nasal (or even oral) vowel plus nasal consonant.[27] If they become too oral, they cannot be distinguished from their oral counterparts.[28]

7.4 INTEGRATION INTO THE THEORETICAL FRAMEWORK

Several findings in the preceding sections of this chapter should be integrated into my phonological theory, viz. the difference in velic behaviour between lower oral vowels and higher oral vowels in nonnasal environment in 7.3.1 above; the difference in height between low nasal vowels and low oral vowels in 7.3.2 above; and the influence of nasality upon the perception of other vowel properties in 7.3.3 above.

1. The difference in velic behaviour between lower oral vowels and higher oral vowels in nonnasal environment can be captured in a physical diagram or a universal phonetic constraint. The tentative physical diagram is given in fig. 7-3. It indicates the domain of possible low vowels in human language.

The corresponding universal phonetic constraint can roughly be worded as:

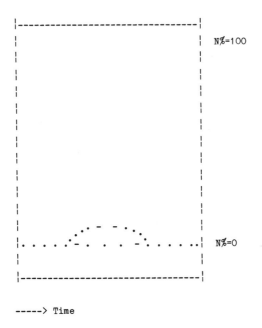

-----> Time

Fig. 7-3. Tentative universal physical diagram of low oral vowels.

Speakers may produce their lower oral vowels with N% slightly higher than zero.

This is so, because speakers attempt to keep their higher oral vowels in non-nasal environment more oral than their lower oral vowels.

Fig. 7-3 serves as the source of possible language-specific differences among lower oral vowels. In AmEng and CanFr, N% may be greater than zero. The low level phonological rules in these languages should state that lower oral vowels in nonnasal environment are produced with N% somewhat greater than zero. It should explicitly be stated that symbols of low vowels in phonetic transcriptions in these languages refer to low vowels as described in the physical diagram for nasality of that language. In other languages, the low level phonological rules state that N% in low vowels is zero, just as it is in high oral vowels.

2. The difference in height between nasal low vowels and oral low vowels can be captured in terms of a physical diagram or a universal phonetic constraint. The tentative physical diagram is given in fig. 7-4 (in which I have not ela-borated the specific feature constellation of **SPE** in any detail). It indicates the domain of possible high and low vowels in human language. The universal physical diagram of the feature LOW of a nasal low vowel has a smaller value than that of the feature LOW of an oral low vowel.

ORAL VOWELS   NASAL VOWELS

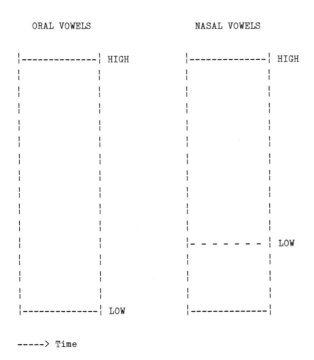

-----> Time

Fig. 7-4. Tentative universal physical diagram of the features HIGH and LOW in oral and nasal vowels.

The corresponding universal phonetic constraint can roughly be worded as:

Speakers produce their low nasal vowels higher than the corresponding low oral vowels.

If they do not, they cannot make their low vowels sufficiently nasal. As the increase in N% in nasal vowels may be different in various languages, the influence of nasality on the features LOW and HIGH may be different as well. This difference should be stated in language-specific low level phonological rules. Symbols of low nasal vowels in phonetic transcriptions of specific languages should refer to the state of affairs described in the physical diagram for nasality of that language.

3. The influence of nasality upon the perception of other vowel properties has to be captured in a physical diagram or a universal constraint. With nasal vowels, the perceptual distance of the physical diagrams of the features LOW, HIGH and BACK is smaller than with oral vowels. The tentative physical diagram is given in fig.7-5, to which I have added two perceptual scales. In fig.7-4 I

had not taken into account the overall influence of nasality on the perception
of vowel height. Therefore, fig. 7-4 has to be substituted by fig. 7-5.   The
perceptual scale A was implicitly present in the case of fig. 7-4. The fact
that nasality makes vowel height less well perceived, is expressed by means of
the short perceptual scale B.

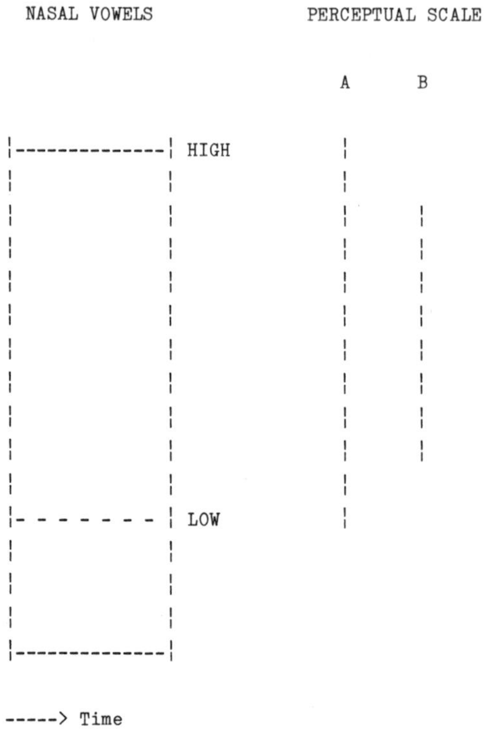

```
         NASAL VOWELS              PERCEPTUAL SCALE


                                   A       B

     |--------------| HIGH         |
     |              |              |
     |              |              |       |
     |              |              |       |
     |              |              |       |
     |              |              |       |
     |              |              |       |
     |              |              |       |
     |              |              |       |
     |              |              |       |
     |              |              |       |
     |              |              |       |
     |              |              |
     |- - - - - - - | LOW          |
     |              |
     |              |
     |              |
     |--------------|


     -----> Time
```

Fig. 7-5. Tentative universal physical diagram of the features HIGH and LOW in
nasal vowels with added perceptual scale.

   The corresponding universal phonetic constraint can roughly be worded as:

Vowel height in nasal vowels is less well perceived than it is in oral vowels.
(It should be added that the same holds for the front/back dimension).

When N% starts to be high early in the vowel, the physical diagrams of the
features LOW, HIGH and BACK are perceptually more limited than when it starts
late. Symbols of low nasal vowels in phonetic transcriptions should refer to
the relevant physical diagram of that language.

NOTES TO CHAPTER 7

1. Other references can be found in Ohala (1975:299) to which I add: Paris
   (1898:301 note 1), de Saussure (1918:75), Jespersen (1913:59), Delattre
   (1970:224).

2. See also Chen (1973), Ferguson (1975:182), Straka (1955). Especially for
   EurFr many references can be found in Rochet (1976), who does not agree
   with statements of the nature of (2), however.

3. The same trend is visible in a set of Dutch data (see Eijkman 1902, table
   III) and in the Hindi utterance [kan] (see Ohala (M.) 1975:324).

4. We have to make an exception for vowels occurring in utterance-final
   position, see chapter 6.

5. It should be added that in data set 6 the amount of nose coupling is
   slightly greater than zero. Lubker (1968) gives averages in terms of
   velopharyngeal distance and adds standard deviations, the highest VP
   being that of [...pipipi...] = 0.1 mm with the highest standard deviation
   = 0.34. This results in an average amount of nose coupling of 0.04 mm^2.

6. It should be added that in data set 6 the amount of nose coupling may be
   much greater than 42 mm^2. Lubker (1968) gives as highest VP 3.4 mm
   (corresponding with 57 mm^2 after application of equation IX) with a standard deviation of 2.21. The VP measure used by Lubker may be slightly
   different from the one used in the present study, especially in the case
   of the higher values (cf. Lubker 1968:17). With respect to AmEng low oral
   vowels Ohala (1975:299) observes: "It would seem that a little bit of
   nasalization is not just tolerated on these vowels, it is required." As
   appears from the data under discussion, this observation is correct under
   specific conditions only.

7. Speech rate is proposed as an explanation in Bzoch (1968:217); evidence
   in favour of it is offered in Moll and Shriner (1967), in Kent et al.
   (1974:484) and in Kuehn (1976:99). That sex may explain the difference
   can be inferred from Schwartz (1968a); it accounts for the differences
   found in Schwartz's own data based on vowels produced by 15 males and 15
   females, as well as for differences found in the data in Moll (1962) - as
   Schwartz (1968a:199) reports. That the nature of the nonnasal environment
   may play a part can be inferred from statements in Moll and Daniloff
   (1971:683) and from the discussion on the perceptual results in Lintz and
   Sherman (1961:391, 394).

8. Moll (1962) has selected three X-ray photographs per vowel maximally
   (p.31). I assume that on an average these photographs were situated in
   the central phase of the vowel. In total, he has analysed 20 high and 20
   low vowels before a nasal consonant, produced by 10 speakers. The

difference he found between the two environments [N-] and [-N] can be compared with other data. In CanFr and EurFr the amount of nose coupling in vowels in [NV̂(?)] syllables is about half the amount of nose coupling found in vowels in [V̂(N)] syllables (cf. Appendices 2, 3 and 4, tables A2-2, A2-3, A2-4, A3-1, A3-2, A4-2). The same holds for the nasograph data in Ohala (1971:33 = 1975:304), but not for the data in Lubker and Moll (1965): here the amount of nose coupling N in the vowel of [nip] is extremely high (see Appendix A3-3).

9. Lubker (1968) has analysed 15 high and 15 low vowels produced by two females and three males. He has made tracings and measurements of "all frames exposed during the vowel portion of all three repetitions of each utterance type" (p.5). I assume that on an average his frames (photographs) were situated in the central phase of the vowel.

10. The values for MC in table 7-3 below, which concern the EurFr and CanFr subjects discussed in chapter 6, are considerably lower.

11. Any consistent way of taking measurements in the second half of these vowels leads to the same result: the amount of mouth constriction in nasal vowels is lower than that in oral vowels. However, this trend is not visible in Delattre 1965, fig 3. The measure "Tongue constriction" used by Lubker and Moll (1965:264) is not equivalent to my measure "smallest mouth distance SM", since tongue constriction is measured between the hard palate or alveolar ridge and the tongue, but not between the tongue and the soft palate.

12. There are more extreme differences, but in the case of Wood we are sure that the same method has been applied with both subjects.

13. See Delattre (1965:94; 1968:69; 1970:222;) Brichler-Labaeye (1970) and Charbonneau (1971). In Simon (1967) tracings of four unstressed lower nasal vowels are presented. These vowels - which are short or very short - are not always produced with a clearly lowered velum.

14. As we have seen in 4.2 above, the results in Carney and Morris (1971) confirm what we expect for AmEng speakers. However, these speakers are slightly deviant: they are nasal speakers without cleft palate (see section 5.1 above.)

15. Ali et al. (1971) do not mention whether the vowels are nasal or not. My notation of the ·syllables as [CVC] and [CV̂N] is based upon the results mentioned in chapter 6 and 7.1 above that AmEng vowels before a nasal consonant are nasal vowels. In addition, I have adapted the terminology they use, since it is not always appropriate. For instance, they conclude: "Consonants which followed the low back vowel /a/ were perceived

as nasal with a significant greater frequency than the vowels /u/, /eI/, and /i/." (p.539). However, the consonants in question were cut off, and the authors did not intend to compare consonants with vowels.

16. The way they present the results requires some reanalysis. In the experiment 9 females and 1 male produced isolated vowels with different degrees of nasality: "extreme", "moderate", and "natural" (p.46). Ten students of "a speech class of Duke University" judged whether the vowels sounded "nasal" or "normal" (i.e. nonnasal) (cf. p.47). In the last column of table 7-4 I had to make guesses as to the number of vowels judged, because Massengill.& Bryson do not mention how many vowels were produced without nose coupling. They observe: "Each S(=subject, PvR) phoneted each of these vowels three times, simulating an extreme amount of nasality for the first phonation, a moderate for the second, and the vowel in a natural manner in the third... During the first and the second phonation... the velum lacked contact with the pharyngeal wall... In a few cases the third phonation was not recorded because velar closure was obtained during the second phonation." (p.46-7). Though this quotation suggests that one vowel with N% zero was produced in each set of two or three, the values in table 7-4 point in a different direction. As the score for [i, u] and [æ] is a fraction, and the listeners judged the vowels in terms of the integers 0 or 1, the values in table 7-4 must be averages based upon the sum of the scores "1". Since no more than 10 vowels of a certain type without nose coupling were produced (cf. the quotation above), the sum of the scores "1" is either 4 or 8 times as much, i.e. either 29 or 58 judgements in the case of [i, æ], or 35 or 70 in the case of [u]. In all cases the total number of scores (both "1" and "0") must have been a multiple of 10, i.e. 40 or 80, and the number of vowels judged 4 or 8. For [a] no guess of the preceding kind can be made. It must be assumed that a reasonable number of [a] vowels has been produced without nose coupling.

17. The difference between front and back vowels, falling outside the scope of this study, is greater.

18. Mohr and Wang (1968:33-4) mention that these vowels were produced by a "speaker" and that listeners were "native speakers of (American? PvR) English". The authors do not comment on the way the speech samples were produced.

19. Listeners were twelve graduate students in linguistics (p. 375) - besides two bilinguals, all native speakers of AmEng (p.382). Wright does not mention whether the speakers, too, are AmEng.

20. Wright (1975) has analysed the vowels of his two speakers spectrographically as well. A comparison of the spectrographic analysis and the perceptual results shows that the latter are not well predictable on the basis of the former.

21. In Rochet (1974,1975,1976) and Van Reenen (to appear) the same claim is made.

22. Explanations which attribute the lower position of the velum during the production of low oral vowels "to some mechanical connections between the tongue body and the soft palate" (as Ohala 1975:299 has worded it) have been given in Moll (1962:34), Lubker (1968:13) and others. In the light of recent electromyographic studies such explanations do not hold, see Ohala (1975:299) for some discussion and references. According to Delattre (1965, 1968, 1970) the dimensions of the pharyngeal cavity during the production of high vowels would not favour the nasalization of these vowels. In his view it would be inexplainable why high nasal vowels occur so frequently in human language.

23. X-ray photographs tell us now that the argument does not hold for [i].

24. Another reason why they need this high amount of nose coupling is the fact that the nasal vowels are produced without any increase in N%.

25. See Appendix 2, tables A2-1, A2-2, A2-3 for CanFr and Delattre and Monnot (1968) for EurFr.

26. For discussion concerning the position of EurFr nasal vowels as compared with their oral counterparts see Linthorst (1975:88-9), Straka (1955:247) and Strenger (1969), for CanFr see Charbonneau (1971).

27. This has occurred in the history of a series of Rumanian words. An example is Latin **genuculum** "knee" which changed into [genŭk] and later in [genuŋk]. For more details, see Nandrish (1963).

28. See Greenberg (1966:514 and passim). One of the perceptual experiments in Mohr and Wang (1968:37, table V) shows that the perceptual distance between [i - ĩ, u - ũ, a - ã] is small as compared with the perceptual distance between other pairs of sounds.

CHAPTER 8

Nasal consonants and their relation to vowels

Until now it has been assumed that in terms of N% the physical reality of nasal consonants is less complicated than that of nasal vowels. Yet they do not form a homogeneous class in all respects.

The amounts of nose coupling with which nasal consonants are produced may vary considerably. The variation is systematically determined by the environments in which the nasal consonants occur. This is the subject of 8.1.

A comparison between nasal consonants as a class and nasal vowels, discussed in 8.2, reveals not only systematic differences in N% and in the amount of nose coupling, but also in velic behaviour. See 8.2.

When in real speech a nasal consonant and a vowel occur next to each other, they influence each other. I will show that a nasal consonant has to be defined otherwise than it has been until now, see 8.3.

Integration of the results into my phonological framework will be discussed in 8.4.

8.1 NASAL CONSONANTS

This section concerns only the most common type of nasal consonants: the nasal stops. Other nasal consonants will not be dealt with, as was stated in 3.4 above. By a nasal consonant, therefore, I understand a nasal stop. According to Chomsky and Halle (1968: 317, 316), "in stops the air flow through the mouth is effectively blocked" and as the stops are nasal, they "are produced with a lowered velum". In other words: in a nasal stop the amount of mouth constriction MC is zero and the amount of nose coupling N is greater than zero. Application of equation (I) (see chapter 4, section 4.2) shows that for a nasal stop:

$$N\% = \frac{N}{0 + N} \cdot 100 = 100 \qquad \text{for any value of } N > 0 \qquad (I)$$

That is why the amount of nose coupling N may vary considerably, in fact almost freely, in a nasal consonant, without affecting the value of N% = 100, and N and N% are mutually independent, provided N is greater than zero. The position of the velum need not be a specific one, as long as the nasal port is not obstructed. Therefore we may expect that nasal consonants are not characterized by a specific amount of nose coupling, and that the velum moves quite freely and may adopt a great variety of shapes and positions.

This expectation is not in agreement with the opinions of the few phoneticians who have explicitly dealt with the question. As we have seen in section 3.2 above, Jespersen (1913:56-63) distinguishes four degrees of velic opening, which may be labelled as **very open** (delta 3) or the velum is very much lowered, **open** (delta 2) or the velum is lowered, **slightly open** (delta 1) or the velum is slightly lowered, and **closed** (delta 0) or the velum is not lowered. Jespersen considers nasal consonants to be produced with the nasal port **open** (the velum lowered), whereas I expect that the nasal port may be **slightly open** and **very open** as well. Something of the same kind may apply to the sound classification described in Ladefoged (1975:270-1) in section 3.2. On Ladefoged's physical scale, nasal consonants in English are as nasal as possible, i.e. the velum is as low as is possible in speech sounds.

From many data it appears, however, that my expectation is correct. First, there is no specific amount of nose coupling for nasal consonants. It is clear from data in Lubker (1968: 8, 9, 15), Bjoerk (1961:40), Petursson (1974:297, 298, 311, 312, 320, 325, 332, 333), Rochette (1973 passim), Simon (1967:318-20) that the amount of nose coupling in nasal consonants may vary considerably. In Rochette, for instance, I estimate that for one of his subjects the greatest amount of nose coupling per nasal consonant varies between 14 mm^2 and 273 mm^2.[1] Clearly, such variations cannot be described by expressions like "the nasal port is **open** (delta 2)" or "the velum is lowered" (Jespersen) or "the velum is in as low a position as is possible in speech" (Ladefoged).

Secondly, what is also visible in X-ray tracings is that the velum moves rather freely and may adopt a great variety of shapes and positions.

However, with respect to the velum Delattre (1965:95-6) observes in his X-ray tracings that only one of its movements and shapes is typical for nasal consonants:

"...l'ouverture vélique des consonnes se fait non par un abaissement du voile, mais par un repliement latéral, en accordéon."

Indeed, in the X-ray tracings of Delattre the velum is folded sidewards and the nasal port is opened by means of a fronting movement. The fronted position of the velum can be observed in the X-ray tracings in Rochette (1973) as well and he may even conclude that during the production of a nasal consonant the velum "s'avance plus qu'il ne s'abaisse" (p.399). The X-ray tracings in Delattre and Rochette prove that expressions containing the term "lowered" in connection with the position of the velum are misleading and should be avoided.

Yet, the velum may adopt other shapes and positions, although it is true that in the X-ray tracings published by Delattre (1965:103; 1968:69) the nasal consonants are never produced with the velum lowered. This appears from a comparison of the X-ray tracings in Fant (1960:140), Simon (1967:318-20), Petursson (1974:297, 298, 311, 312, 320, 325, 332, 333) and also Rochette (1973). Here we see that nasal consonants may be produced with a lowered velum as well.

Therefore, there is no specific amount of nose coupling characteristic for nasal consonants, and the velum may move quite freely and adopt a great variety of shapes and positions. This result is what we expect on the basis of equation I above: provided the amount of nose coupling N is greater than zero, N may vary freely.

Since the amount of nose coupling N of a nasal consonant actually varies independently of N% - as long as it is greater than zero - and the velum may move quite freely, it is not surprising that the velic behaviour and the amount of nose coupling may be strongly influenced by adjacent sounds. I will now examine the influence of different kinds of environment on velic behaviour and nose coupling.

1. Isolated nasal consonants.
In isolated nasal consonants there is no influence from the environment apart from silence, and during silence the velum is typically in rest-position, because we expect the amount of nose coupling to be high. This prediction is supported by results in Lubker (1968:8, 9).[2] Lubker observes that for his five speakers, "on the average, palatal elevation during the production of the sustained /m/ was slightly above physiologic rest ... (approximately 2mm)" and concludes that "nasal consonants can be produced with little or no velar elevation", although "there was considerable between-subject variability" (p.15). During speech, however, the velum is well above the physiological rest-position as appears from all the relevant X- ray tracings I have examined.[3]

2. Nasal consonant next to nonnasal consonant: [CN] and [NC].
Since the [C]'s, as a rule, are produced without nose coupling, we expect a relatively small amount of nose coupling N during the part of the nasal consonant next to the nonnasal consonant. This is indeed what we usually find in X-ray tracings. It appears very clearly in those in Rochette (1973:passim) (EurFr)[4]. It is especially in this environment that the velum is often fronted instead of lowered.

3. Nasal consonant adjacent to high and low vowels.
As we have seen in chapters 6 and 7 above, the vowels may be more or less nasal. As lower vowels are produced with a greater amount of nose coupling

than higher vowels in various languages (see chapter 7 above), we expect a nasal consonant preceded by a low vowel to be produced with a greater amount of nose coupling than when preceded by a high vowel. The scarce data on this point confirm this expectation. The results of Kuehn (1976:98-9) and Bell-Berti et al. (1979:190-2) bear it out for AmEng. With respect to [V̂N] and [NV] or [NV̂] syllables Kuehn (ibidem) concludes: "The results ... suggest that, during velar lowering for the nasal consonant, the velum is ... higher within a high vowel context than within a low vowel context. It appears that the entire locus of normal palatal movement between lowered and elevated position is shifted depending on the particular vowel category within the phonetic environment." From the tracings in Rochette (1973) I have drawn the same conclusion for EurFr. Here syllables occur which may be noted as [VN] and [NV], [NV̂] and [V̂N]. The portion of the [N]'s next to the higher oral vowels is produced with a smaller amount of nose coupling than the portion of the [N]'s next to lower oral vowels. That portion, in turn, is produced with a smaller amount of nose coupling than the portion of the [N]'s next to (lower) nasal vowels.

Therefore, although there is no specific amount of nose coupling and no typical movement of the velum during the production of nasal consonants in general, there may be specific amounts of nose coupling N and typical movements of the velum per environment.

8.2 NASALITY IN CONSONANTS AND VOWELS

Nasal (or nonnasal) consonants can be considered as a group, and as such be compared to nasal (or nonnasal and oral) vowels, in which comparison the following aspects are relevant:
1. The possible degrees of nasality.
2. The behaviour of the velum.
3. The values of the amount of nose coupling and N% as functions of time.
4. The status of the so-called nasal consonant segment and its relation to nasal vowels.

Ad 1. The possible degrees of nasality.
It follows from the nature of consonants and vowels that they do not exhibit the same number of degrees of nasality. From the equation:

$$N\% = \frac{N}{N + MC} \cdot 100 \qquad \text{(cf. chapter 4, equation I)}$$

we may deduct that consonants are trinary as to nasality and vowels multivalued. For vowels the amount of mouth constriction MC is always greater

than zero, for stops the amount of mouth constriction MC is zero and for continuants it approaches to zero. So there are many values for N% possible for
the vowels (cf. chapters 4, 6 and 7), but only three for consonants.[5] For
nasal consonants N% is 100; and for nonnasal continuants, in which MC
approaches to zero, N% is zero. However, for nonnasal stops, in which the
amount of nose coupling N = 0 and the amount of mouth constriction MC = 0, the
resulting value for N% is indefinite. This is an unsatisfactory result,
because these stops are perceived and transcribed as nonnasal, independently
of the value of the mouth constriction. Therefore, nonnasal stops and nonnasal
continuants are equally nonnasal and consonants are, in fact, binary.

Therefore, a first difference between vowels and consonants concerns the
possible values of N%: 100 and zero or indefinite for consonants, all values
smaller than 100 for vowels. Thus, with respect to the feature NASAL, consonants are essentially binary and vowels multivalued. Vowels may be nasal in
many degrees (at least nonnasal, oral and nasal), whereas consonants are
either nasal or nonnasal.

Ad 2. Velic behaviour.
It is the merit of Delattre to have been the first to signalize a difference
in velic behaviour between nasal vowels and nasal consonants, I should add
nasal consonants next to a nonnasal consonant, as we have seen in 8.1 above.
In his X-ray tracings Delattre (1965:95-6) (see also above) noticed that:

"La forme arquée de l'abaissement du voile du palais... est caractéristique
des VOYELLES nasales, mais pas des consonnes nasales. ... l'ouverture vélique
des consonnes se fait non par un abaissement du voile, mais par un repliement
latéral, en accordéon, et cette ouverture est plus étroite que pour les voyelles nasales."

Rochette (1973:399) observes something of the same kind in his X-ray tracings:

"Sans toucher le dos de la langue, le voile du palais est très bas pour les
voyelles nasales pour lesquelles il s'éloigne de la paroi pharyngienne vers
l'avant et vers le bas... Il est plus élevé quand il s'agit de consonnes
nasales; il s'avance plus qu'il ne s'abaisse. Les muscles plus tendus le main-
tiennent plus élevé que pour les voyelles nasales."

The observation in Delattre that in nasal consonants the opening of the nasal
port is smaller than in nasal vowels has not been repeated by Rochette.
Indeed, as far I can judge from the tracings in this latter study, there is no
such difference: both the fronting and the lowering movement of the velum may
result in considerable amounts of nose coupling.

Delattre and Rochette have not proposed an explanation for the difference
between nasal consonants and nasal vowels, at least the lower nasal vowels. In
subsection 7.3.2 above I have attempted to provide the reason why the velum is

134

lowered during the central part of the lower nasal vowels and why it takes the shape of an arch parallel to the back of the tongue. This is because it fulfils a double function. In lower nasal vowels the velum regulates not only the opening of the nasal port in order to create the right amount of nose coupling N, but also - together with the back of the tongue - the access to the mouth cavity in order to create the right amount of mouth constriction MC.

In nasal consonants the velum does not fulfil this double function. Here it does not regulate the amount of nose coupling N, but it causes the amount of nose coupling to be greater than zero, if the influence of surrounding sounds is not taken into account. As I have observed above, the statements of Delattre and Rochette concern nasal consonants in specific environments. Therefore they are not complete: the velum, which forms a sharp angle near the uvula when the nasal port is closed, may during a nasal consonant not only be fronted in the direction of the hard palate without any lowering or change in the sharp angle, but it may also be lowered in the form of an arch. It may even be in physiological rest-position. The reason is that during the production of nasal consonants the velum does not play a part in the formation of the mouth constriction (except - together with the back of the tongue - during the production of the uvular and, sometimes, velar nasal consonants[6]). If we take into account the influence of the environment, the strategy behind velic behaviour in nasal consonants is to a large extent to create an amount of nose coupling greater than zero by staying as close as possible in the position it was in during the adjacent nasal or nonnasal sounds or during silence. The more firmly the nasal port is obstructed in the surrounding sounds, the less the velum will be lowered and the more it will be fronted in the nasal consonant.

Therefore, the difference in velic behaviour between nasal consonants and nasal vowels is this: for nasal consonants the shape and position of the velum are determined to a large extent by the environment, as long as the amount of nose coupling is greater than zero; for nasal vowels its position is determined by the proportion between the various amounts of nose coupling and mouth constriction. In the latter case more precision is needed, especially because the velum has a function in the regulation of the two values in order to create the change in N%.[7]

Ad 3. The values of N% and nose coupling as functions of time.
During the production of a nasal consonant the nose coupling N is greater than zero from the very beginnihg of the consonant to its end, though the amount of nose coupling may vary considerably. If the nasal consonant occurs before or after a vowel, we may even add that the amount of nose coupling N is also greater than zero during the adjacent portion of the vowel, as we have seen in chapter 7. This is illustrated in the X-ray tracings in Rochette (1973) (EurFr), Petursson (1974) (Icelandic) and Simon (1968) (EurFr). However, as we

have seen in chapter 6, during the production of a nasal vowel the nose coupling N is not always necessarily greater than zero. Especially when preceded by a nonnasal sound, a nasal vowel is produced with a change in N% from (almost) zero to about 75.

Delattre (1965:102) observed at least part of this difference between nasal consonants and nasal vowels:

"...le voile du palais s'abaisse avec anticipation pour les consonnes nasales, mais s'abaisse avec retardement pour les voyelles nasales."[8]

Delattre might have added as well that, when nasal consonants are followed by a vowel, the nasal port is usually closed with a certain delay. That the time dimensions of the nose coupling N and N% in nasal consonants are different from those in nasal vowels has also been noticed by some investigators who studied nasality from an acoustic point of view. Stevens (1979: 56) mentions the "rather steady" character of nasal murmurs [m n ŋ]. Actually Jakobson et al. (1952, §2.441) observed already that the typical "formants of the murmur part (of a nasal consonant, PvR) are relatively stable". Therefore, the nose coupling N and N% in nasal vowels are different from those in nasal consonants with respect to time dimensions. Nasal vowels display a change in N% from (almost) zero to about 75 and an increase in the amount of nose coupling N, whereas nasal consonants have the constant value 100 for their N% and a variable, mainly determined by context, amount of nose coupling N, which is greater than zero.

Ad 4. Nasal consonant segments.
Phoneticians frequently mention the existence of so-called nasal consonant segments which are said to occur after nasal vowels.[9] We may wonder (a) why these segments always follow a nasal vowel or are the final portion of such vowels; (b) whether they are consonants in their own right or part of the nasal vowel; (c) whether these segments, if they are consonants in their own right, are nasal stops or nasal continuants. The following observations may throw some light on these questions.

Within the framework of the present study it is quite understandable that, when nasal consonant segments occur, they always follow the nasal vowel and never precede it. A nasal vowel is characterized by a change in N% from (almost) zero to about 75. But it may happen that during the vowel the amount of mouth constriction approaches to zero at a moment at which the amount of nose coupling is still greater than zero. Consequently, N% does not increase from (almost) zero to about 75 but to about 90 or 100. In this way we obtain a vowel portion with ambiguous status, since it may be viewed as part of the vowel or as a nasal consonant in its own right, and in the latter case either as a continuant - when N% is about 90 - or as a stop - when N% is 100.

If we want to determine the status of such ambiguous vowel portions, the

136

following considerations are to be taken into account.

If in nasal vowels before a nonnasal stop incidentally a vowel portion occurs with N% increasing from about 75 to about 90 or 100 (see for instance the CanFr speaker in chapter 6 and Appendix 4, tables A4-3), there is no reason to transcribe this portion as a nasal consonant.[10]

If in nasal vowels before nonnasal stop there is an average nasal vowel portion with N% increasing from about 75 to 90 or 100, there is a reason to insert a nasal continuant in phonetic transcription, although it may be captured in the convention which interprets the physical diagram of the feature NASAL in that language. If in the said vowel portion N% is 100, it has to be noted as a nasal stop.

If nasal consonant segments with N% 100 precede or follow fricatives, semivowels, vowels or silence, the only possible conclusion is that they are real nasal consonants. The same holds for nasal consonant segments which are stops and occur normally homorganically before nonnasal stops.

8.3 NASAL CONSONANTS, SEGMENTATION AND COPRODUCTION

This section concerns the relations between nasal consonants and vowels adjacent to each other. Investigators refer to these relations in terms of coproduction (coarticulation, sometimes assimilation). These notions presuppose views of how sounds would look like without being influenced by other sounds, and how they react on the presence of other sounds. In 8.3.1 I will point out a problem of coproduction, in 8.3.2 I will discuss two views on the segmentation of sounds, in 8.3.3 I will present a solution of the problem and propose a different conception of the notion "nasal consonant".

8.3.1 AN UNSOLVED PROBLEM OF COPRODUCTION

We have found in chapter 7 that in all languages examined higher vowels before or after nasal consonants are produced with a smaller amount of nose coupling N than lower vowels in the same position, no matter whether the amount of nose coupling in the vowels is relatively high, as in AmEng and Portuguese, or not, as in EurFr and Amoy.

We have found as well, in section 8.1, that a nasal consonant before or after a higher vowel is produced with a smaller amount of nose coupling than one before or after a lower vowel, at least in languages such as AmEng and EurFr.

At first sight these findings may seem to be the results of articulatory restrictions on successive sounds, viz. examples of coproduction.[11] This may be correct, but when they are explained in terms of coproduction, they lead to a problem which has not been noticed until now.

Investigators generally will agree that, when a vowel occurs next to a

nasal consonant and is produced with a greater amount of nose coupling than it
would have had in nonnasal environment, this is the result of coproduction
(coarticulation or assimilation) of the vowel and the nasal consonant.

　However, investigators never explain why

(a) before or after a nasal consonant a higher vowel is produced with a
smaller amount of nose coupling than a lower vowel;

(b) before or after a higher vowel a nasal consonant is produced with a
smaller amount of nose coupling than a nasal consonant before or after a lower
vowel.

　Within the framework I have developed in the present study, I may provide
an answer for AmEng nasal vowels before a nasal consonant, but not for the
EurFr oral vowels in that environment.[12] In chapter 6 above I have concluded
that in AmEng both higher and lower vowels before nasal consonants are nasal
in their own right, independently of these nasal consonants. As higher nasal
vowels are produced with less nose coupling than lower nasal vowels in order
to be characterized by the same change in N%, the difference between the subsequent nasal consonants can be explained quite naturally as an example of
left-to-right coarticulation: the amount of nose coupling in the nasal consonants is influenced by the amount of nose coupling in the preceding nasal
vowels, not vice versa.

　However, my explanation does not hold for those vowels before a nasal consonant which are not nasal in their own right, for instance the oral vowels in
this position in EurFr.

8.3.2 TWO VIEWS ON SEGMENTATION

Until now I have assumed that vowels are produced without blocking of the
vocal tract (with an amount of mouth constriction greater than zero) and that
nasal consonants are produced with the vocal tract effectively blocked (with
mouth constriction zero) (cf. 8.1 above). I will call the blocking or not
blocking of the vocal tract the primary articulatory gestures of consonants
and vowels (cf. Fowler 1980:131), the opening or closing of the nasal port the
secondary articulatory gestures of these sounds.

　When this view is applied to real speech, it implies that a nasal consonant
before a vowel ends the moment at which the mouth passage ceases to be completely blocked and that the vowel begins at the same moment. This has the
great advantage that - just as in phonetic transcription (or representation) -
real speech sounds follow each other, per definition, without any coproduction. Coproduction has to be expressed in terms of the influence of one sound
within the domain of the adjacent sound. The vowel and the nasal consonant
themselves - whether or not influenced by each other - have their own domain
clearly separable in real time.

　Some investigators seem to have chosen the primary articulatory gesture of

the nasal consonant and the adjacent vowel as the only criterium for segmentation. As long as primary and secondary articulatory gestures are made simul-
taneously, there is no problem. But, as we have seen in sections 6.2 and 6.3,
there is good reason to suspect that they are not. In nasal consonants the
secondary articulatory gesture, the opening of the nasal port, may occur both
earlier and later than the primary articulatory gesture. It follows that the
overlap of the secondary articulatory gesture of the nasal consonant in the
domain of the vowel (the opening of the nasal port) is a property of the vowel
which should be noted - and actually has been noted by some investigators - in
the phonetic transcription of the utterances. Investigators who, more or less
implicitly, have adopted this view are Straka (1955:266, 269-70), Rueter (1975
:14, 21), Hooper (1976:86) and, even more implicitly, Delattre (1965:104).[13]
It may be the view of Chomsky and Halle (1968) as well, this would explain why
they represent the vowel in **inn** as [2 nasal], i.e. partially nasal, cf.
chapter 3 above. Fant (1973:155)also seems to suggest that the nasality is a
property of the vowel, not of the nasal consonant, see the following quotation: "The perceptual importance of nasalization of a vowel as a cue for identification of an adjacent nasal phoneme is considerable".

Other investigators adopt the view that both the primary and the secondary
articulatory gestures are characteristic for a nasal consonant, which implies
that vowel and nasal consonant are necessarily (partly) coproduced. This view
is proposed for instance in Ohala (1975:302) (rather implicitly), in Hyman
(1972:169f) (see 6.2.1 above), in Kent and Minifie (1977:118)[14] and very
clearly in Fowler (1977, 1980).

Fowler (1980) argues that the failure of the theories on coarticulation is
a result of the conception that sounds are segmented in real time, and that
the conception of segmenting sounds in real time - "extrinsic timing" in her
terminology - has to be replaced by another one: segmentation by means of
intrinsic timing. Her basic idea is that vowels and consonants belong to different layers which are necessarily (partly) coproduced. In this view at least
some of the nose coupling found in a vowel adjacent to a nasal consonant is
not a property of the vowel, but part of the nasal consonant. In that case, I
think, there is no reason why this nose coupling should be noted in phonetic
transcriptions as a property of the vowel. Vowels in [CVN] and [NVC]
sequences are then rightly noted as nonnasal, since these vowels are necessarily (partly) coproduced with the secondary articulatory gesture of the
nasal consonant. Phonetic transcriptions need not specify real time properties
of sound sequences. By comparing phonetic transcriptions and the physical
reality they describe, we have to take into account that the successive segments of phonetic transcriptions refer to necessarily (partly) coproduced
sounds in physical reality.

I have found one perceptual experiment - reported in Mårtony (1964) and

Mårtony and Fant (1964) - on this subject. Its result confirms that there is
necessarily (partial) coproduction of vowel and nasal consonant with respect
to nasality. The experiment concerns the question whether or not a nasal consonant can be produced without being necessarily coproduced with an adjacent
vowel. Mårtony and Fant discussed acoustic properties of artificial [NV]
syllables (N = [n] or [m]; V = [i], [a] or [u]), made to resemble real Swedish
syllables as much as possible. Especially in the case of [a], but also in the
case of [i] and [u], it appeared that the vowel has to be produced with nasal
formants, the acoustic correlates of nose coupling. If these nasal formants
were absent in the **vowels**, the nasal **consonants** [n] and [m] were perceived as
[l], [d] or [nd] and [b] or [mb] by Swedish listeners. In brief, the nose coupling in the vowel was necessary to make the nasality of the adjacent nasal
consonant perceptible for the Swedish listeners.[15]

I conclude from this experiment that the secondary articulatory gesture of
a nasal consonant must still be present in the subsequent vowel, in other
words that vowel and nasal consonant are necessarily (partly) coproduced.

8.3.3 THE PROBLEM SOLVED

The view that vowels and consonants are necessarily (partly) coproduced can
help us to find an explanation for the problem described in 8.3.1. One of the
consequences of this view is that it is possible to reconsider the notion
"nasal consonant" as defined in 8.1 above. It seems to be necessary to replace
this notion by the following one:

A nasal consonant is characterized by
- an on-glide in which N% increases from zero onwards;
- a central phase in which N% is 100 (since MC is zero);
- an off-glide in which N% decreases to zero;

Phoneticians do not assign on- or off-glide status to the secondary articulatory gesture of nasal consonants as they do to nonnasal plosives (cf. Gimson
1970:150).[16] Yet, I think it justified to propose that nasal consonants have
an on- and an off-glide, which are necessarily (partly) coproduced with a
preceding, respectively following, vowel. Next to another consonant or next to
silence the on- or off-glide are not produced, however.

The question why the amount of nose coupling is smaller in a high vowel
before a nasal consonant than in a low vowel in the same environment (see
8.3.1 above) can now be answered. The smaller amount of nose coupling in the
high vowel serves to make N% equally high as in low vowels during the on-glide
of the nasal consonant - which is necessarily (partly) coproduced with the
last phase of the high or low vowel, i.e. in which the nasal port is open
already. In order for N% to be equally high in the two kinds of vowels, the
amount of nose coupling N in the high vowels is made smaller than that in the

low vowels.

The question why the amount of nose coupling in a nasal consonant preceded by a high vowel is smaller than in a nasal consonant preceded by a low vowel (see 8.3.1 above) can be answered as well. It is a result of the fact that in the last phase of a preceding high vowel - which at the same time is the on-glide of the nasal consonant - the amount of nose coupling is smaller than in the last phase of a preceding low vowel (see 8.3.1 above).

The question why vowels before a nasal consonant are produced with more nose coupling than when occurring in nonnasal environment can be answered by pointing out that the nasal consonant necessarily starts its realisation already during the oral vowel.

The view that vowels and nasal consonants are necessarily (partly) coproduced has a practical disadvantage, viz. that in speech utterances we cannot isolate vowel and consonant.

In addition, my alternative notion of "nasal consonant" (see above) implies an ambiguity. If the nose coupling of a nasal consonant is necessarily (partly) coproduced with the vowel, the question arises whether we can always attribute the nasality in the vowel to the nasal consonant alone. If the nasality in the vowel is only the result of the presence of the nasal consonant (as in EurFr), we might argue that the vowel is nonnasal and that the correct notation is $[VN]$. But if the nasality in the vowel is part of both the nasal consonant and the vowel (since they are necessarily (partly) coproduced), we might argue that the vowel is slightly nasal in its own right.

Something similar holds in the case of $[\tilde{V}N]$ (as in AmEng). We might argue that the nose coupling during the on-glide of the $[N]$ (which is necessarily (partly) coproduced with the vowel) should be subtracted from the nasality of the vowel. After the subtraction the vowel may be regarded as slightly nasal, not as nasal. As soon as the $[N]$ were added again the result would be $[\tilde{V}N]$ again. In this view, vowels followed by nasal consonants will never be more than slightly nasal in their own right. This would be in agreement with the fact that Chomsky and Halle (cf. chapter 3 above) assign to the vowel in **inn** the value $[2 \underline{nas}]$. In a diachronic perspective this view would imply that for a vowel to become nasal in its own right ($[\tilde{V}]$), the following nasal consonant should be dropped.[17]

But again another view is possible, viz. that values should not be added up but may play a double role. Then the on-glide of the nasal consonant cannot be distinguished from the vowel nasality, which is present in the vowel independently of the nasal consonant.[18]

Some aspects of the preceding discussion on segmentation and coproduction are illustrated in the hypothetical examples of fig. 8-1. In these examples vowels and consonants - succeeding symbols in phonetic transcription - are partly coproduced, i.e. the vowels and consonants partly overlap in real

time. In these examples we cannot see the amount of nose coupling with which
the individual sounds are produced; what we can observe is the moment at which
the amount of nose coupling starts or stops to be greater than zero. The earlier the nose coupling starts before a nasal consonant (or the later the nose
coupling ends after it) (cf. chapter 6 and section 7.1) the greater the amount
of nose coupling.

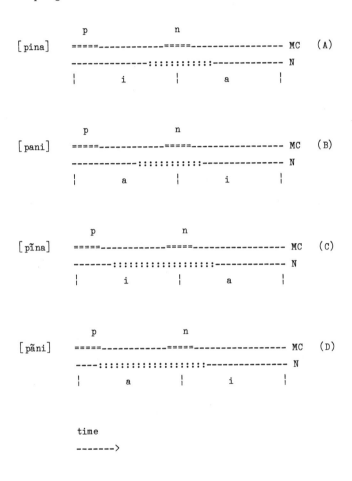

Fig. 8-1. Hypothetical examples of (partly) coproduction of consonants and
vowels in four nonsense words. The horizontal lines are time axes indicating
whether the amount of mouth constriction is zero or not (upper line) or whether the amount of nose coupling is zero or not. "=====" = The amount of mouth
constriction MC is zero; ":::::" = The amount of nose coupling N is greater
than zero; "-----" = The amount of mouth coupling MC is greater than zero or
the amount of nose coupling N is zero.

142

The primary articulatory gestures of the various $[n]$'s in the examples - during which the amount of mouth constriction MC is zero ("=====") - and their secondary articulatory gestures - during which the amount of nose coupling N is greater than zero (":::::") - do not coincide, i.e. vowels and nasal consonants are partly coproduced. In (A) and (B) the duration of the secondary articulatory gestures is slightly longer than that of the primary articulatory gestures. When the nasal consonant occurs adjacent to a low vowel, the nasal port is slightly longer open (or the on- and off-glides are longer) than when the nasal consonant occurs adjacent to a high vowel.

In (C) and (D) the primary articulatory gestures of the nasal consonants have the same duration as in (A) and (B), but the secondary articulatory gestures start earlier in the preceding vowel. This implies that the preceding extra amount of nose coupling belongs exclusively to the vowel. And as the vowel is nasal in its own right, the nose coupling in the on- glide of the nasal consonant may have a double role. It may be part of both the vowel and the nasal consonant. In the extrinsic view of segmentation, nose coupling cannot have this double role: it belongs either to the vowel or to the consonant. Although the examples are hypothetical, they are constructed in such a way that they might represent speech samples produced by an Amoy speaker ((A) and (B)) and by a speaker of AmEng ((C) and (D)).[19]

8.4 INTEGRATION OF CONCLUSIONS

In this section a number of conclusions which concern the presence or absence of nasality in sounds will be integrated into my phonological framework.

As a definition of the feature NASAL I have proposed: nasal sounds are produced with N% higher than in oral sounds. N% gives the proportion between the amount of nose coupling N and the sum of the amounts of nose coupling N and mouth constriction MC. Investigators specify nasality and orality in segments and symbols. Segments are usually characterized by either [+nas] or [-nas], rarely something else (like [2nas]). Symbols - such as [m, ĩ, N, V̂] or [b, i, C, V] - can be analyzed in terms of [+nasal] and [-nasal]. Nasal segments or symbols refer to various types of physical states of affairs, i.e. various types of nasal sounds, just as oral segments and symbols refer to various types of oral sounds.

The various types of nasal and oral sounds are represented in fig. 8-2. Fig. 8-2 is a universal physical diagram of nasality. The interpretation is: "I" represents the nasal consonant line: N% increases from zero to 100 during its on- glide, is 100 during its central phase and decreases from 100 to zero during its off-glide. "II" represents the nasal vowel line: N% increases from (almost) zero to about 75 and stays at that level. "III" represents a possible line for low oral vowels which are not nonnasal: N% increases from zero to about 10 and decreases again to zero. "IV" is the nonnasal vowel and consonant line: N% is zero.

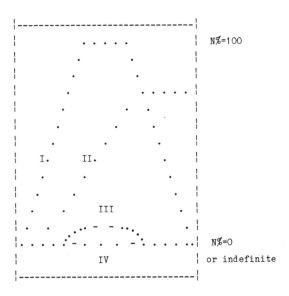

-----> Time

Fig. 8-2. Physical diagram of the feature NASAL.

Like feature definitions, physical diagrams are universal. They are less abstract than feature definitions, since they take into account the way the feature interferes with other features in the sounds. In one respect fig. 8-2 is too precise to be universal. Instead of the lines III and IV and the on- and off-glides of lines I and II, we should have presented approximately parallel bundles of lines, since there are more possibilities than fig. 8-2 suggests. In addition, physical diagrams should contain borderlines. The areas delimited by these borderlines should represent what is covered by symbols of phonetic transcription systems. For instance, as far as nasality is concerned, three different areas (not lines) should represent what is covered by tran- scriptions such as [ĩ], [m], [i, b] respectively. Thus, the [m]'s in various languages would not need to be represented by the same line, but would only be in the same area. For nasal consonants may start their on-glide earlier (or stop their off-glide later) in one language than in another, and nasal vowels may start their increase in N% from (almost) zero to about 75 earlier or later in the vowel, or they may have more than one degree of nasality. Low oral vowels may be nonnasal in one language and slightly nasal in another.

Universal physical diagrams have to be supplemented by language-specific interpretation conventions. Such conventions interpret feature coefficients such as "+" and "-" (see section 2.1 above), i.e. relate them to the physical diagrams. As an example of a language-specific interpretation convention I give the one for CanFr.

144

[+nasal] refers to nasal consonants and nasal vowels;
[-nasal] to oral vowels and nonnasal consonants in the physical diagram
representing N% in CanFr.

Language-specific low level phonological rules introduce the precise values
of this physical diagram into phonetic representation of CanFr. In relative
time these sounds can be characterized as follows:

Nasal consonants	0-50-100-100-50-0
Nasal vowels	0-20-75
Low oral vowels	0-20-0
Other oral vowels	0-0-0
Nonnasal consonants	0-0-0

Segments succeed each other in phonetic representations and symbols in
phonetic transcriptions. However, in physical reality, sounds do not simply
succeed each other, they are necessarily (partly) coarticulated or coproduced.
Fig. 8-3 to 8-6 represent several examples of coarticulation or coproduction.

Fig. 8-3 represents the sequence [NC]. When they occur adjacent to a nonnasal consonant, the on- or off-glide of a nasal consonant are elided. Fig.
8-4 represents the sequence [NV̂]. The off-glide of the [N] is imposed on the
first phase of the [V̂] in which N% should be (almost) zero. This coproduction
or coarticulation between nasal consonant and nasal vowel causes the decrease
in N% to be small.

In fig. 8-5 nonnasal vowel and nasal consonant are (partly) coproduced.
Consequently, the nasal consonant imposes on the nonnasal vowel an increase in
N% from zero to 100. It follows that the nonnasal vowel obtains a structure
which resembles that of a nasal vowel. The differences from a nasal vowel are
the fact that the increase in N% is not from (almost) zero to about 75, but
from zero to 100, and that the N% starts to be greater than zero late in the
vowel. Yet, the nonnasal vowel has obtained some N%, i.e. some nasality.

In fig. 8-6 the increase in N% starts earlier in the nasal vowel. The on-
glide of the nasal consonant has almost completely been overruled by the N% of
the central phase of the nasal vowel. Or, alternatively, the nasality of the
vowel has to be attributed partly to the nasal consonant. The point where the
vowel ends and the nasal consonant starts is actually more difficult to distinguish than fig. 8-6 suggests.

In fact, fig. 8-5 and 8-6 are ambiguous. The problem is that we do not know
to what extent speaker-hearers consider the vowels to be nasal. In fig. 8-5
they may consider the nasality to belong to the nasal consonant only, or to
belong to the vowel as well. In fig. 8-6 they may subtract the nasality of the
nasal consonant from that of the nasal vowel. Sequences or notations like
- [VN] suggest that the nasality in fig. 8-5 belongs to the nasal consonant

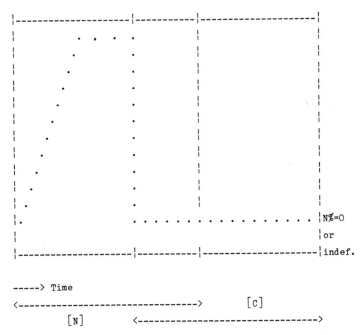

```
                                                            |N%=0
                                                            |or
|----------------------------|----------|-------------------|indef.
```

```
-----> Time
<-------------------------------->          [C]
      [N]              <-------------------------------->
```

Fig. 8-3. Physical diagram of the feature NASAL in the sequence [NC].

alone;

- [2nas] (Chomsky and Halle) that the nasality in fig. 8-5 or 8-6 does not belong to the nasal consonant alone, but that the vowel is partly nasal as well;

- [ṼN] that the nasal vowel in fig. 8-6 is nasal in its own right, i.e. the on-glide of the nasal consonant has almost completely disappeared into the vowel nasality.

As fig. 8-5 and 8-6 represent extreme possibilities, there may occur many configurations in between.

Until now, we have seen the feature definition and the corresponding physical diagram. The physical diagram is less abstract than the feature definition, since it concerns types of sounds. The physical diagram may be viewed as derived from more concrete physical data like nose coupling N and mouth constriction MC. The N% in the physical diagram does not tell us the value of N or MC, except when N% is zero or indefinite, which implies that N is zero, or when N% is 100, which implies that MC is zero. In addition, in nasal vowels and in on- or off- glides of nasal consonants, we know the proportion between MC and N. When N% is 100 we only know that the amount of nose coupling N is greater than zero and when N% is zero, we know nothing about MC.

In one respect physical diagrams representing values of nose coupling N (or

146

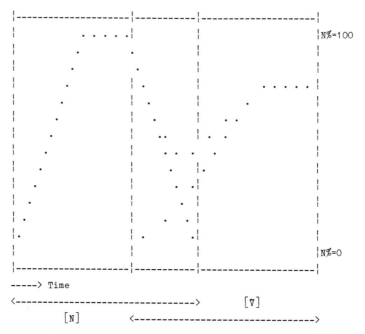

-----> Time

<-------------------------------->   [Ṽ]

     [N]   <-------------------------------->

Fig. 8-4. Physical diagram of the feature NASAL in the sequence [NṼ].

mouth coupling MC, which I will not consider here) are closer to physical reality than physical diagrams representing values of N% are. They include more sound properties than physical diagrams in terms of N% do, viz. differences in the amount of nose coupling between higher and lower nasal vowels (see chapter 7) and between consonants in different environments. Physical diagrams of nose coupling N would not need include individual properties of speakers, because the maximal variation in nose coupling per speaker can be stated to be from zero to 100, cf. chapter 3.

On the basis of what we have found in 8.1 and 8.3.3, the physical properties of the central phase of nasal consonants can be stated in such diagrams, viz.

1. In isolation a nasal consonant has no vowel medium to realize itself in. On-glide and off-glide are produced in silence. The amount of nose coupling N in the central phase may vary freely.

2. Next to a nonnasal consonant the on- or off-glide of a nasal consonant is dropped (see fig. 8-3), that is why the nose coupling in the nasal consonant will tend to be lowest next to the nonnasal consonant.

3. When (partly) coproduced with a low vowel, the on- or off- glide of a nasal consonant will be produced with a greater amount of nose coupling (or will start earlier and stop later respectively) than when (partly) coproduced with

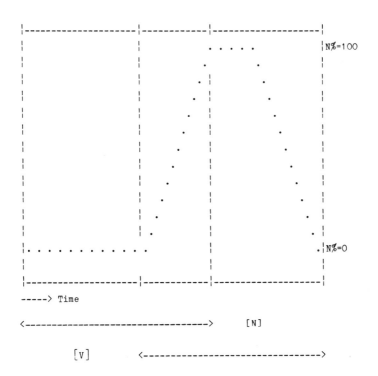

----> Time

<------------------------------------>   [N]

[v]   <------------------------------------>

Fig. 8-5. Physical diagram of the feature NASAL in the sequence [VN].

a high vowel. This will have make that the central phase of the nasal consonant next to a high vowel is produced with a smaller amount of nose coupling
than the central phase of a nasal consonant next to a low vowel.

4. If the vowel followed by a nasal consonant is nasal in its own right, the
amount of nose coupling during the on-glide of the nasal consonant is overruled by ("submerges" in) the amount of nose coupling of this nasal vowel, and
the central phase of the nasal consonant will be produced with a greater
amount of nose coupling than when it follows an oral vowel.

148

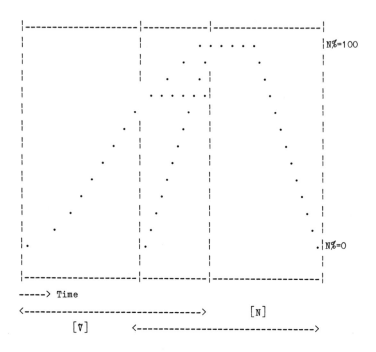

Fig. 8-6. Physical diagram of the feature NASAL in the sequence [ṼN].

NOTES TO CHAPTER 8

1. Some more details: in the X-ray tracings in Rochette (1973), which are
    85% of real size, I have measured the maximal velopharyngeal distance VP
    per nasal consonant. I found as most extreme cases 1.9mm (Plate 14) and
    10.6mm (Plate 20), which correspond with $14mm^2$ and $273mm^2$ nose coupling
    (subject T); 3.4 mm (Plate 77) and 8.8 mm (Plates 33, 74), which
    correspond with 57^2mm and 229 mm^2 nose coupling (subject B). The values
    in mm^2 have been obtained after application of equations IX or X men-
    tioned in chapter 5 above.

2. Lubker's results are expressed in terms of velopharyngeal distance VP
    plus standard deviations. As has been observed in subsection 7.1.1 (note
    6) above, the VP distance used by Lubker (1968:17) as a measure may be
    slightly different from the one used in the present study, especially
    when higher values are concerned.

3. However, when the [m] in Bjoerk (1961:40) is produced in isolation
    (Bjoerk does not provide any details), it has much less nose coupling
    than when the velum is in rest-position. We cannot rule out the possibil-
    ity that some subjects produce isolated nasal consonants after having
    more or less adjusted the different articulators to speech position, i.e.
    after having raised the velum.

4. Of the 28 sequences [VNC] or [CNV] in Rochette (1973), 21 (or 75%) show
    this tendency, whereas 7 (or 25%) do not. The tendency is also visible in
    tracings in Petursson (1974: fig. 95, 102, 130, 137, 138, 148a, 149)
    (Icelandic), Simon (1968:82 and passim) (EurFr). See also the observa-
    tions in Kent et al. (1974: 477-8) (AmEng) and Bell-Berti et al.
    (1979:190-2) (AmEng).

5. I leave out of consideration the consonants listed in section 3.4.

6. X-ray tracings of velar nasals are to be found in Delattre (1965:103;
    1968:69) and Petursson (1974:332, 333). For only one out of the four
    [ŋ]'s the mouth closure might have been brought about not only by means
    of raising the tongue body but also by means of lowering the velum.

7. As I have observed in chapter 7, high nasal vowels may be different from
    low nasal vowels, however.

8. It is surprising that Delattre uses the expression "abaisser le voile du
    palais" and not a more neutral expression like "to open the nasal port"
    in connection with the nasal consonants, since according to his own
    observations: "... l'ouverture vélique des consonnes se fait, non par un
    abaissement du voile, mais par un repliement latéral, en accordéon...",
    as we have seen in the quotation (7) earlier in this section.

9. See, for instance, Avram (1968, 1972) and Petrovici (1930:24-5,35-55,72) mainly with respect to Rumanian; Almeida (1971:33-7, 1976:350-4), Barbosa (1962), Brito (1975:49) with respect to Portuguese; Andersen (1972:19-21) with respect to Polish.

10. Such examples are mentioned in Straka (1955:246, 267-8), Charbonneau (1971:297), Hattori et al. (1953:274). Charbonneau ibid. observes that nasal consonant segments occur in CanFr but not in EurFr. This is not in agreement with the observation in Straka (1955:246). In Durand (1953:42-47) many cases from several languages are discussed. As to AmEng, Malécot (1960) concludes that before plosives a nasal consonant is reduced to an insignificant consonantal segment which may even be absent.

11. Though coarticulation (coproduction) may concern other factors such as lip rounding, I will focus on the relation between the obstruction in the oral cavity and nose coupling (velic behaviour) only. For references and discussion on coarticulation (coproduction) in general I refer to Bonnot (1978) and Fowler (1980).

12. In the following I will hardly consider nasal consonants before vowels. What will be said about nasal consonants after vowels applies to them as well.

13. Instead of "coproduction" some of these authors use the term "assimilation".

14. Kent and Minifie (1977) show that all efforts to explain coarticulation in speech sounds segmented in real time fail. As we have seen in chapter 3, not all the evidence they present can be accepted: vowels followed by nasal consonants in AmEng are, at least to some extent, nasal in their own right.

15. In section 6.4 above I have interpreted the perceptual experiment reported in Linthorst (1973) along the same lines.

16. In the passage of Delattre (1965:102) quoted above, an interesting ambiguity occurs in the expression "avec anticipation" ("...Le voile du palais s'abaisse avec anticipation pour les consonnes nasales, mais s'abaisse avec retardement pour les voyelles nasales"). Would Delattre agree that nasal consonants have an on-glide? In the passage of Kuehn (1976:99) quoted above, it seems as if the idea of coproduction of consonant and vowel is implicitly present: "during velar lowering for the nasal consonant, the velum is ... higher within a high vowel context than within a low vowel context. It appears that the entire locus of normal palatal movement between lowered and elevated positions rather than just the highest point of elevation is shifted depending on the particular vowel or vowel category within the phonetic environment."

17. If this latter line of thought is correct, we would arrive at the conclu-
    sion that the creation of a nasal vowel depends on the disappearance of a
    following nasal consonant. Following a completely different direction we
    would thus arrive at the same conclusion as Durand (1953:41-2).

18. I think that phonologists and phoneticians will agree with this reasoning
    in examples such as [vɛ̃ndø] "twenty two" in French.

19. See in particular the data presented in appendix 5, table A5-8.

Retrospect

In the preceding pages I have given my view on phonetic feature definitions, their place in generative phonology and the way they relate to speech.

I have suggested that
- feature definitions have only two correlates which are physical (articulatory and acoustic) in nature;
- these correlates are related to two-dimensional physical diagrams, which contain information on relative time, and not to one-dimensional physical scales, which do not contain such information;
- physical diagrams give information with respect to a feature in specific (groups of) speech sounds;
- the relation between the physical coefficients in physical diagrams and their mental reflexes remains as constant as possible;
- several physical diagrams may be needed for one and the same feature;
- the same universal physical diagrams may have more than one perceptual scale for different groups of sounds;
- universal physical diagrams represent graphically what is stated in universal phonetic constraints;
- two levels of phonetic representation - a binary and a multivalued - are to be distinguished;
- these two levels are related to each other by means of language-specific low level phonological rules, which convert binary coefficients into multivalued specifications;
- the binary specifications are interpreted by means of language-specific interpretation conventions;
- universal physical diagrams (or universal phonetic constraints) determine the interferences of feature specifications with other features of the same sound or with feature specifications in adjacent sounds;
- symbols used in phonetic transcriptions of specific languages are related to the language-specific physical diagrams (or low level phonological rules);
- phonetic representations and phonetic transcriptions are testable against physical speech properties, after they have been supplemented with what is stated in the relevant universal constraints (or the universal physical

diagrams);

- the phonological component of a generative grammar contains a sound component consisting of the universal physical diagrams and the universal phonetic constraints.

Appendix 1

In the appendices 2 to 4 many data are presented in the form of tables based on two sets of published X-ray tracings: Brichler- Labaeye (1970) and Charbonneau (1971). Brichler-Labaeye (1970) contains hundreds of tracings based upon lateral X-ray films of vowels transcribed as [V] and [V̂] of a European French (EurFr) speaking male. Charbonneau (1971) contains such tracings of the vowels of a Canadian French (CanFr) speaking male. I have carried out measurements in these tracings and the results are to be found in the tables A2-1, A2-2, A2-3, A2-4, A3-1, A3-2 and A4-2.

In this appendix I give some general information on these studies, followed by details with respect to the measuring method I have used in order to obtain the values mentioned in the tables. I add some observations on the reliability of the tracings in the two studies and on the reliability of the measurements I have taken.

The two studies present in the form of tracings 5 to 15 lateral X-ray photographs of each vowel, from beginning to end. An example of such a tracing has already been given: fig. 5-1 in section 5.1 above. In the tracings I have taken several measurements: one of the velopharyngeal distance VP and one of the smallest mouth distance SM in the different mouth cavity regions (unless VP is zero, in which case N% is zero anyhow). In addition, by means of the equations (III) to (X) introduced in section 5.2 above, I have estimated the amount of nose coupling N and the mouth constriction MC per tracing. And when we know MC and N, we can determine N% by means of equation (I) in 4.1 above. Since per vowel 5 or more tracings are available, the values found for N, MC and N% can be followed throughout the whole vowel, and average values can be calculated per speaker. In this manner I have determined the changes in MC, in N and in N% for the vowels of the two speakers.

I have not used all the tracings. Quite a number of speech samples in Charbonneau (1971) end in [Vr]. The tracings of the vowels in these speech samples have not been taken into consideration. This [r] - the properties of which are hardly visible in the tracings and which, as Charbonneau observes, may not always be pronounced - seems to behave as a nasal consonant, i.e. the preceding vowel can hardly be distinguished from [V̂] in [V̂N] or [CV̂C].

The amounts of nose coupling and mouth constriction have been established as follows:

1. I have taken measurements from the tracings in Charbonneau (1971) and Brichler-Labaeye (1970) by means of a ruler with a 0.5 mm scale. The tracings in the two studies are 2/3 of real size pictures (cf. Charbonneau 1971:22; Brichler-Labaeye 1970:20). Therefore the results had to be multiplied by a factor 3/2 in order for me to obtain the smallest mouth distance SM and the velopharyngeal distance VP in mm. These values were converted into amounts of nose coupling N and amounts of mouth constriction MC in m^2 by means of the

equations III to VIII (cf. section 5.2 above). When N and, consequently, N%
were 0, I have not taken measurements of SM and I have noted the corresponding
MC as "-" in the tables.

2. In fig. 5-1 (cf. section 5.2 above) I have indicated the various regions of
the mouth cavity: the incisors, the hard and the soft palate. In the tracings
of the EurFr subject the labial region is visible as well. After the measuring
of SM in the different regions and the application of equations III to VIII,
the lowest value found is the amount of MC. Values measured between the incisors by means of equation VII, especially in the case of the EurFr subject,
often turned out to be the lowest amounts of MC. In fig. 5-1 VP is indicated
as well. It has been measured at at least 15 mm (real size) from the tip of
the uvula in the case of the CanFr subject, at least 7.5 mm (real size) from
the tip of the uvula in the case of the EurFr subject.

3. Wherever in Brichler-Labaeye two tracings of the same vowel segment are
given, I have measured both and taken the mean value. But in some cases
apparent mistakes occurred in the tracings which I have not taken into consideration. For a list of the mistakes see below.

4. As to the tracings of Charbonneau (1971), some series are not complete. In
such cases I have introduced MC and N values intermediate between the values
measured for the preceding and the following tracing. In the tables these
values are preceded by a "?".

The following problems, inaccuracies or mistakes have to be signalized.

1. According to Brichler-Labaeye (1970:17-9), the end of a vowel which occurs
in utterance-final position could not always be determined with certainty,
since the sound track corresponding to the film did not work.

2. There are problems with the labial regions in the tracings. In the case of
the CanFr subject no measurements could be taken of this region since his lips
have not been drawn. This may have caused the values for mouth constriction MC
mentioned in the tables to be somewhat higher than what they would have been
if measurements had been taken also in the labial region. This will occur
especially when the nasal vowel is preceded or followed by a labial consonant.
Fortunately, for labial consonants preceding the nasal vowel, values for MC
often do not need to be measured, because the amount of nose coupling N usually is zero during the first phase of the vowel. And if N=0, N%=0 as well
(as follows from equation I in 4.1 above). Labial consonants which follow the
vowel are rare in the data.

In the tracings of the EurFr subject the lips of the subject are visible,
but not always completely and in most of them no estimates can be made of the
lip protrusion. It follows from equation VII in 5.2 above that if the lip protrusion is feeble, the labial area is rather large and the area of smallest
mouth constriction is situated elsewhere in the mouth cavity. In as far as
estimates could be made, lip protrusion was small indeed and the smallest

mouth constriction was not situated in the labial area. I have selected the labial region only once in a tracing as the area of smallest mouth constriction.

3. The tracings in Brichler-Labaeye (1970) are sometimes incorrect. Since in the majority of cases the tracing of one and the same vowel segment is given twice in her study, the two tracings can be compared. The comparison reveals two kinds of incompatibilities, which I label as (a) mistakes and (b) inaccuracies.

(a) Mistakes are the following tracings, which concern the smallest mouth distance SM or the velopharyngeal distance VP. The smallest mouth distance SM in 47:7 (= fig. 47, tracing 7), 49:8, 53:11, 56:9; and the velopharyngeal distance VP in 6:3, 46:7, 47:7, 53:11 are mistakes. To this list I add VP: 52:3, which concerns a different subject. Between the two tracings of 52:3 I estimate the difference in N to be more than 100 mm^2.

(b) Inaccuracies are differences in mm between measurements of the two tracings which are 0.4 =< x =< 2.7 (real size) as I have measured them. The total number of tracings which can be compared is 79 for nasal vowels [Ṽ], 30 for oral vowels preceded by nasal consonant [NV] (apart from the list of mistakes signalized above and fig. 52 which concerns another subject).

mm	SM in [Ṽ],	in [NV];	VP in [Ṽ],	in [NV]
0.4-0.7	20	8	9	10
0.8-1.1	8	1	11	2
1.2-1.5	14	1	15	3
1.6-1.9	1	0	3	1
2.0-2.3	1	0	1	1
2.4-2.7	1	0	0	0
	---	---	---	---
total	45 (out of 79)	10 (out of 30)	39 (out of 79)	17 (out of 30)

This table reads as follows: first row of figures: a difference of 0.4 to 0.7 mm has been measured in the SM in 20 nasal vowels [Ṽ], and in 8 oral vowels preceded by a nasal consonant [NV]; in the VP of 9 nasal vowels [Ṽ], and of 10 oral vowels preceded by a nasal consonant [NV]. Last row: in 79-45=34 nasal vowels [Ṽ] the difference between SM in the two tracings is smaller than 0.4mm. Etc.

For the CanFr subject of Charbonneau (1971) tracings have only been made once. This makes comparisons of the kind just described impossible. However, the regularity of the successive tracings in his study makes a more accurate impression than the tracings of Brichler-Labaeye.

Appendix 2

CANADIAN FRENCH ORAL VOWELS

No	29	30	31	50	66	27	49	64
	tɛːt	kɛːt	fɛːt	pɑːt	koːt	lɛ	*gɑ*	so

Mouth constriction MC in mm²

	29	30	31	50	66	27	49	64
1	-	-	-	84	-	-	-	-
2	-	-	-	84	-	-	-	-
3	79	-	-	72	-	-	-	-
4	58	-	-	60	-	-	38	-
5	47	-	-	71	-	-	41	-
6	47	41	-	79	28		49	-
7	47	33	-	79	-		47	
8	38	43	49	-	-			
9	19	-	47	-	-			
10	20	-	38	-	-			
11		-	18	-				
12				-				

Nose coupling N in mm²

	29	30	31	50	66	27	49	64
1	?0	?0	0	?1	?0	?0	0	?0
2	0	0	0	3	0	0	0	0
3	9	0	0	3	0	0	0	0
4	13	0	0	?13	?0	0	3	0
5	24	0	0	13	0	0	9	0
6	24	?0	0	13	1		21	0
7	24	1	0	?3	0		54	
8	9	6	3	0	0			
9	3	0	13	0	0			
10	?1	0	13	?0	0			
11		?0	27	0				
12				?0				

N%

	29	30	31	50	66	27	49	64
1	0	0	0	1	0	0	0	0
2	0	0	0	4	0	0	0	0
3	10	0	0	4	0	0	0	0
4	18	0	0	18	0	0	7	0
5	34	0	0	18	0	0	18	0
6	34	0	0	16	3		31	0
7	34	3	0	4	0		53	
8	19	12	6	0	0			
9	14	0	22	0	0			
10	5	0	25	0	0			
11		0	60	0				
12				0				

Table A2-1. Values for mouth coupling MC, nose coupling N and N% estimated on the basis of measurements in X-ray tracings. The first row refers to the numbers of the figures in Charbonneau (1971), for details see Appendix 1. The second row contains the syllable in which the oral vowel occurs. The first column refers to the number of the tracing of the vowel of which 5 to 12 tracings were made with an interval of about 28ms.

CANADIAN FRENCH NASAL VOWELS (UTTERANCE FINAL)

no	8	9	10	11	12	32	33	34	35	36	52	53	54	55	56	67	68
	pɛ̃	tɛ̃	kɛ̃	fɛ̃	sɛ̃	pɑ̃	tɑ̃	kɑ̃	fɑ̃	sɑ̃	pɔ̃	tɔ̃	kɔ̃	fɔ̃	sɔ̃	kœ̃	fœ̃

Mouth constriction MC in mm^2

	8	9	10	11	12	32	33	34	35	36	52	53	54	55	56	67	68
1	-	-	-	-	-	-	-	-	-	-	-	-	-	-	-	-	-
2	-	-	-	-	-	-	-	-	57	23	-	83	-	-	-	-	-
3	-	-	15	-	63	-	-	53	57	23	-	130	-	-	41	47	77
4	43	73	14	-	49	84	57	28	22	50	-	54	19	-	49	43	77
5	22	22	24	-	22	77	57	33	15	77	60	28	22	43	33	33	60
6	12	33	14	47	5	47	60	22	14	47	38	33	22	73	33	28	47
7	2	33	5	54	11	22	22				43	22	14	28	22		15

Nose coupling N in mm^2

	8	9	10	11	12	32	33	34	35	36	52	53	54	55	56	67	68
1	?0	?0	0	?0	?0	0	?0	0	?0	0	?0	0	?0	0	?0	?0	?0
2	?0	?0	0	0	0	?0	?0	0	6	3	0	12	0	0	0	0	0
3	0	0	3	0	6	0	0	9	45	27	0	69	0	0	27	9	6
4	?12	9	9	0	69	1	24	54	54	?60	0	90	24	0	42	45	45
5	45	24	72	0	81	12	63	90	114	90	1	90	33	78	69	45	45
6	90	45	?72	13	114	27	90	90	159	90	24	117	54	90	69	72	69
7	?105	45	72	24	114	69	90				36	117	69	114	?78		99

N%

	8	9	10	11	12	32	33	34	35	36	52	53	54	55	56	67	68
1	0	0	0	0	0	0	0	0	0	0	0	0	0	0	0	0	0
2	0	0	0	0	0	0	0	0	10	12	0	13	0	0	0	0	0
3	1	0	17	0	9	0	0	15	44	54	0	35	0	0	40	16	7
4	22	11	39	0	58	1	30	66	71	55	0	63	56	0	46	51	37
5	67	52	75	0	79	13	53	73	88	54	2	76	60	64	68	58	43
6	88	58	84	22	96	36	60	80	92	66	39	78	71	55	68	72	59
7	98	58	94	31	91	76	80				46	84	83	80	78		87

Table A2-2. Values for mouth coupling MC, nose coupling N and N% estimated on the basis of measurements in X-ray tracings. The first row refers to the numbers of the figures in Charbonneau (1971), the source of the tracings. The second row contains the syllable in which the nasal vowel occurs. The first column refers to the number of the tracings of the vowel of which 6 to 7 tracings were made with an interval of about 28 ms. All vowels occur in utterance-final position.

CANADIAN FRENCH VOWELS (FOLLOWED BY PLOSIVE)

	no	13	14	15	16	17	37	38	39	40	57	58	59	60	69
		pɛ̃:t	tɛ̃:t	kɛ̃:t	fɛ̃:t	sɛ̃:t	pɑ̃:t	tɑ̃:t	kɑ̃:t	fɑ̃:t	pɔ̃:p	pɔ̃:t	kɔ̃:t	fɔ̃:t	fœ̃:t
MC	1	-	-	-	-	-	-	63	2	-	-	-	-	-	-
	2	-	-	14	-	-	-	73	22	-	-	-	19	-	-
	3	50	-	36	-	-	60	73	33	-	84	-	84	33	53
	4	86	-	28	-	64	47	22	27	120	73	67	27	49	43
	5	41	92	19	49	33	33	28	27	47	60	53	15	36	43
	6	28	43	19	54	12	12	11	14	24	33	54	5	22	43
	7	22	43	19	33	12	12	19	14	18	19	33	12	14	43
	8	30	15	15	19	19	3	18	5	15	5	24	11	5	28
	9	18	12	8	11	19	3	5	2	14	28	15	15	19	30
	10	18	12	4	11	9	22	5	5	12	33	22	14	28	39
	11	-	12	8	6	6	22	0	14	14	47	12		12	18
	12	-	2	0	6	2	33	0	14	19		57			8
	13		2	0				0	0	18					0
	14			0					0						0
	15			0					0						
N	1	0	?0	?0	?0	0	?0	?1	5	?0	0	0	0	?0	0
	2	?0	?0	1	0	?0	0	3	5	0	0	0	6	0	0
	3	3	?0	15	?0	0	1	3	63	0	18	0	6	9	9
	4	12	0	36	0	15	9	69	99	3	45	24	12	15	24
	5	63	9	63	?1	60	63	105	99	36	63	60	27	?33	60
	6	96	60	?63	3	90	78	105	117	72	69	69	54	51	90
	7	96	69	63	18	72	63	72	117	60	81	99	105	?51	90
	8	96	81	51	45	105	78	72	69	90	81	90	87	51	96
	9	72	81	?42	114	60	78	105	69	?81	36	117	15	69	?81
	10	27	45	27	114	90	150	105	72	69	3	99	3	51	63
	11	0	9	69	45	54	108	90	63	60	?1	45		3	?45
	12	0	3	27	24	15	18	72	27	45		3			27
	13		?1	27				45	51	6					9
	14			?12					51						3
	15			?6					81						
N%	1	0	0	0	0	0	0	2	71	0	0	0	0	0	0
	2	0	0	7	0	0	0	4	19	0	0	0	24	0	0
	3	6	0	29	0	0	2	4	66	0	18	0	7	21	15
	4	12	0	56	0	19	16	76	79	2	38	26	31	23	36
	5	61	9	77	2	65	66	79	79	43	51	53	64	48	58
	6	77	58	77	5	88	87	91	89	75	68	56	92	70	68
	7	81	62	77	35	85	84	79	89	77	81	75	90	78	68
	8	76	84	77	70	85	96	80	93	86	94	79	89	91	77
	9	80	87	84	91	76	96	95	97	85	56	89	50	78	73
	10	60	79	87	91	91	87	95	94	85	8	82	18	65	62
	11	0	43	90	88	90	83	100	82	81	2	79		20	71
	12	0	60	100	80	88	35	100	66	70		5			77
	13		33	100				100	100	25					100
	14			100					100						100
	15			100					100						

Table A2-3. Values for mouth coupling MC, nose coupling N and N% estimated on the basis of measurements in X-ray tracings. The first row refers to the numbers of the figures in Charbonneau (1971) (for details see Appendix 1). The second row contains the transcription of the syllable in which the nasal vowel occurs. The first column refers to the number of the tracing of the vowel of which 10 to 15 tracings were made with an interval of about 28 ms. All vowels are followed by [c].

EUROPEAN FRENCH NASAL VOWELS

no	44	45	46	54	55	56	51	53	47	48	49	50
	pɛ̃:	kɛ̃:t	pɛ̃:s	pã	vã:v	kã:t	tõ	bõ:b	kœ̃:	fœ̃:	œ̃:b	fœ̃:t

Mouth constriction MC in mm^2

no	44	45	46	54	55	56	51	53	47	48	49	50
1	-	-	-	-	96	-	-	-	-	?50	105	105
2	-	-	117	-	31	-	51	-	-	103	63	128
3	119	83	96	150	28	24	24	-	86	93	67	72
4	123	54	123	76	17	100	5	46	111	93	97	83
5	111	38	96	33	26	33	6	17	86	76	120	111
6	112	25	96	19	22	28		17	24	86	105	31
7	104	43	96		28	19		10	12	63	86	64
8	83	40	61		5	38		11	36	79	33	59
9	49	47	54		5	22		12	103	5	40	
10	49	49	45			24		9	130		22	
11	12	22	27			33		19			13	
12						33		5			21	

Nose coupling N in mm^2

no	44	45	46	54	55	56	51	53	47	48	49	50
1	0	0	0	0	3	0	0	0	0	72	9	13
2	0	0	3	0	41	0	45	0	0	79	108	90
3	9	75	45	6	95	9	104	0	59	140	140	72
4	75	90	126	45	86	36	95	48	135	135	180	117
5	162	158	158	126	95	78	153	71	180	180	203	162
6	149	171	171	135	117	90		117	162	211	203	120
7	171	162	175		104	93		135	180	180	158	152
8	180	162	162		159	99		139	144	180	147	63
9	180	184	144		159	146		117	131	180	130	
10	180	135	135			149		113	117		150	
11	207	13	99			117		180			189	
12						54		108			135	

N%

no	44	45	46	54	55	56	51	53	47	48	49	50
1	0	0	0	0	3	0	0	0	0	59	7	11
2	0	0	3	0	57	0	47	0	0	43	63	41
3	7	47	32	4	77	27	81	0	41	60	68	50
4	38	63	51	37	83	26	95	51	55	59	65	59
5	59	81	62	79	79	70	96	81	68	70	63	59
6	57	87	64	88	84	76		87	87	71	66	79
7	62	79	65		79	83		93	94	74	65	70
8	68	80	73		97	72		93	80	69	82	52
9	79	80	73		97	87		91	56	97	76	
10	79	73	75			86		93	47		87	
11	95	37	79			78		90			94	
12						62		96			87	

Table A2-4. Values for mouth coupling MC, nose coupling N and N% estimated on the basis of measurements in X-ray tracings. The first row refers to the numbers of the figures in Brichler-Labaeye (1970), for details see Appendix 1. The second row contains the syllable in which the nasal vowel occurs. The first column refers to the number of the tracing of the vowel of which 5 to 12 tracings were made with an interval of about 20 ms.

Appendix 3

MC in mm²

no	46 nɑ:3	25 mɛs	23 nɛl	65 no	44 ma:3	47 ma:ʃ	22 nɛ:3	73 nø
0	0	0	0	0	0	0	0	0
1	64	47	12	18	24	86	24	49
2	60	33	35	49	24	67	67	49
3	58	12	-	43	28	73	58	33
4	73	12	-	24	28	58	33	47
5	84	14	-	12	38	49	33	43
6	71	12	-	5	33	49	22	53
7	58	-	-	5	15	47	12	
8	49	-			33	36	27	
9	24				18	27	-	
10	24				18	12	-	
11	-				15	-	-	
12	-				19	-		
13	-				-	-		
14	-				-	-		
15	-				-	-		

N in mm²

no	46	25	23	65	44	47	22	73
0	90	18	?63	?98	?27	63	?10	27
1	90	54	45	36	36	108	10	27
2	90	54	9	18	45	114	10	27
3	?45	54	0	13	69	99	3	42
4	45	33	0	3	24	99	45	36
5	45	6	0	0	69	114	15	36
6	45	0	0	0	33	?96	?15	24
7	?27	0	0	(13)	33	72	15	
8	13	0			27	?33	5	
9	12				27	9	0	
10	3				9	3	0	
11	0				8	0	0	
12	0				1	?0		
13	?0				0	?0		
14	?0				?0	?0		
15	0				0	0		

N%

no	46	25	23	65	44	47	22	73
0	100	100	100	100	100	100	100	100
1	58	54	79	67	60	56	29	36
2	60	62	21	27	65	63	13	36
3	44	82	0	23	71	58	5	56
4	38	73	0	11	46	63	58	43
5	35	33	0	0	65	70	31	46
6	39	0	0	0	50	66	41	31
7	32	0	0	(72)	69	61	56	
8	21	0			45	48	16	
9	33				60	25	0	
10	11				33	20	0	
11	0				35	0	0	
12	0				5	0		
13	0				0	0		
14	0				0	0		
15	0				0	0		

Table A3-1. Values for mouth coupling MC, nose coupling N and N% in oral vowels preceded by nasal consonant estimated on the basis of measurements in X-ray tracings of the CanFr subject. The 1st row refers to the numbers of the figures in Charbonneau (1971), see Appendix 1 for details. The 2nd row contains the syllable in which the vowel occurs. The 1st column refers to the number of the tracing of the vowel of which 6 to 15 tracings were made with an interval of about 28 ms. The 0 in this column concerns the last tracing of the nasal consonant.

no	6	12	25	27	15	42
	ɲe	mɛːr	møt	møʒ	mal	maːʃ

Mouth constriction MC in mm^2

	6	12	25	27	15	42
1	33	84	68	68	125	105
2	38	96	57	68	127	96
3	60	93	57	66	209	126
4	53	87	48	66	200	93
5	35	93	-	68	-	130
6		87	-	-	-	107
7		78		-		107
8		84		-		79
9		87				96
10		68				78
11		58				63
12		58				

Nose coupling N in mm^2

	6	12	25	27	15	42
1	33	117	135	114	162	135
2	8	84	135	67	194	126
3	14	149	36	72	107	126
4	5	71	23	1	15	126
5	(36)	50	0	5	0	104
6		32	0	0	0	81
7		27		0		99
8		36		0		72
9		45				27
10		50				36
11		54				45
12		12				

N%

	6	12	25	27	15	42
1	50	58	67	63	57	56
2	17	47	70	50	60	57
3	19	62	39	52	34	50
4	9	45	32	1	7	58
5	(51)	35	0	7	0	44
6		27	0	0	0	43
7		26		0		48
8		30		0		48
9		34				22
10		42				32
11		48				42
12		17				

Table A3-2. Values for mouth coupling MC, nose coupling N and N% estimated on the basis of measurements in X-ray tracings of the EurFr subject. The first row refers to the numbers of the figures in Brichler-Labaeye (1970), see Appendix 1 for details. The second row contains the syllable in which the vowel occurs. The first column refers to the number of the tracing of the vowel of which 5 to 12 tracings were made with an interval of about 20 ms.

164

T	N	MC	N%
0	111	0	100
1	114	57	66
2	15	74	17
3	0	88	0

Table A3-3. Nose coupling N, mouth coupling MC and N% in the vowel [i] and in the last phase of the preceding nasal consonant of the nonsense word [nip] occurring in the frame "Say ... again". The numbers in the left column refer to the moment the measurements have been taken. The interval between two moments of measurements is 41.7 ms. Though this interval is rather large, the changes in N and MC seem to be quite regular. Data have been extracted from the graphic representation in Lubker and Moll (1965:266, fig. 6). They measure smallest mouth distance SM - tongue constriction T-C - differently than I do. They define it as "the point of greatest constriction between the tongue and hard palate or alveolar ridge" (p.264). However, in the case of high and mid front vowels and [n] this measure is the same as my measure SM, so that I can estimate the amount of mouth constriction MC by applying equation (IV) in 5.2 above.

BRETON NASAL VOWELS PRECEDED BY NASAL CONSONANT

1.Pinvidig eo bremañ   "He is rich now"
  [pin'vidig ɛo bRɛ̃mɛ̃]

2.Pehed eo skoi anezañ   "It is sinful to beat him"
  [pɛ́həd ɛo 'skwe 'nɛ̃]

3.Poan peuh en ho tent?   "Do your teeth hurt?"
  ['pwã̃n 'pœx nɛ̃ o tɛn]

4.Pa vefe mamm   "When she will be mother"
  [pa 'vefə 'mã̃m]

5.Pa veve mamm   "When mother was still alive"
  [pa 'vevə mã̃m]

6.Pa vevhe mamm   "Since his mother is alive"
  [pa 'vev i mã̃m]

7.Diaoulou moan zo en ivern   "There are skinny devils in hell"
  ['djɑulu 'mwã̃n zo ã̃n 'ivən]

8.Peɟ emaint? Pemp pe c'hweh. "How many are they? Five or six."
  [ped mã̃iɲ 'pæm pe hwex]

9.Pad hañv vez kalz heol   "In summer there is a lot of
  [pad 'nã̃ɔ̃ vɛ kalaz 'ɛɔl]   sunshine"

Table A3-4a.Orthographic representation, phonetic transcription and English translation. Adapted from Bothorel (1978). The utterances 1 to 9 are numbered 8, 57, 120, 27, 40, 80, 9, 51 and 55 respectively in Bothorel.

BRETON NASAL VOWELS PRECEDED BY NASAL CONSONANT

Transcription	N in nasal sound(s) before nasal vowel		N in nasal vowel or in nasal diphthong		MC in nasal vowel or in nasal diphthong		N% in nasal vowel or nasal diphthong	N in nasal subsequent sound
	first	last	first	last	first	last		
1. [mã̂#]	+	-	+	+			(+)	
2. [nɛ̃#]	+	-	+	+			(+)	
3. [nɛ̃o]			+	-			(+)	-
4. [mã̃m]	+	-	+	+			(+)	+
5. [mã̃m]	+	-	+	+			(+)	+
6. [mã̃m]			+	+			(+)	
7. [mwã̃n]	+	-	+	+			(+)	
8. [mã̃iɲ]			=	=	-		+	=
9. [nã̃ɔ̃]			=	=	-	-	+	

Table A3-4b. Movements of the velum indicating changes in the amount of nose coupling N and changes in the amount of mouth constriction MC, as I have observed them in the X-ray film of the Breton speaker in nasal vowels preceded by nasal consonant and adjacent sounds (see table A3-4a). A "+" indicates that the amount of nose coupling N, mouth constriction MC or N% increases, a "-" that it decreases, a "=" that it is constant. A "(+)" concerns a change which was not directly observed, but which I have inferred from the increase in the amount of nose coupling N. The terms "first" and "last" refer to either the first or the last part of the sound(s) in question. For instance, in the preceding sound(s) - a nasal consonant or the sequence [mw] - I have always observed a closing movement of the velum during the last part; during the nasal vowels the velum makes always an opening movement from begin to end; during the nasal diphthongs it either is in stable position (in 8 and 9) or makes an opening and a closing movement (in 3). When nothing has been mentioned as to the movement of the velum, its movement was not visible on the X-ray film.

Appendix 4

Language	No of subjects	Average percentage of the vowels produced with open nasal port
Amoy	2	37
French	3	65
Hindi	1	72
Swedish	3	75
Portuguese	1	98
Am. English	4	101

Table A4-1. Time of opening of the nasal port in vowels before a nasal consonant in 6 languages. In the 3rd column the average time during which the vowels are produced with some amount of nose coupling as a percentage of the total vowel duration is presented. The percentages represent averages of groups of high vowels, mid vowels (except in Amoy) and low vowels, as they are found in Clumeck (1976). (In the case of Swedish I have neglected the difference made by Clumeck between short and long vowels.) Note that in AmEng the nasal port is already open before the vowel begins. The number of vowel tokens measured per language varies from 30 to 225. See Appendix 5, table A5-8, for Clumeck's data in unreduced form.

no	18	19	20	21	41	42	43
	pɛn	pɛɲ	tɛn	sɛn	taɲ	kan	fam

Mouth constriction MC in mm²

	18	19	20	21	41	42	43
1	-	-	-	-	33	-	-
2	-	-	-	27	112	-	-
3	93	77	58	27	-	47	-
4	73	73	93	73	49	79	49
5	60	60	32	60	79	54	77
6	47	54	24	60	38	33	24
7	53	43	38	48	33	43	43
8	33	28	14	4	28	38	24
9	38	12	0	0	9	12	27
10	38	12			0	0	33
11	0	0					28
12							24
13							0

Nose coupling N in mm²

	18	19	20	21	41	42	43
1	?0	?0	?0	?0	?9	?0	?0
2	0	0	0	3	1	0	?0
3	12	6	6	18	0	27	0
4	5	6	13	36	36	27	3
5	24	36	54	72	36	45	9
6	54	63	45	72	63	69	36
7	108	51	18	81	99	45	72
8	117	63	?18	63	99	33	108
9	117	81	13	63	90	33	?114
10	?117	81			72	33	117
11	117	90					126
12							135
13							180

N%

	18	19	20	21	41	42	43
1	0	0	0	0	21	0	0
2	0	0	0	10	1	0	0
3	11	7	9	40	0	37	0
4	6	8	12	33	42	26	6
5	29	38	63	55	31	46	11
6	54	54	65	55	62	68	60
7	67	54	32	63	75	51	63
8	78	69	56	94	78	47	82
9	76	87	100	100	91	73	81
10	76	87			100	100	78
11	100	100					82
12							85
13							100

Table A4-2. Values for mouth coupling MC, nose coupling N and N% in oral vowels followed by nasal consonant estimated on the basis of measurements in X-ray tracings. The first row refers to the numbers of the figures in Charbonneau (1971), for more details see Appendix 1. The second row contains the syllable in which the vowel occurs. The first column refers to the number of the tracing of the vowel of which 6 to 15 tracings are made with an interval of about 28 ms. The last tracing in this column concerns the first tracing of the following nasal consonant. Note that the presence of nose coupling in the first phase of the [a] of [taɲ] (no 42) is probably due to the preceding [~], the whole word being [mɔ̃taɲ] with a "nasal" [t].

Source	vowel and preceding context	no of tokens	% of the vowel produced with nose coupling	subjects
1.	[sæ]	2	75 to 85	1 male
2.	[#i]	1	0	1 female
3.	[#a]	1	100	1 female
4.	[pi]	1	63 to 88	1 male
5.	[se]	1	64 to 79	1 male
6.	[tæ]	4	90	4 males

Table A4-3. Oral vowels followed by a nasal consonant [m, n, ŋ] in AmEng. In the first column the sources: 1. Delattre (1965:102-3) 2 and 3. Moll (1960:235) 4 and 5. Lubker and Moll (1965:266) 6. Moll and Daniloff (1971:680) 2nd column: vowel and preceding context; 3rd column: number of vowels examined; 4th column: the percentage of the total vowel duration produced with nose coupling (I have estimated the percentages on the basis of tracings or diagrams in the case of source 1, 4 and 5); 5th column: number and sex of the subjects. The subject of Delattre has been chosen by Delattre as representative out of three subjects.

STATE OF THE NASAL PORT IN SWEDISH VOWELS

1	2	3	4
nasal port is	number of subjects (absol.)	number of subjects (percent.)	utterance, gloss, vowel and reference
closed	4	9	['fi:na] "fine",
closed/open	11	26	stressed [i:]
open	28	65	(p.69-70)
closed	0	0	[pu'li:sən] "the
closed/open	7	16	police", unstressed
open	39	85	[ə] (p.71)
closed	4	9	['bu:vən] "the
closed/open	5	11	convict", unstressed
closed	37	80	[ə] (p.71)
closed	2	4	['ga:tan] "the street",
closed/open	5	11	unstressed [a]
open	40	85	(p.73-4)
closed	3	6	['va:kən]
closed/open	8	17	"awake", unstressed
open	36	77	[ə] (p.76-7)

Table A4-4. Closed, open or partly closed/partly open nasal port during the production of oral vowels before a nasal consonant in Swedish. The first column concerns the state of the nasal port during the vowel; the second column gives the number of speakers in absolute terms, the third column as a percentage; in the last column the vowel and the utterance in which it occurs, the translation of the utterance and the reference to pages of the source from which I have extracted the data: Bjoerk (1961). The total number of vowels is not always the same. In addition, since the data in Bjoerk are presented in terms of graphs, the numbers I mention may not be completely correct.

	Following nonnasal consonant removed		Following nasal consonant removed		Nasal vowel	
	number of vowels	% of nasal answers	number of vowels	% of nasal answers	number of vowels	% of nasal answers
high front	5	34	5	37		
mid front	2	35	4	18		
mid back	2	28.5	4	32		
low	1	28.5	3	38	4	57

Table A4-5. Nasality of French vowel stimuli judged by 7 (American) English listeners. Source: Clumeck 1971. Clumeck presented French stimuli to five male and two female students, all of the University of California, Berkeley, which were registered as majors in linguistics, and had received a sufficient phonetic training in the recognition of the phonemes used (p.30). The stimuli consisted of [CVN], [CVC] and [CV̇] sequences. The last consonants were spliced away and "approximatily half of the duration of each of the four nasal vowels in final position."(p.29).

Appendix 5

HIGH AND LOW VOWELS IN NONNASAL ENVIRONMENT

		Number of subjects	Obstruction of the nasal port in the vowels is relatively weak → strong
1	American English	3	*a* i u
2	American English	2	ɔ e o U i u
3	American English	5	a u
4	American English	1	*a* i u
5	American English	11	*a* æ i u
6	American English	5	*a* æ i
7	American English	2	*a* u
8	American English	3	a æ ɔ i u
9	American English	40	a æ e o i u
10	American English	1	a æ U u ɛ I i
11	Japanese	7	a o e i
12	Japanese	1	a e o i u
13	Japanese	5	a e o i u
14	French	1	*a* a œ ɔ e o *ø*
15	French	1	*a* e i
16	French	2	a e o i
17	French	1	a other vowels
18	French	1	no difference observable
19	Czech	10	a o e i u
20	Czech	1	*a* e o u i
21	Italian	many	*a* e o u i
22	Russian	1	*a* e o ɨ i u
23	Australian English	12	a æ i u
24	British English	1	*a* i
25	German	6	*a* ɔ a o ɛ e ø y i u
26	Icelandic	1	a other vowels
27	Dutch	1	*a:* *a* ɔ o: u: ɛ e: i:

Table A5-1. Degree of obstruction of the nasal port in oral vowels in nonnasal
environment (or in isolation). From left to right the obstruction increases.
Among vowels grouped closely together, no difference in velic behaviour has
been observed. The phonetic symbols are those used by the sources to which
the numbers in the first column refer:

1	Bell-Berti 1976	14	Benguerel et al.1977a
2	Bloomer 1953	15	Brichler-Labaeye 1970
3	Bzoch 1968	16	Chlumsky et al.1938
4	Fritzell 1969:38,47	17	Condax et al.1976
5	Fritzell 1969:56,58,62-5	18	Delattre 1965
6	Lubker 1968	19	Boehme et al. 1966
7	Moll and Shriner 1967	20	Polland and Hala 1926
8	Moller et al. 1971	21	Croatto et al. 1959:142
9	Nusbaum et al.1935	22	Fant 1960:48,107,114
10	Perkell 1969:53	23	Bernard 1970
11	Matsuya et al. 1974	24	Calnan 1953
12	Takahashi et al.1962	25	Kuenzel 1977,1978
13	Wada et al.1969	26	Petursson 1974
		27	Eijkman 1902

For American English the list is not complete. We might add Clumeck 1975,
Denes & Pinson 1973:15,65, Kuehn 1976:97, Ladefoged 1962:96-8, Russell
1928:257-66, Skolnick 1970 and the sources mentioned in table 5A-2. The data
not mentioned here exhibit the same trend: more obstruction of the nasal port
with higher vowels than with lower ones.

A. AMOUNT OF NOSE COUPLING N

Source	Nose coupling N in mm² in high/low vowels				number & sex of subjects	number of vowels		speech condition
	mm²	high	mm²	low		high	low	
1	0	i u	0	a	5	225	225	[pVpVpV] syll.
2	–		0	æ	1M	–	1	"say [tVp]"
3	–		0	a	4	–	4	
	–		4	a	1	–	1	Isolated
	–		45	a	1	–	1	vowels
4	–		15	æ	1F	1	1	"say [hVd] again"
	–		0	a	1F	1	1	"say [hVd] again"
5	–		30	æ	1	1	1	"shack"
6	0	i u	42	a æ	3M&2F	30	30	Sustained isol. &
	0	i	42	æ	3M&2F	15	15	short isol.vowels
	0	i	10	æ	3M&2F	15	15	"[...bVbVbV...]"
	0	i	10	æ	3M&2F	15	15	"[...pVpVpV...]"
	0	i	6	æ	3M&2F	15	15	"[...dVdVdV...]"
	0	i	18	æ	3M&2F	15	15	"[...tVtVtV...]"

B. PERCENTAGE OF VOWELS PRODUCED WITH OPENING OF THE NASAL PORT

7	13 i u 38 *a æ*	6M&4F	520	520	[CVC] syllables
8	25 i u 90 *a* 10		60	30	Isol.vowels,[pVp] syll. (isol. & in context)

Table A5-2. A. Amount of nose coupling N (A) and percentage produced with opening of the nasal port (B) during the production of high and low vowels in nonnasal environment. Speech samples in 1 to 7 have been produced by normal speakers of AmEng, in 8 by nasal speakers without cleft palate. I have added F (female) or M (male), when this was mentioned in the source. The values in the sources have been given in terms of velopharyngeal distance VP to which I have applied equations IX and X (see chapter 5). In the case of 5, I have estimated the VP in the tracings drawn in the source. The list of sources is:

1 Bzoch 1968
2 Lubker & Moll 1965
3 Kaltenborn 1948
4 Schwartz 1968a
5 Delattre 1965
6 Lubker 1968
7 Moll 1962
8 Carney & Morris 1971

HIGH AND LOW ORAL OR NASAL VOWELS PRECEDED BY NASAL CONSONANT

	Language	Number of subjects	Opening of the nasal port in the vowels tends to be greater ← → smaller
1	American English	3	*a* ... i u
2	American English	3	*a* æ ɔ ... ɛ ... i u
3	American English	1	*a* ... i ... u
4	American English	1	*a* · i ... u
5	American English	11	*a* ... i
6	American English	5	æ ... i
7	American English	2	ɑ ... u
8	American English	10	*a* æ ... i u
9	Swedish	about 45	ɑ ... i
10	Swedish	1	a ... ɔ ɛ o i
11	French	1	a ... ø
12	French	1	a ... ɛ ɔ
13	French	2	a œ ø ɔ ... i u o
14	Canadian French	1	*a* ... a œ ø ɔ ... o
15	Hindi	1	*a* ɛ ... e ɔ ... i u

Table A5-3. Opening of the velar port in vowels preceded by a nasal consonant. From left to right the opening decreases. The phonetic symbols are those used by the authors. Among vowels grouped closely together, no difference in velic behaviour has been observed. The numbers in the first column refer to the following sources:

1 Bell-Berti 1976
2 Clumeck 1975 (or 1976)
3 Fritzell 1969:38, 47
4 Fritzell 1969:38, 47
5 Fritzell 1969:56, 58, 62-5
6 Lubker 1968
7 Moll and Shriner 1967
8 Moll 1962

9   Bjoerk 1961
10 Clumeck 1975
11 Brichler-Labaeye 1970
12 Benguerel et al.1977a
13 Rochette 1973
14 Charbonneau 1971
15 Clumeck 1975 (or 1976)

HIGHER AND LOWER ORAL OR NASAL VOWELS PRECEDED BY NASAL CONSONANT IN   AMERICAN
ENGLISH

Lower vowels			Higher vowels	
1	ana#	+	11	ini#	+
2	asna	+	12	[mi]	−
3	napple	+	13	mitt	−
4	[m æ]	+	14	an#is	−
5	martin	=	15	[i] (sneered)	−
6	alna	−	16	[mu]	−
7	not	−	17	[mi]	−
8	[nɛ]	−	18	[me]	−

Table A5-4. Vowels preceded by a nasal consonant in American English in which
the degree of opening of the nasal port can be compared with that in the nasal
consonant. "+" = the vowel is produced with more opening than the nasal consonant; "−" = the vowel is produced with less opening than the nasal consonant; "=" = the vowel and the consonant are produced with about an equal degree of opening. Forms have been given in normal orthography or in the phonetic transcription ([   ]) of the sources. The numbers refer to the follows
sources:

1 and 11 Moll 1960
2 and 6 Kuehn 1976
3 Weatherly et al. 1966
4,16,17 and 18 Clumeck 1975
5,7,12,15 Fritzell 1969:57
8 Perkell 1969:72-3
13 Ohala 1975:298,304
14 Ohala 1974a:363

HIGH AND LOW ORAL OR NASAL VOWELS FOLLOWED BY NASAL CONSONANT

Language	Number of subjects	Opening of the nasal port in the vowels tends to be greater	smaller
1 American English	4	a æ ɔ ɛ ʌ	I U i u
2 American English	10	ɑ æ	i u
3 Swedish	3	a ɛ ø o e	y ʉ i u
4 Amoy	2	a	i
5 Hindi	1	a e ɛ ɔ	i u
6 Portuguese (Braz)	1	no clear differences	
7 French	3	a ɛ ɔ œ o	y i u
8 French	2	a	y
9 Dutch	1	a a: ɛ	ɪ u

Table A5-5. The opening of the nasal port in vowels before nasal consonant. From left to right the opening decreases. The phonetic symbols are those used by the authors. Between vowels closely grouped together no difference in velic behaviour has been observed. The numbers in the first column refer to the following sources:

1,3 to 7 Clumeck 1976 and 1975
2 Moll 1962
8 Rochette 1973
9 Eijkman 1902

HIGH AND LOW NASAL VOWELS FOLLOWED BY A NASAL CONSONANT IN AMERICAN ENGLISH

A. The nasal consonant is followed by an obstruent

Lower vowels   Higher vowels

1 ...ample (2x)   +   11 Tim # twice   -
2 Sam(p)son   +
3 pam#p or pam#b   +
4 sank   +
5 belongs to   +
6 tent   +
7 sent or send   +
8 ampa (2x)   +
9 anta (2x)   =
10 home papa   -

B. The nasal consonant is followed by a vowel, occurs utterance-finally or
what follows is not mentioned

Lower vowels   Higher vowels

12 Sam#is   +   18 [im]   -
13 ...an#is (4x)   +   19 [um]   -
14 ana   =   20 [i] of clean   -
15 [æ m]   -   21 ini   -
16 [ɑ m]   -
17 again(2x)   -

Table A5-6. Nasal vowels before a nasal consonant in American English in which
the opening of the nasal port in the vowel can be compared with that in the
nasal consonant. "+" = the vowel is produced with more opening than the nasal
consonant; "-" = the vowel is produced with less opening than the nasal consonant; "=" = vowel and consonant are produced with about equal opening. The
numbers refer to the following sources:

1 Weatherley-White et al. 1966   7 and 11 Ohala 1975
2,3 and 13 Ohala 1974a   8,9 and 17 Kuehn 1976
4 and 12 Delattre 1965   14 and 21 Moll 1960
5 Fritzell 1969:56   15,16,18 and 19 Clumeck 1975
6,10 and 20 Warren & DuBois 1964

In Kent et al.1974 several examples occur which show the same trend: more velic lowering in lower vowels than in the following nasal consonant, even in one
of the higher vowels.

HIGH AND LOW NASAL VOWELS

Language	Number of subjects	Opening of the nasal port in the vowels tends to be	
		greater	smaller
1 Hindi	1	ã́	ũ
2 Hindi	1	no significant difference	
3 Portuguese (Braz)	1	ã ẽ õ	ĩ ũ
4 Amoy	1	ã	ĩ
5 Swedish	1	ə̃	ĩ

Table A5-7. The opening of the nasal port in nasal vowels in nonnasal environment. From left to right the opening decreases. The phonetic symbols are
those used in the sources. Between vowels grouped closely together no difference in opening has been observed. The numbers in the first column refer to
the following sources:

1 Ohala,M. 1975:325
2 to 4 Clumeck 1976:344-6
5 Bjoerk 1961:40

TIME OF OPENING OF THE NASAL PORT IN HIGH, MID AND LOW VOWELS

Language	No of subjects	no of tokens	%	S.D.	vowels: H(igh), M(id) or L(ow)	
Amoy	2	69	0.32	0.16	[i]	H
	2	77	0.41	0.19	[a]	L
Swedish (V:)	3	52	0.47	0.33	[i: y:ɯ: u:]	H
	3	53	0.64	0.27	[e: ɛ: ø: o:]	M
	3	13	0.77	0.24	[a:]	L
Swedish (V)	3	59	0.93	0.53	[I Y u U]	H
	3	60	0.81	0.24	[e ɛ ø ɔ]	M
	3	15	0.87	0.16	[a]	L
French	3	85	0.52	0.19	[i y u]	H
	3	112	0.64	0.29	[ɛ o ɔ œ]	M
	3	28	0.78	0.28	[a]	L
Hindi	1	10	0.46	0.15	[i u]	H
	1	16	0.77	0.15	[e ɛ ɔ]	M
	1	4	0.94	0.04	[a]	L
AmEng	4	74	0.92	0.21	[i I u U]	H
	4	45	1.08	0.39	[ɛ ʌ]	M
	4	95	1.04	0.13	[æ a ɔ]	L
Portuguese (Brazilian)	1	49	1.06	0.22	[ĩ u]	H
	1	81	0.88	0.16	[e o]	M
	1	34	1.01	0.12	[a]	L

Table A5-8. Time of opening of the nasal port in vowels preceding a nasal consonant in 6 languages. 1st column: the language (for Swedish a distinction has
been made between short (V) and long (V:) vowels); 2nd column: the number of
speakers; 3rd column: number of tokens examined; 4th column the percentage of
the vowel in real time produced with an amount of nose coupling greater than
zero; 5th column: the standard deviation S.D.; last column: transcriptions
(note that AmEng [ɔ] is a low vowel) as they have been given in Clumeck
(1976:340-3), the source of the data.

Bibliography

In the bibliography the following abbreviations have been used:

ARIPUC	Annual Report of the Institute of Phonetics, University of Copenhagen
CPJ	The Cleft Palate Journal
FoliaPh	Folia Phoniatrica
JASA	Journal of the Acoustical Society of America
JL	Journal of Linguistics
JPh	Journal of Phonetics
JSHD	Journal of Speech and Hearing Disorders
JSHR	Journal of Speech and Hearing Research
Lg.	Language
LI	Linguistic Inquiry
Proc.Phon.	Proceeding of the nth international Congress of Phonetic Sciences.
Ph	Phonetica
SL	Studia Linguistica
STL-QPSR	Quaterly Progress and Status Report, Speech Transmission Laboratory, Royal Institute of Technology, Stockholm
WPLU	Working Papers on Language Universals

Ali, L., Gallagher,T., Goldstein,J.& Daniloff,R.(1971), "Perception of coarticulated nasality", JASA 49,538-540.

Allen,W.E.S.(1953), Phonetics in ancient India. London: Oxford University Press.(reprint 1965).

Almeida,A.(1971), Die portugiesischen Nasalvokale.Versuch einer phonetisch-phonologischen Untersuchung. Marburg:Philips- Universitaet, Unpublished M. A. Thesis.

Almeida,A.(1976), "The Portuguese nasal vowels: phonetics and phonemics", in: Schmidt-Radenfeldt,J. Readings in Portuguese linguistics. Amsterdam: North-Holland Publishing Company.

Almeida,A.(1978), Nasalitaetsdetektion und Vokalerkennung. Forum Phoneticum 17, Hamburg:Helmut Buske Verlag.

Andersen,H.(1972), "Diphthongization", Lg 48,11-50

Anderson,S.R.(1972), "On the description of 'apicalized' consonants", LI 2,103-107.

Anderson, S.R.(1974), The organization of phonology. New York:Academic Press.

Anderson,R.A.(1975), "The description of nasal consonants and internal struc-ture of segments.",in: Ferguson et al.(1975),1-26.

Avram,A.(1968), "Sur le rapport entre les voyelles neutres et la nasalité", Revue roumaine de linguistique XIII,567-573

Avram,A(1972), "Les phonèmes indéterminés et l'interprétation phonologique des voyelles nasales", Linguistics 80,5-16.

Balasubramanian,T.(1980), "Nasalisation of vowels in colloquial Tamil", JPh 8,261-373.

Barbosa,J.M.(1962), "Les voyelles nasales portugaises: interprétation phonolo-gique", Proc.Phon. 5,691-710

Basbøll,H. (1979), "Phonology", Proc.Phon. 9, I, 103-131.

Bell-Berti,F.(1976), "An electromyographic study of velopharyngeal function in speech", JSHR 19, 225-240.

Bell-Berti,F.,Baer,T.,Harris,K.H. and Niimi,S.(1979), "Coarticulatory effects of vowel quality on velar function", Ph 36, 187-193.

Bell-Berti,F. and Hirose,H.(1975), "Palatal activity in voicing distinctions: a simultaneous fiberoptic and electromyographic study", JPh 3,69-74.

Bendor-Samuel,J.T.(1960), "Some problems in the phonological analysis of Terena", in: Palmer,(1970), 214-222.

Benguerel ,A.-P., Hirose,H., Sawashima,M. and Ushijima,T.(1977a), "Velar coar-ticulation in French: a fiberscopic study", JPh 5, 149-158.

Benguerel,A.-P., Hirose,H., Sawashima,M. and Ushijima,T. (1977b), "Velar coarticulation in French: an electromyographic study", JPh 5, 159-167.

Bernard,J.R.L.-B, "A cine-X-ray study of some sounds of Australian English". Ph 21,138-150

Bibeau,G.(1975), Introduction à la phonologie générative du français. Studia Phonetica 9, Didier,Montréal etc.

Bjoerk,L.(1961), Velopharyngeal function in connected speech. Acta Radiolo-gica, Supplementum 202, Stockholm.

Bloomer,H.(1953), "Observations on palatopharyngeal movements in speech and deglutition", JSHD 18, 230-246.

Boehme,G.,Sram,F. & Kalvodova,E. (1966), "Elektromyographische Untersuchungen ueber das Verhalten der Mm.levator und tensor veli palatini bei der Atmung und bei Phonation von Vokale", FoliaPh 18,9-18.

Bondarko,L.V.(1979), "On the phonological operations ensuring speech communication", Proc.Phon 9,67-73.

Bonnot,J.-F.P.(1978), "A propos de la coarticulation en français et en Nèerlandais: quelques remarques préliminaires à une étude expérimentale", unpublished.

Borel-Maisonny,S.(1967), "Analyse tomo-acoustique; applications possibles", International Audiology 217-225.

Botha,R.P.(1971), Methodological Aspects of Transformational Generative Phonology. Mouton, The Hague, Paris.

Bothorel,A.(1978), Etude phonètique et phonologique du Breton parlè à Argol (Finistère-Sud). Strassbourg, Thèse d'Etat.

Brichler-Labaeye,C.(1970), Les voyelles françaises. Paris:Klincksieck.

Brito,A.G.(1975), "The perception of nasal vowels in Brazilian Portuguese: A pilot study", in: Ferguson et al.(1975),49-66.

Bzoch,K.R.(1968), "Variations in velopharyngeal valving: the factor of vowel changes", CPJ 5, 211-218.

Calnan, James S.(1953), "Movements of the soft palate", British Journal of Plastic Surgery 5, 286-296.

Canu,Gaston (1975), La langue mo:re. Dialecte de Ouagadougou (Haute-Volta). Description synchronique. Paris: SELAF.

Carney,P.J.& Morris,H.L.(1971), "Structural correlates of nasality", CPJ 8, 307-321.

Carney,P.J. Sherman,D.(1971), "Severity of nasality in three selected speech tasks", JSHR 14,396-406.

Charbonneau,R.(1971), Etude sur les voyelles nasales du français canadien. Quèbec: Presses de l'Université Laval.

Chen,M.(1973), "On the formal expresion of natural rules in phonology", JL 9, 223-250.

Chiba,T. & Kajiyama,M. (1958), The vowel, its nature and structure. Tokyo: Phonetic Society of Japan.

Chlumsky, J., Pauphilet, A., Polland, B. (1938), Radiografie francouzskych samohlasek a polosamohlasek V Praze: Nakladem ceske Akademie ved a umeni.

Chomsky,N.(1964), "Current issues in linguistic theory", in: Fodor and Katz (1964), 50-118).

Chomsky,N.(1965), Aspects of the theory of Syntax. MIT Press, Cambridge, Massachussets.

Chomsky,N.and Halle,M. (1968), The sound pattern of English. New York: Harper & Row.

Clarke, W. M. and Mackiewicz-Krassowska, H. (1977), "Variation in the oral and nasal sound pressure level of vowels in changing phonetic contexts", in: JPh 5, 195-203.

Clumeck, H. (1971), "Degrees of nasal coarticulation", Monthly International Memorandum, Phonology Laboratory, University of California, Berkely, July.

Clumeck, H.(1975), "A cross-linguistic investigation of vowel nasalization: an instrumental study", In:Ferguson et al. (1975), 133-151.

Clumeck,H.(1976), "Patterns of soft palate movements in six languages", JPh 5, 337-351.

Condax,I.D., Howard,I.,Ikranagara,K.,Lin,Y.C,Crosetti,J. and Yount,D.E.(1974), "A new technique for demonstrating velic opening: application to Sundanese", JPh 2, 297-301.

Condax,I.D.,Acson,V.Miki,C.C. and Sakoda,K.K.(1976), "A technique for monitoring velic action by means of a photo- electric nasal probe: application to French", JPh 4, 173-181.

Croatto, L. et Croatto-Martinolli, C. (1959), "Physiopathologie du voile du palais", FoliaPh 11, 124-166.

Curtis,J.F.(1970), "The acoustics of nasalized Speech", CPJ 7,380-397.

Debrock, M. (1974), "La structure spectrale des voyelles nasales", Revue de Phonètique appliquèe 29, 15-31.

Delattre,P.(1954), "Les attributs acoustiques de la nasalitè", SL 7, 103-109.

Delattre,P.(1965), "La nasalitè vocalique en français et en anglais", The French Review 39, 92-109.

Delattre,P.(1968), "Divergences entre nasalités vocalique et consonantique en français",, Word 24, 64-72 (=Linguistic studies presented to André Martinet).

Delattre,P.(1970), "Rapports entre la physiologie et la chronologie de la nasalité distinctive",in: Actes du 10e congrès international des linguistes 4, 221-227.

Delattre,P.and Monnot,M.(1968). "The role of duration in the identification of French vowels", IRAL 6, 267-288.

Dell, F.(1973), Les règles et les sons. Introduction à la phonologie générative. Herman:Paris.

Denes,P.B. & Pinson,E.N.(1973), The speech chain. 2nd edition, New York: Doubleday.

Dickson,D.R.(1962), "An acoustic study of nasality", JSHR 5, 103-111.

Durand,M.(1953), "De la formation des voyelles nasales", SL 7, 33-53.

Entenman,G.(1976), The development of nasal vowels. diss. University of Texas at Austin, reproduced by Un.Microfilms International.

Essen,O. von(1961), "Die phonetische Documentation der Nasalitaet und des offenen Naeselns", FoliaPh 13, 269-275.

Eijkman,L.P.H.(1902), Les mouvements du voile du palais. Extraits des Archives Teyler,Serie II,tome VIII,Haarlem.

Eijkman,L.P.H.(1926), "The soft palate and nasality", Neophilogus 11, 207-218.

Eijkman, L.P.H.(1928),"More soft palate and nasality", English Studies, 114-118.

Eijkman,L.P.H.(1934), "Nasality again", Neophilologus 20,25-30.

Fant,G.(1960), Acoustic theory of speech production, with calculations based on X-ray studies of Russian articulations. The Hague: Mouton.

Fant,G.(1973), Speech sounds and features. Cambridge (Mass.): The MIT Press.

Feinstein,M.H.(1979), "Prenasalisation and Syllable Structure", LI 10,243-278

Ferguson, Ch.A. (1963), "Assumptions about nasals: a sample study in phonological universals", in: Greenberg, J.H. (ed.), Universals of language, MIT Press: Cambridge (Mass.).

Ferguson,Ch.A.(1974), "Universals of nasality", WPLU 14, 1-16.

Ferguson,Ch.A.(1975), "Universal Tendencies and 'normal' Nasality", in: Ferguson et al.(1975),175-196.

188

Ferguson, C.A.,Hyman,L.M.,Ohala,J.J. (eds.)(1975), Nasalfest. Papers from a symposium on nasals and nasalization, Language Universal Project, Department of Linguistics, Stanford University, Stanford.

Fodor,J.A. and Katz,J.J.(eds.)(1964), The structure of language. Readings in the philosophy of language, Englewood Cliffs (N.J.): Prentice-Hall.

Fowler,C.A.(1977), Timing control in speech production. Bloomington: Indiana University,Linguistics Club.

Fowler,C.A.(1980), "Coarticulation and theories of extrinsic timing", JPh 8, 113-133.

Francard,M.(1975), Aspects de la phonologie générative du français contemporain. Travaux de la Fac.de Phil. et Lettres de l'Université Cath. de Louvain, XIV, Section de Philologie Romane II, Louvain,Leiden: Bibl. de l'Univ.,E.J.Brill.

Fritzell,B.(1969), The velopharyngeal muscles in speech. An electromyographic and cineradiographic study, Goeteborg: Acta Oto-Laryngologica. Supplementum 250.

Fujimura,O.(1962), "Analysis of nasal consonants", JASA 34, 1865-1875.

Gelder,L. van(1965), Het zachte gehemelte bij de spraak. Haarlem: Bohn.

Genet,E.(1971), "Une double nasalisation en Mo:re?", Ph 24, 175-187.

Gimson,A.C.(1970), An introduction to the pronunciation of English. Edward Arnold,London.

Goldsmith,J.(1976), "An overview of autosegmental phonology", Linguistic Analysis 2,23-68.

Greenberg,J.H.(1966), "Synchronic and diachronic universals in phonology", Lg. 42, 508-517.

Greene,M.C.L.(1955), "The cleft palate patient with incompetent palatophar-yngeal closure", FoliaPh 7, 172-182.

Halle,M.(1964), "On the basis of Phonology", in: Fodor and Katz (1964),324-333.

Halle,M. and Stevens,K.N.(1964), "Speech recognition: a Model and a Program for Research", in: Fodor and Katz,604-612.

Hattori,S. Yamamoto ,K.,.Fujimura,O(1958), "Nasalization of vowels in relation to nasals", JASA 30, 267-274.

Herbert,R.K.(1979), "Typological universals,aspiration and post-nasal stops", Proc. Phon 9,19-26.

Hewlett,N.(1981), "Phonetic realisation rules in generative phonology", JPh 9,63-77.

Hirano,M.,Takeuchi,Y. and Hiroto,I.(1966), "Intranasal sound pressure during utterance of speech sound", FoliaPh 18, 369-381.

Hooper,J.B.(1976), An Introduction to natural generative phonology. Academic Press,New York.

House,A.S.(1957), "Analog studies of nasal consonants", JSHD 22, 190-204.

House,A.S. and Stevens,K.N.(1955), "Auditory testing of a simplified description of vowel articulation", JASA 27, 882-887.

House,A.S.and Stevens,K.N.(1956), "Analog studies of the nasalization of vowels", JSHD 21, 218-232.

Hyman,L.M.(1972), "Nasals and Nasalization in Kwa", Studies in African Linguistics 3,167-205.

Jakobson,R. and Halle,M.(1956), Fundamentals of Language. Mouton, The Hague.

Jakobson,R.C.,Fant,G.M. and Halle,M.(1952), Preliminaries to Speech Analysis, The distinctive features and their correlates. MIT Press, Cambridge, Massachussets.

Jensen,O.K.(1967), "Features of the acoustical and physiological structure of the French nasal vowels", ARIPUC 1, 59-66.

Jespersen,O.(1913), Lehrbuch der Phonetik. Leipzig etc: Teubner.

Jones,D.(1956), An outline of English phonetics. 8th edition, Cambridge:Heffer and Sons.

Kaltenborn,A.L.(1948), An X-ray study of velopharyngeal closure in nasal and non-nasal speakers. M.A.thesis, Evanston:North-Western University.

Kacprowski,J.(1977), "A simulative model of the vocal tract including the effect of nasalization". Archives of Acoustics 2,4,235.

Karttunen,F.and Lockhart,J.(1976), "Nahuatl nasals", LI 7, 380-383.

Kaye,J.D.(1971), "Nasal harmony in Desano", LI 2,27-56.

Kenstowicz, M. and Kisseberth, C. (1979), Generative phonology, Description and theory. Academic Press, New York etc.

Kent,L.M.R.(1966), The effects of oral-to-nasal coupling on the perceptual, physiological and acoustical characteristics of vowels. Ph.D.of the University of Iowa (Reproduced by University Microfilms International).

Kent,R.,Carney,P. and Severeid,L.(1974), "Velar movement and timing: Evaluation of a model for binary control", JSHR 17,470-488.

Kent,R.D. and Minifie,F.D.(1977), "Coarticulation in recent speech production models", JPh 5, 115-117.

Kenyon,J.S. and Knott,T.A.(1944), A pronouncing dictionary of American English. Springfield (Mass.):Merriam.

Klingholz,F. und Meinhold,G.(1975), "Spektrale Intensitaetsver teilung deutscher Phonem-realisationen", Ph 32, 81-88.

Kohler,K.(1978), "Review of : Ladefoged 1975", Ph 35,112-114.

Kuehn,D.P.(1976), "A cineradiographic investigation of velar variables in two normals", CPJ 13, 88-103.

Kuenzel,H.J.(1977), "Photoelektrische Untersuchung zur Velumhoehe bei Vokalen: erste Anwendung des Velographen", Ph 34, 352-370.

Kuenzel,H.J.(1978), "Reproducibility of electromyographic and velographic measurements of the velopharyngeal closure mechanism", JPh 6, 345-351.

Kuenzel,H.J.(1979), "Roentgenvideographische Evaluierung eines photoelektrischen Verfahrens zur Registrierung der Velumhoehe beim Sprechen", Folia Phoniatrica 31, 153-166.

Labov,W.(1971), "Methodology", in: Dingwall(ed), College Park: University of Maryland Linguistics Program , p. 412-497.

Labov,W.(1972), Sociolinguistic patterns, Philadelphia: University of Pennsylvania Press.

Ladefoged,P.(1962), Elements of acoustic phonetics. Chicago and London: The University of Chicago Press.

Ladefoged,P.(1974), Preliminaries to linguistic phonetics. Chicago and London: The University of Chicago Press.

Ladefoged,P.(1975), A course in phonetics. New York: Harcourt Brace Jovanovich.

Ladefoged,P.(1979), "Articulatory parameters", in: Proc.Phon 9, Vol.I, 41-47.

Lahti.I(1953), "La dénasalisation en français", Neuphilologische Mitteilungen LIV Jahrgang,1-33.

Lanher,J.(1972), "Une graphie curieuse dans les chartes des Vosges antérieures à 1270" in: Straka,G., Les dialectes de France au moyen-âge et aujourd'hui, Domaines d'oil et domaines franco-provençal, Paris: Klincksieck, 337-348.

Lass,R.(1976), English Phonology and Phonological Theory, Synchronic and Diachronic Studies. Cambridge univ.Press, Cambridge etc.

Lindblom, B.E.F.,Lubker,J.F. and Pauli,S.(1977), "An acoustic- perceptual method for the quantitative evaluation of hypernasality", JSHR 20, 485-496.

Linthorst,P.(1973), Les voyelles nasales du français. Etude phonétique et phonologique, Groningen: V.R.B. Offsetdrukkerij.

Lintz,L.B. and Sherman,D.(1961), "Phonetic elements and the perception of nasality", JSHR 4, 381-396.

Lovins,J.B.(1978), " "Nasal reduction" in English syllable codas", Papers from the fourteenth regional meeting, Chicago Linguistic Society, 14-25.

Lubker,J.F.(1968), "An electromyographic-cinefluorographic investigation of velar function during normal speech production", CPJ 5, 1-18.

Lubker,J.F. and Moll,K.L.(1965), "Simultaneous oral-nasal air flow measurements and cinefluorographic observations during speech production", CPJ 2, 257-272.

Luecksinger, R.(1954), "Klanganalytische Untersuchungen des offenen Naeselns im Vergleich zu den manometrisch-phonetischen Registrierungen", FoliaPh 6, 233-239.

Lunt,H.G.(1973), "Remarks on nasality: the case of Guarani",in: Anderson S.R. and Kiparsky,P. (eds.), Festschrift for Morris Halle. New York: Holt, Rinehart and Winston, 131-139.

Malécot,A.(1960), "Vowel nasality as a distinctive feature in American English", Lg 36, 222-229.

Malécot,A. and Metz,G.(1972), "Progressive nasal assimilation in French", Ph 26,193-209.

Martony,J. and Fant,G.(1964). "Information bearing aspects of formant amplitude",Proceedings of the fifth International Congress of Phonetic Sciences. Muenster,409-411.

Martony,J.(1964), "The role of formant amplitudes in synthesis of nasal consonants", STL-QPSR 3,28-31.

Massengill,R. and Bryson,M.(1967), "A study of velopharyngeal function as related to perceived nasality of vowels,utilizing a Cinefluorographic Televison monitor", Fol.Phon. 19,45-52.

Matsuya, T.,Miyazaki,T. and Yamaoka,M.(1974), "Fiberscopic examination of velopharyngeal closure in normal individuals", CPJ 11,286-291.

192

McDonald,E.T. and Baker,H.K.(1951), "Cleft palate speech: an integration of research and clinical observation", JSHD 16,9-20.

Meinhold,G.(1970), "Nasal und Orale Vokale - Struktur und Perzeption", Proc.Phon 6,(1967),641-662.

Mermelstein,P.(1973), "Articulatory model for the study of speech production", JASA 53,1070-1082.

Merrifield,W.R(1963), "Palantla Chinantec syllable types", Anthropolocal Linguistics 5,1-16.

Mohr,B. and Wang,W.S.-Y.(1968), "Perceptual distance and the specification of phonological features", Ph 18,31-45.

Moll,K.L.(1960), "Cinefluorographic techniques in speech research", JSHR 3,227-241.

Moll,K.L.(1962), "Velopharyngeal Closure on Vowels", JSHR 5,30-37.

Moll,K.L. and Daniloff,R.G.(1971), "Investigation of the Timing of Velar Movements during Speech", JASA 50,678-684.

Moll,K.L.and Shriner,T.H.(1967), "Prelimimary investigation of a new concept of velar activity during speech", CPJ 4,58-69.

Moller,K.T.,Martin,R.R. and Christiansen,R.L.(1971), "A technology for recording velar movement" CPJ 8,263-276.

Mrayati,M.(1975), "Etudes des voyelles nasales françaises", Bulletin de l'Institut de Phonètique de Grenoble IV,1-26

Nandrish,O.(1963), Phonètique historique du roumain, Klincksieck,Paris.

Nihalani,P.(1975), "Velopharyngeal opening in the formation of voiced stops in Sindhi", Ph 32,89-102.

Noske,R.(1979), "Een onderzoek naar het mogelijk diftongale karakter van nasale klinkers", bijvakscriptie,Instituut voor Fonetische Wetenschappen, Universiteit van Amsterdam.

Nusbaum,E.A.,Foley,L.and Wells,C.(1935), "Experimental studies of the firmness of the velo-pharyngeal occlusion during the production of English Vowels", Speech Monographs 2,71-80.

Oftedal,M.(1956), The Gaelic of Leurbost Isle of Lewis, A linguistic survey of the Gaelic dialects of Scotland .Vol VII,H.Aschehoug,Oslo.

Ohala,J.J.(1971), "The Role of Physiological and Acoustic Models in Explaining the Direction of Sound Change" POLA 15,Berkeley,25-40.

Ohala,J.J.(1972), "Physical models in phonology", Proc.7th ICPS. 1166-1171.

Ohala,J.J.(1974a), "Experimental historical Phonology", Proceedings of the first International Conference on Historical Linguistics. Edinburgh,North-Holland Press 2, 353-389.

Ohala,J.J.(1974b), "Phonetic explanation in Phonology",in: Papers from the Parasession on Natural Phonology, Chicago Linguistic Society, 251-274.

Ohala,J.J.(1975), "Phonetic explanations for nasal Sound Patterns", in: Ferguson et al.(1975),289-316.

Ohala, M.(1975), "Nasals and nasalization in Hindi", in: Ferguson et al.(1975),317-332.

Palmer,F.R.,(1970), Prosodic Analysis.London: Oxford University Press.

Paris,G.(1898), "Review of Uschakoff 1897", in: Romania 27,300-304.

Perkell,J.S.(1969), Physiology of Speech production, Results and Implications of a Quantative Cineradiographic study. The MIT Press,Cambridge(Mass) and London.

Petrovici,E.(1930), De la nasalité en roumain. Lucrari de Fonetica Laboratorului de Fonetica Experimentala al Universitatii din Cluj 6.

Petursson,M.(1974), Les articulations de l'Islandais à la lumière de la radiocinématographie. Paris,Klincksieck

Pike,K.L.(1968), Phonemics. The University of Michigan Press, Ann Arbor.

Polland,B.and Hala,B.(1926), Les radiographies de l'articulation des sons tchèques, V PRAZE: Nakladem CESKE AKADEMIE VED A UMENI.

Reenen, P.T. van(to appear) "A propos de la formation des voyelles nasales en ancien français ou la fiabilité des données linguistiques", Actes du 16e congrès international de linguistique et philologie romanes, Palma.

Reenen, P.T. van, and Voorhoeve,J.(1980), "Gender in Limbum" in: van Alkemade, D.J.van,Feitsma,A.,Meys,W.J.,van Reenen,P.T.,Spa,J.J. (eds) (1980), Linguistic Studies offered to Berthe Siertsema. Amsterdam, Rodopi

Robins,R.H.(1953), "The phonology of the nasalized verbal forms in Sundanese", in: Palmer(1970),104-111.

Robins,R.H.(1957), "Aspects of prosodic analysis", in: Palmer,188-200.

Rochet,B.(1974), "A morphologically-determined sound change in Old-French", Linguistics 135,43-56

Rochet,B.(1975), "About a pseudo-linguistic universal: That Nasal Vowels Have a Tendency to Lower", Proc.Ling.11. vol.II,727-730.

Rochet,B.L.(1976), The formation and the evolution of the French nasal vowels, Beihefte zur Zeitschrift fuer romanische Philologie 153, Max Niemeyer Verlag, Tuebingen.

Rochette,C.(1973), Les groupes de consonnes en français. Klincksieck-Laval, Paris-Quebec.

Rueter,G.(1975), Vowel Nasality in the speech of rural Middle Georgia, Dissertation of Finory University.

Ruhlen,M.(1973), "Nasal Vowels", in: Working Papers on Language Universals. 12,1-36

Ruhlen,M.(1974), "Some comments on vowel nazalisation in French", JL 10, 271-275.

Ruhlen,M.(1975), "Patterning of nasal vowels",in: Ferguson et al.(1975),333-352.

Ruhlen,M.(1978), "Nasal Vowels",in:Greenberg,J.H.(ed), Universals of human language 2, Phonology, University Press, Stanford,203-241.

Russel,G.O.(1928), The Vowel, Its physiological Mechanism as shown by X-ray, McGrath Publ.Comp.Maryland (1970).

Saussure, F. de (1918), Cours de linguistique génèrale , pp. Bally,C., Sechehaye,A., Riedlinger,A., Payot, Paris.

Schane,S.A.(1973), Generative Phonology. Englewood Cliffs (New Jersey): Prentice Hall.

Schourup,L.(1972), "Characteristics of Vowel Nasalisation", Glossa 5,4.

Schourup,L.C.(1973), "A cross-language study of vowel nasalization",in: Working Papers in Linguistics 15,Department of Linguistics, The Ohio State University,190-221.

Schwartz,M.F.(1968a), "Relative intra-nasal sound intensities of vowels" Speech Monographs ,196-200.

Schwartz,M.F.(1968b), "The acoustics of Normal and Nasal Vowel Production" PJ 5,125-140.

Schwartz,M.F.(1971), "Acoustic measures of nasalization", Cleft lip and palate, 56,Boston,798-804.

Simon,P.(1967),Les consonnes françaises Klincksieck,Paris

Simon,P.(1968), "A propos de la désarticulation de la consonne palatale n dans la prononciation du français d'aujourd'hui" in: Mèlanges Straka, Phonètique et Linguistique romanes I, Lyon-Strasbourg,67-98.

Simon,P.,Bothorel,A.,Wioland,F.,Brock,G.(1979), "Méthode de synchronisation image-son pour l'étude radiologique des faits de parole - application au français", in: Proc.Phon.9, Vol I, 213.

Skolnick,M.L.(1970), "Videofluoroscopic examination of the velopharyngeal portal during phonation in lateral and base projections - A new technique for studying the mechanics of closure", CPJ 7,803-816.

Skolnick,M.L.,McCall,G.N.and Barnes,M.(1973), "The sphincteric mechanism of velopharyngeal closure", CPJ 10,286-305.

Smith,S.(1951), "Vocalization and added nasal resonance", FoliaPh 3,165-169.

Spriesterbach,D.C. and Powers,G.R.(1959), "Nasality in isolated vowels and connected speech of cleft palate speakers", JSHR 2,40-45.

Stevens,K.N.(1979), "Basis for Phonetic Universals in the properties of the Speech Production and Perceptual Systems", in: Proc.Phon 9,vol 2,

Stevens,K.N. and House,A.S.(1955), "Development of a quantative description of vowel articulation", JASA 27,484-493.

Stevens,K.N.,Kalikow,T.R. and Willemain,T.R.(1975), "A miniature accelerometer for detecting glottal waveforms and nasalization", JSHR 18,594-599.

Stevens,K.N.,Nickerson,R.S.,Boothroyd,A.,Rollins,A.M.(1976), "Assessment of nasalization in the speech of deaf children", JSHR 19,393-416.

Straka,G.(1955), "Remarques sur les voyelles nasales,leur origine et leur évolution en français", Revue de Linguistique Romane 19,245-274.

Strenger,F.(1969), Les voyelles nasales françaises.Tr. de l'Institut de Phon. de Lund VIII, Gleerup,Lund.

Takahashi,H.,Honjo,I.,Azuma,F. and Yanagihara,N.(1962), "Studies on the movement of the nasopharyngeal wall related to speech", Studia Phonologica 11,47-60.

Ternes,E.(1973), The phonemic analysis of Scottish Gaelic. Based on the dialect of Applecross, Ross-shire. Forum Phoneticum, vol 1. Hamburg:Buske.

Trenschel,W.(1977), Das Phaenomen der Nasalitaet. Schriften der Phonetik, Sprachwissenschaft und Kommunikationsforschung 17, Akademie Verlag, Berlin.

Troubetzkoy,N.S.(1967), Principes de Phonologie, traduit par J.Cantineau, Paris: Klincksieck.

Ushijima,T. and Hirose,H.(1974), "Electromyographic study of the velum during speech", JPh 2,315-326.

Wada,T.,Yasumoto,M.,Ikeoka,N.,Fujiki,Y. and Yoshinaga,R.(1970), "An approach for the Cinefluorographic study of articulatory movements", CPJ 7,506-522.

Warren,D.W.and DuBois,A.B.(1964), "A pressure-flow technique for measuring velopharyngeal orifice area during continuous speech", CPJ 1,52-71.

Weatherley-White,R.C.A.,Stark,R.B. and De Haan,C.R.(1966), "Acoustic analysis of speech;Validation Studies", CPJ 3,291-300.

Wood,S.(1979), "A radiographic analysis of constriction locations for vowels", JPh 7,25-43.

Wright,J.(1975), "Effect of Vowel nasalization on the perception of vowel height", in: Ferguson et al.(1975),373-387.

Zagorska-Brooks,M.(1968), Nasal Vowels in contemporary standard Polish.An acoustic-phonetic analysis. Mouton,The Hague,Paris.